James Bellini studied at Cambridge University, going on to submit his doctoral thesis at the London School of Economics. He then joined the Harvard Institute for Economic Affairs, to become Head of Political Studies at the Institute's Paris headquarters. Since 1975 he has worked in British television, notably on *Panorama* and as the presenter of *The Money Programme*. He recently presented the ATV series *Rule Britannia*.

James Bellini

RULE BRITANNIA

A progress report for Domesday 1986

ABACUS edition published in 1982
by Sphere Books Ltd
30–32 Gray's Inn Road, London WC1X 8JL

First published in Great Britain by
Jonathan Cape Ltd 1981

Printed and bound in Great Britain by
Cox & Wyman Ltd, Reading

Melius est reprehendant nos grammatici quam non intelligant populi

It is better that the professors should reproach us than that the people not understand

St Augustine

Contents

KEEPING DOWN THE PEASANTS

APPENDIX

Acknowledgments

My thanks go to Alan Bell and Clive Fleury for invaluable discussions held in the course of producing a documentary series for ATV based on the themes set out in this book. The conclusions, errors and omissions are nevertheless mine alone.

Important contributions to Part Five, *Keeping Down the Peasants*, were the work of Robert Harris.

Introduction

This is not a book of prescriptions. It does not offer a programme of reform that could transform Britain's social structure so as to lay the foundations of a more egalitarian society. It was written to mark the ninth centenary of the Domesday Survey conducted during the reign of William the Conqueror, the point at which the history of England as a cultural entity really began. This book is, therefore, a progress report.

The picture of Britain in the 1980s is a provocative one. It describes a country in which a century of economic failure has had a marked effect on the way millions of people live. Because of this failure, and because of the peculiarly dated social structure that has long been a feature of British life, the country is now returning to a pre-industrial social framework. In short, Britain is losing its industrial façade – which has existed for little more than a century – and is creating a new feudal lifestyle, a mixture of medieval social relationships and the revolutionary impact of those high technologies that are rapidly transforming sectors of the economy.

Britain's economic failure is reflected in the collapse of its industrial base. It was the creation of this industrial foundation, during the nineteenth century, which put Britain at the forefront of world economic power and which lit the fuse on a process of comprehensive social change that created a huge industrial population, urban concentration, and a new kind of politics. But the social revolution was never to run its course. Britain's industrial momentum began to slow in the late nineteenth century and by the Second World War had reached a point of near-stagnation from which it has never really recovered. Yet it was at this precise point, as the war drew to a close, that the country embarked on an experiment in egalitarian politics. The Education Act of 1944 and the vast apparatus of the welfare state were products of this new post-war ambition to eliminate Britain's pre-industrial social framework and replace it with a meritocratic, mobile society of open opportunity. This ambition was shared by all the major political parties. But it needed the success and expansion of Britain's economy to provide the resources that could underpin such a long-term transformation. And that success was never to come.

As the facts of Britain's economic crisis have become more apparent, a glittering array of learned studies and reports has testified to a growing concern for Britain's future. An early example was, indeed, the work of an overseas organisation. In 1968 the Brookings Institution, in the United States, published *Britain's Economic Prospects*. This attempt to diagnose the causes of Britain's malaise was followed by a series of equally comprehensive surveys that punctuated the decade of the 1970s with a note of professional alarm at the decline of Britain's economy. In 1971 a British group, the Trade Policy Research Centre, responded with *Britain's Economic Prospects Reconsidered*. In 1976 two Oxford economists, R. W. Bacon and W. A. Eltis, published *Britain's Economic Problem: too few producers*. And there were many more besides. But the problem persisted, and Britain's situation grew more dire with each passing year.

Indeed, it is a sad comment on Britain's condition that in the autumn of 1980 the Brookings Institution returned to the issue, as if to set the scene for the new decade. Their report, *Britain's Economic Performance*, looked at the same intractable problem. It is significant, perhaps, that the title of the 1968 study, with its emphasis on 'prospects', has given way to one using the word 'performance'. The earlier interest in the future for Britain has been overtaken by a concern only for the statistical past.

The analysts from Brookings, in this new study, nevertheless included a striking observation among their list of conclusions about Britain's poor economic record. 'The productivity problem originates deep within the social system.' Unfortunately, professional reluctance prevented them from pursuing the point. Yet it is now clear that the reasons for Britain's economic crisis are, indeed, primarily social. Britain's social system – pre-industrial, immobile, resistant to change – stands in the way of creating an economic structure that can fit the country for the challenges and dangers of the twenty-first century. Unlike counterparts in the industrialised world of Western Europe and North America, Britain has had no social revolution. Apart from the unfinished process begun by the Civil War of the 1640s, there has been no fundamental change in the structure of social power. Britain is thus unique amongst industrial societies for the social and political influence granted to its aristocracy. The pattern of Britain's life-style, with its unwritten taboos and its hidden codes of social conduct, is little different from an informal apartheid based on social rank rather than on race – although there are points where the two become synonymous. And it is this feudal pattern that stands in the way of economic success.

Britain's feudal lifestyle has economic effects for very basic reasons. A stratified society limits mobility. It places social limits in the way of economic innovation; in other societies that innovation would be judged on practical grounds alone. These social limits put barriers in the way of improvement within the professions, from engineers to lawyers. The recent inquiry into the status of the British engineer, supervised by Sir Monty Finniston, is a symptom of a deep-rooted social phenomenon, coming as it has more than a century after the engineering profession became recognised as the pivotal group in the process of industrial modernisation. Because of Britain's feudal social mentality, however, groups and professions associated with industry have been relegated to a second class level in the ordering of political influence and in the machinery of economic management. The long-term consequences of this ostracism of practical specialists from the mainstream of decision-making are profound, and account for many of the observable weaknesses that affect the operation of British industry. Most of these weaknesses are identifiable – a poor record of production engineering is a typical one. But the underlying causes are elusive, precisely because they stem from social practices that cannot be readily defined.

In 1979 I published, along with James Morrell, *The Regeneration of British Industry*, under the aegis of the Henley Centre for Forecasting. The book is an attempt to analyse the social, as well as the practical, barriers that stand in the way of a transformation of Britain's industrial base. Curious readers are directed to the various chapters of that book for precise details and for a series of recommendations aimed at reforming the structure of British industry. These recommendations include changes to the education system to allow better provision for practical studies suited to the technological challenges of the new industrial revolution now under way. Proposals are made to provide incentives for high-technology production. Changes are suggested in the way British governments prepare for regional growth and restructuring, and for the encouragement of new businesses. The financial system, together with fiscal policies, is examined in the context of the need for funds for new industries. The importance of rigorous, but flexible, national planning is stressed consistently. The book is, in other words, a blueprint for industrial change to make Britain's economy modern and efficient.

Alas, the task of transforming Britain's industrial base has not yet begun. Indeed, the collapse of industry has, if anything, accelerated. There are many in Britain who will accept the demise of industry as part of an inexorable process of true modernisation. There is, for example, a powerful school of thought which sees industrial growth as only an intermediate stage on the way to 'post-industrial' life, and which argues that the passing of British industry is a sign that the country is approaching a real maturity where service activities and intellectual skills will become the dominant form of work.

It is the contention of this book that such a post-industrial lifestyle, in which manufacturing industry has been eliminated, is not an option that is available to Britain. Two hundred years of industrialisation have created an enormous dependent population that is being impoverished by the steady disintegration of the industrial base. The decline of industry will place an ever-growing burden on Britain's trade performance, since the goods that are no longer produced by local industry will need to be imported. In the immediate future the costs of this will, unfortunately, continue to be obscured by the transitory financial benefits of North Sea oil. Above all, the progressive collapse of industry will leave only one major area for employment, namely the service sector. And since this service sector – financial activities, insurance, advisory services and other knowledge-based work – is the one most directly affected by the social codes, class considerations and other taboos of feudal Britain, the increasing domination by services of the job market will magnify the feudal flavour of Britain's economic system.

Already, the signs of social tension and rebellion are there. In the words of the Supplementary Benefits Commission, in its 1980 annual report: 'In view of the unemployment forecast it would be dangerously optimistic to assume that the recent riots in Bristol could not be repeated elsewhere.' It seems inevitable that, with forecasts of 4 or 5 million British unemployed by the mid-1980s, the steady decline of industry will create a vast, alienated subgroup of working people deprived of work. And, for the first time since the beginning of the age of industry, these millions will slowly realise that their workless state could become a permanent one. Violence, the Commission concluded, is the inevitable consequence of massive unemployment of a long-term nature.

Economic theory now lies helpless in the face of this gathering industrial crisis. Good planning, the redirecting of resources, the development of new skills and new products, the freeing of initiative and enterprise from the heavy hand of social conventions – all would help change the climate of Britain's future. Ironically, those social barriers to economic success are cherished and preserved by the same groups who now clamour for a new age of opportunity. Britain's crisis remains rooted in the social domain.

Withdrawn from empire, Britain now confronts its last colony – itself. Within its borders the natives grow restless. Growing numbers feel an overwhelming disillusionment with the economic harvest that two hundred years of industrial toil have brought them. Many of them may recall the words of Britain's other anthem: 'Rule, Britannia! Britons never, never, never shall be slaves.' One day, if the conditions of British everyday life continue to be eroded by failing industry and glaring inequalities, they may decide that the impossible has happened – and that the slave-masters are close to home. But that, I am sure, is a long way off. Perhaps five or six years, at least. The policies currently being implemented in an effort to avoid social disaster may, indeed, succeed. This book has been written on the assumption that they will fail.

THE DRIFT TO PRUTOPIA

1

The drift to Prutopia

There was once a country called Britain that grew rich and powerful by discovering the art of making things on a vast scale with the help of machines. Huge factories soon covered the landscape and an immense empire spread itself across the world. Its citizens dreamed of a future of comfort and saw themselves as destined to a life of privilege in the international community.

But after two hundred years the factories began to disappear. And the dreams of Utopia fell apart. One day in 1986 the people woke up to find that all the factories had gone and the country was being run by the Prudential Assurance Corporation with a little help from its friends in high places.

The name of the country was changed to Prutopia. Even ordinary place-names were altered to keep up with the times. Milton Keynes was changed to Milton Friedman. By A.D. 2010, the memories of factories and machines had faded away. Meanwhile, the rest of the world carried on as before and never even noticed that Britain wasn't there any more.

2

Backwards into the future

Can a country turn back the clock and become once again a feudal society, with peasants, princes and lords of the manor? The suggestion seems absurd. Yet the Britain of the 1980s is proof that it is possible to go backwards in time, to re-create the social order of the Middle Ages behind the misleading appearance of a modern façade.

This book looks at the social consequences of economic failure, something that professional economists seldom do and professional politicians cannot do if they wish to survive in the marketplace of voting politics. The pace of Britain's economic decline is now so rapid and the spread of industrial collapse so wide that the entire social framework is breaking down. The coming of high-technology systems has only added to a process which is simplifying Britain's social groups into a hierarchy of status and economic roles that bears the hallmark of the old feudal order. Economic failure is not unknown elsewhere in the world – Argentina, Haiti and Weimar Germany are obvious examples – but each society reacts in an individual style. In Britain the underlying characteristics of the society have always been feudal. Now that the modern face imposed by industry is crumbling away, it is inevitable that this latent feudal spirit should struggle to reassert itself. That is the prospect for Britain as it enters the twenty-first century. The motto of this new Britain could be taken from its medieval past: the rich man in his castle, the poor man at his gate.

In the 1080s, some nine centuries ago, William the Conqueror ordered a study of his newly acquired territory. The picture that emerged from the Domesday Survey of 1086 was of a strictly ordered society in which a ladder of privilege, rank, status, wealth, power and subservience was clearly defined. Daily life was governed by the needs of the landed gentry. The relationship between the powerful few and the masses they governed was summed up in the simple word *servus* – hence the existence of the serf in feudal times. His job was to provide for the maintenance of the gentry's lifestyle. It was, in essence, a 'service' society. Knowledge was monopolised by a priestly class who exerted immense social and political influence through their command of learned texts and ancient ritualistic ceremonies. They explained the law and dominated the administration.

The more individual tasks of service to the powerful were entrusted to loyal stewards. The system was held together by bonds of ritual, taboo, mystery and magic, all based on appeals to the 'irrational' impulses of the ordinary man and woman in the fields. Above them stood the commanding ethos of the medieval world – the cult of the military. The knight was the man on horseback; his elevated station and the war machine he rode set him apart.

In the nine centuries that have elapsed since Domesday I, only the words have changed in this description of Britain's condition. Behind the outward appearance of bustling commerce, picket lines, gentlemen's clubs and elected parliaments there is another country, a country in which the old feudal order has survived and waits only for Britain's flirtation with factory culture to run out of passion before resuming its place as the true expression of Britain's rural dream.

The rise of industry in Britain brought new forms of wealth and new kinds of work. For two hundred years from 1750, the factory culture prospered. The traditional feudal order was temporarily diluted by a factory class of manual workers and a managerial group who supervised the mechanical activities of this new age. Britain's industrial revolution triggered off a chain reaction around the world. The social consequences were unlimited. A new business class emerged, while the business ethic became the morality which governed everything. The slogan of the New York stockbroker, 'What is good for General Motors is good for America', set the tone of this new international climate.

But in Britain the coming of industry was greeted with mixed sentiments. The factory brought an unwelcome intrusion upon a habit of rural conduct that had been raised to the status of religion:

> And did those feet in ancient time
> Walk upon England's mountains green? . . .
>
> And was Jerusalem builded here
> Among those dark Satanic mills?

William Blake's popular hymn summed up the tension between modern times and the deep nostalgia for a pre-industrial lifestyle.

'In 1958 the United Kingdom's annual wealth or gross domestic product was ahead of that of Germany and France – and twice that of Italy and Japan. In 1976 Italy's gross domestic product alone was lower than our own. That of France was 50 per cent higher while that of Germany and Japan was well over twice that of the U.K.'

Peter Shore, Secretary of State for the Environment, in 1978

The dream proved strong enough to fend off the challenge of industry. It guaranteed that the industrial revolution was, for Britain at least, merely a passing phase before the country reverted to its traditional pattern. And it worked through the subtle operation of a feudal sub-consciousness, which dictated that the object of success in business was to resurrect the qualities of medieval life, no matter what the consequences for the mass of ordinary individuals. The process has largely escaped the attention of the economists, with their love of numbers and charts, even though it lies at the very foundation of Britain's crisis. It did not escape a more sensitive observer, however, and in the work of the novelist Thomas Mann the theme has been set out with simple clarity. In *Buddenbrooks* the dream is given shape through the rise of a family from humble beginnings to a state beyond vulgar industry. The book is a study of three generations: the first sought money; the second, born to money, sought social and civic position; the third, born to comfort and prestige, looked to the life of music. This process of seduction has been the prime cause of Britain's economic demise and the guarantee of the rise of its new feudal order.

In Lancashire, where the cotton mills played a vital role in the surge of Britain's industrial empire, Thomas Mann's elegant phrases have a more basic counterpart: clogs to clogs in three generations. But the differing expressions stand for the same inexorable drive that pushes Britain backwards. The coming of those dark satanic mills marked a revolutionary break with a social structure that had existed since the Conquest, a structure in which landed power had stood unchallenged. The mass production of household goods, equipment and clothes now meant that there would be universal access to the physical symbols of affluence. This was truly 'democratic' wealth. The wages that came with the factory promised a future in which poverty would be eliminated. And the emergence of a popular consciousness, based on large urban populations pushed together in the factory and the street, linked by cheaper transport and mass literature, would lead to a popular politics that would end the influence of privileged minorities. That was the promise; it was to last just two hundred years.

'The relative industrial decline of this country is now widely seen as a matter of grave concern. If allowed to continue it would seem only too likely to lead to growing impoverishment and unemployment in years to come.'

Bank of England, 1979

In Richard Hoggart's book of the 1950s, *The Uses of Literacy*,[1] we catch a glimpse of the era of democratic wealth in Britain as it reached its high point. Through the educational impact of cheaply printed literature, we were told, the popular mind had reached a stage of mass sophistication. Britain was approaching a condition of classlessness. Just as important, the reforms in education enshrined in the 1944 Education Act were beginning to work through to the functioning of the elites who governed the country. We were advised, by Michael Young in *The Rise of the Meritocracy*,[2] that the best and the brightest of the Hoggart generation would become the principal components in those new elites. Democratic wealth would have its parallel in the political domain. But this vision of future Britain was a mirage. Britain in 1960 was at its pinnacle of economic and social progress. The journey into the past was just beginning.

Two families, the Levers and the Pearsons, feature in later parts of this survey of Britain in the 1980s, especially in Chapter 13, 'The LeverPearson Effect'. In their very different ways they add flesh and bones to the theory of 'Buddenbrook economics' sketched out by Thomas Mann. They also illustrate the feudal undercurrents that run through British life and somehow manage to carry off the successful individual into a euphoria that saps the vitality of the industrial structure. William Lever rose from the social limbo of a small-town grocery business in Lancashire to the aristocratic heights of becoming Lord Leverhulme of the Western Isles. It was an elevation achieved almost entirely through the production of soap. The third Lord Leverhulme fits the Buddenbrook image to the letter: in 1980 he was one of the four stewards at Royal Ascot, welcoming the Queen as she made her progress through the ranks of top-hatted subjects. His titles and civic offices suggest a loyal knight, edging ever closer to the glory of the throne.

The Pearson family displays in its social evolution a second trait in the Buddenbrook style, that of dynastic power increasingly divorced from humble factory work. From a swashbuckling, pioneering grandfather who grew rich on oil, construction and a taste for the quick profit, a vast business empire was built. The prize for that conquering energy was the title of Viscount Cowdray and a steady absorption into the aristocratic fabric. The business style was more striking: the Pearson empire was to be expanded through the employment of family members in key positions to a degree unrivalled in any other part of British business. Today the Cowdray dynasty, the wealthiest of the aristocratic economy, spreads across a breathtaking array of newspapers, journals, banking institutions, land and craft industry. The *Financial Times*, *The Economist*, Penguin Books, the *Investors Chronicle* and a long list of provincial papers give the Pearson family an awe-inspiring purchase on the popular mind, not least in the vital area of high finance. In three generations it has laid down the rock-hard foundations of a truly medieval lifestyle which embraces half a dozen noble titles and a score of estates. And in keeping with the Buddenbrook pattern, that third generation seems to mark a high point. Cowdray has six children but his eldest son, heir to the title, has so far shown little interest in the business and divides his time between Ibiza and Monte Carlo. A recent purchase was a £100,000 yacht called *The Hedonist*.

Thus, this Britain of the fourth generation now faces its Buddenbrook demise. Two hundred years of industry can now be seen only as the means of creating a new aristocracy to enrich and extend the aristocracy of old landed wealth. Leverhulme built his palaces and art galleries, his feudal settlements; Cowdray indulges in the passions of the knightly class, the world of the horse. (Ironically, much of the evidence used in this book is drawn from the specialist publications of the Cowdray commercial empire.)

'There is a dragon around. He is inside and not outside the walls of the Castle of the Kingdom. The name of the dragon is Attitude – the adverse attitude of the majority of people in Britain to making things . . . Charity, compassion, sympathy, a burning desire to help – all those without the actual material stuff that people require, or the means to help them to produce that stuff for themselves, are useless.'

Kenneth Adams, in a lecture to the Royal Society of Arts, St George's Day, 1980

The Britain they own and therefore govern has the outward appearance of a modern state. But beneath the surface the pre-industrial dream lives on. As the thinning fabric of industrial modernity crumbles, this nostalgic schizophrenia wells up to everyday level. The vocabulary is sometimes new, the dress might be the most modern that Carnaby Street and Chelsea can provide. But that is where the modernity ends. It is not surprising that it was an outsider, the Australian Richard Neville, who defended himself in the High Court with a striking image of twentieth-century Britain:

I have felt at times as though I had got caught in one of Dr Who's time machines: that I had been transported back in time to a wonderland of wigs and starched collars, of liveried courtiers and secret passageways; that I had been deposited amidst an eternal, antique stage play.[3]

Neville's observations could have been made at any point in the last five hundred years – or the next.

Take a typical day in May, when the villages of olde England resounded to the songs and dances of the maypole and the coming of summer heralded a season of optimism. Is it really any different today? The Court Circular announces that the Queen received in audience a Mr Grady and a Mr Rich, who kissed hands on their appointments as Her Majesty's Ambassadors Extraordinary and Plenipotentiary to some distant rulers. The Prince of Wales, Duke of Cornwall, visited his estates in Gloucestershire. The Duke of Gloucester left to attend a seminar on 'Prince Albert and the Victorian Age' at Bayreuth University in Coburg. At Leeds Castle in Kent a garden named after Lord John Culpeper, companion in exile to the future Charles II, was opened with a brief ceremony during which an American gentleman hailed the 'cultural sophistication, intellectual brilliance and enlightened taste which we have inherited in no small measure from you'. And in the elegant surroundings of Grosvenor House in London's Mayfair the gilded youth of polite society gathered for the Rose Ball, an annual celebration of the 'list' of proper young folk as they entered the world of adult privilege. *Suprême de volaille princesse* and *profiteroles au chocolat* were washed down with several thousand bottles of the better wines. The date is 22 May 1980.

But behind the news from the courts – those of royalty as well as those that had tried Mr Neville for his transgressions in the pages of *Oz* – another Britain struggled against a mounting crisis of confidence. Could those liveried courtiers, the secret passageways and the government that went with them deliver the goods? The lead story in *The Times* that day referred to the comments of the Prime Minister, Mrs Thatcher, at a Conservative Conference in London. She told party supporters that British citizens now faced a drop in real incomes; she invoked, in true nostalgic spirit, the image of Drake before Cadiz in 1587. She derided the 'patronage state' that she had inherited from the previous Labour government. Within a month she had sanctioned a Birthday Honours List crammed full with gifts of patronage to trusted friends: Lord Matthews of the *Daily Express*, Sir Ian Trethowan of the BBC, Sir Larry Lamb of the *Sun* joined the ranks of Britain's feudal wonderland.

Other news items of 22 May 1980 highlighted the gathering momentum of Britain's crisis. The Central Policy Review Staff made public a critical report on 'artificial restrictions on entry into certain industries', in which an antiquated training system was condemned as a primary cause of the shortage of skilled people that is strangling industry. Three new books were reviewed; they dealt with the immensity of the technological challenge posed to Britain's creaking industrial structure by micro-processors and other electronic systems. The reviewer seemed beset by doubt:

> The danger is that Britain will stay well clear of the edge of this revolution. We seem to be good at buying micro-based television games and to some extent at developing new micro-based information services. But at modernizing industry to compete in world markets . . . ?

Meanwhile, elsewhere that same day, the liveried courtiers and secret passageways lived on. A document produced by a group of Labour peers called for the abolition of the hereditary peerage; they chose to ignore the possibility that their own mass rejection of their aristocratic status could have been an effective first step. And in the secret corridors of Whitehall a sixty-paragraph document was being circulated which set out rules about how much, and how little, senior civil servants might disclose to Parliament. The rules made it impossible for a civil servant to tell an MP what advice had been given to a Minister, to hold policy discussions with officials of another department, to say anything that might confirm the existence of a Cabinet committee or even to reveal such seemingly harmless details as the name of the committee chairman.

That May day was not unusual. The government could have been of a different political persuasion. The personalities could have had different names. But the snapshot would capture the same flavour of ritualised decline, the 'antique stage play' that has no humour, no energy and no horizons.

This book is inevitably an essay of anger. It is also an essay of reckoning, as was the Domesday Survey those nine centuries ago. Since the high point of the 1960s the pendulum has swung away from the euphoria of the Hoggart generation. Spasms of unease have thrown up a long series of self-examining reports, studies and surveys every bit as comprehensive as the one in 1086. The Fulton Committee on the Civil Service, the Diamond Commission on wealth, Peter Townsend's massive work *Poverty*,[4] the researches of John Goldthorpe and his Oxford colleagues into class, social mobility and education, the Northfield Committee on land, the reports of the committee under Sir Harold Wilson dealing with the immense power of the City and its financial institutions: together they represent a detailed reappraisal of Britain as it is about to enter the twenty-first century. The picture they paint is of a Britain that is fast becoming two nations, separated by wealth and privilege and pushed further apart by the uncontrollable pressures of a technological revolution that is without parallel in social history.

The point was put most eloquently by the man who, perhaps fittingly, was to be given the job – as Chancellor of the Exchequer – of carrying Britain's ageing economy into the 1980s. Sir Geoffrey Howe, in a speech at the Waterman's Arms in East London, spelt out the future with simple clarity:

> Look out of the window on a train journey to any corner of Britain, and you can literally see the dangerous extent to which we have been living off the industrial and social capital that was accumulated by earlier generations – and failing to amass our own. Resources have been diverted to maintain consumer living standards today. But no seedcorn has been saved for tomorrow. This is the key to understanding the developing sickness of our society. The consequent lack of economic success is breeding social tensions and threatening to destroy the framework of civilised existence.[5]

Richard Neville's bemused observations take on a familiar ring. The 'antique stage play' of his courtroom summary is, in fact, a tragedy with a story line by Thomas Mann. Three generations of economic democracy have ground to a halt; the pastoral under-currents of British life are reasserting themselves, flowing steadily into the spaces left behind by the collapse of industry. The wigs and starched collars of privilege are acquiring a new power as mass prosperity fades away. As Britain flicks through the pages of its new Domesday Book it will see a country of growing social con-trasts. The ownership of land is little changed from the days of the Conqueror. The ranking of privilege is still rooted in the mystical formulae of the medieval court. It is still necessary to fill more than 400 pages, as does Debrett's *Correct Form*, with closely reasoned explanations of Britain's social rules before any of these mysteries are even partly understood. And in the end, a country that still tolerates the absurdities of Sir Iain Moncreiffe of that Ilk, as he sets out the minutiae of courtly etiquette, is not a serious place. It is this lack of seriousness that has helped drive the idea of democratic wealth into oblivion.

These remarks may appear out of step with the general climate of optimism that has persisted throughout the economic turmoil of the past ten years. The oil crisis shook long-held ideas of prosperity. The collapse of the Shah's regime in Iran raised major doubts about the stability of the international order. The onset of inflation at 10 and 20 per cent has caused widespread alarm. There are millions out of work across the developed world. But through it all there has shone a faith in the long-term; that Britain is robust enough to withstand the shocks and adjust to high-priced oil, lengthening dole queues and steadily rising prices in the supermarkets. This book is based on the premise that this optimism is misplaced. It argues that the international economy is entering a new stage of deep uncertainty and dangers. Above all, it describes a Britain which is no longer equipped to face the challenge. After two hundred years of industry the country is abandoning its factories; the economy is dividing into two sectors based on land and services. And in this new stage the latent feudal character of Britain will find its hidden strength.

3

The post-industrial rip-off

Millions of ordinary people across the industrial world have been the unsuspecting victims of a gigantic intellectual con trick. That trick has been pulled by the economists and professors at a thousand universities and institutes who have painted pictures of Utopia and called them The Future. The child-like visions were coated in the sophisticated veneers of the academic style, which did nothing more than, to borrow a phrase from George Orwell, give an appearance of substance to pure wind. This Utopian dream goes by the name of Post-industrial Society. The many learned books and articles extolling its virtues and setting out its details would fill a small library. But they are works of pure fiction.

The theme of these Utopians is that industrial society progresses without fail to a state of advanced prosperity, where the problems of everyday economics are solved and where each and every one of us lives in a condition of unparalleled plenty. Alas, there was no room in these flights of fancy for the tragedy of Britain's collapse, or for the vast industrial deserts of Britain's old factory regions, now in decay. Post-industrial society seemed to know no failure, at least for the learned prophets. There was no room in the optimistic scenarios of the post-industrial pioneers such as Rostow, Daniel Bell and Herman Kahn for the awkward idea that their exciting theories might not work in the real world. They even suggested that the rise of technology would sound the death knell for any remnants of the old feudal order of landed privilege. In the society of the future, the old power structure would be swept aside by the revolutionary impact of high knowledge. According to Bell:

If the production and maintenance of the scientific mastery of the future society requires the presence of a highly trained research elite, supported by a large technical staff, does not all this define the attributes of a new potential ruling class?[1]

The answer is No.

As we shall see, the march of high technology will restore pride of place to the old ruling class and bypass the skilled technocrats, who will be replaced by the super-intelligent machines of Bell's future society.

For Britain this discovery has a special poignancy. After all, the godfather of post-industrial belief, W. W. Rostow, had given us pride of place in his early blueprints. According to Rostow's sketches of the future, every country could follow the path to plenty. The model was that of Britain, passing out of its agricultural and feudal lifestyle into the age of industry and eventually into a millenium of unparalleled wealth and individual freedom.[2]

In truth, the post-industrial dream was not a British invention, polished and presented by more imaginative cousins across the Atlantic. It was little more than an intellectual version of the obsession with wealth and expansion that had characterised American life since the birth of the United States. Post-industrial society was an extension of the business ethic that had pushed back the frontiers of the American West, bred Henry Ford and built vast multinational enterprises around the globe. That ethic had already overwhelmed the American mind back in the 1860s, when de Tocqueville was writing of the United States: 'I know of no country indeed where the love of money has taken stronger hold on the affections of men.'

By the time the modern academics sat down to rediscover this urge for plenty a new factor had intervened. The model might be Britain, but the goal now was to follow the example of the United States. Post-industrial society would be a wonderful world of Walt Disney and kitchen gadgetry, courtesy of Factory Town, USA. Nowhere is the message spelt out more clearly than in *Things to Come* by Herman Kahn:[3]

These Westernistic states will have westernised bureaucracies, military, intellectuals, skilled workers, managers . . . They will drink Coca Cola, wear western clothes, have transistor radios,

ride bicycles then motorcycles, and eventually drive privately
owned automobiles . . . the people of the world will be more
culturally similar than they have been at any time in the history
of mankind. To a remarkable degree this global metropolis will
be Americanised in that it will be a mass culture, mechanistic,
pragmatic and cheerfully anarchistic.

In a single paragraph the beauty of the post-industrial rip-off is
laid bare. No room here for the alternative, of a deep failure in the
economic system leading to growing poverty, mass unemployment
and the re-emergence of a truly feudal spirit. Indeed, the very
thought is summarily dismissed: 'Not only has the bourgeoisie
been expanding at the expense of the "feudal" classes, it is
aggrandizing itself at the expense of the proletariat and the
peasantry.' That, at least, is the theory.

Britain's example now stands in sharp contrast to the Utopian
dreams of the showbiz professors of the 1960s. As the statistics
of decline pile up, Britain offers a depressing warning of things to
come for others who have followed the blueprint for post-
industrial society. Even though the rules of the game have been
religiously observed, the prosperity has not followed.

The new serfs

The blueprint called for a shift of resources from industrial production to service activities such as banking, insurance and entertainment. The birth of industry itself had, indeed, been fostered by a
massive exodus from Britain's farms. In 1800 the country had 95
per cent of its population working in the fields. By 1980 the figure
had fallen to 2 per cent. But food production had been increased
through greater efficiency on the farms and with the help of new
technologies. Now a repeat performance was required, this time
with labour moving from industry to services.

The blueprint was applied with admirable zeal by a generation
of British civil servants. Through government agencies such as the
Industrial Reorganisation Corporation the growth of the service
sector was actively encouraged. And the peculiar system of stigma
and status that governs Britain's employment market did the rest.

Educated people have needed little extra incentive before opting for the better paid, more highly regarded and more leisurely occupations of the City of London and their counterparts in offices and commercial premises around the country. Coupled with the rise in jobs in government, this drift to services created a vast new service class. In 1956 some 44 per cent of the British working population earned its living through service activities. By 1980 the figure had risen to more than 55 per cent. In human terms, more than 14 million Britons now spend their working lives with paper, typewriters and filing cabinets. By 1990 the figure may have grown to over 18 million, if their jobs survive.

This massive growth of a service class has feudal overtones, not least because it means a growing subservience to the invisible information technologies that are overtaking the world of business and administration. But it has also been the most critical cause of Britain's industrial decline, itself the very reason for the country's new feudal conditions. As the service class grew, the factories experienced an exodus of workers on an almost catastrophic scale. In the ten years to 1974 some one million jobs were lost in industry. By 1977 Britain's industrial army stood at just over 7½ million people. Reliable forecasts point to a continued downward trend in the years to the end of the century. By the year 2000 a further 2 million jobs will have evaporated, giving Britain an industrial strength of just over 5½ million – less than one-tenth of the population by then struggling to produce goods for a vast national market-place of more than 55 million. Industry will have all but died.

This shrinking industrial workforce seemed ample evidence that Britain was, indeed, entering the millenium of post-industrial prosperity. Had not the professors told us in simple terms that the badge of maturity was the rise of a new breed of service workers? Herman Kahn had summed it up in *Things to Come*: 'Industrial activities that have dominated the economy for the past two hundred years will play an ever-decreasing role . . . the most important economic activities in 1985 will be quaternary [service] activities.'

But the professors had overlooked a vital point. The luxury of this drift into the service state had to be paid for. The exodus from the farms around 1800 had been accompanied by better methods of cultivation and improved farming technologies. Until recently,

British farmers could boast some of the most productive farm units in the world. The loss of agricultural manpower had been, if anything, a stimulus to a better farm industry. Alas, the example was not to be repeated when industry began to lose its labour to the service sector.

For more than a century, British manufacturing has been in decline. Its quality of product has fallen, its capacity to invent new ideas and carry them through to the market has slipped steadily. New money has been invested in the fast-growing opportunities in banking and insurance, where profits are high, while factories have

Figure 3:1

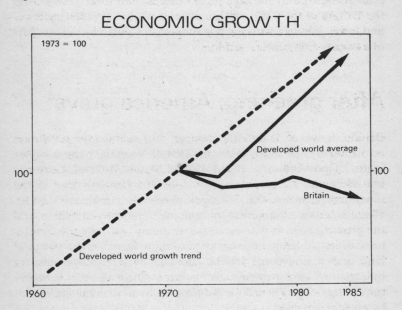

ECONOMIC GROWTH

decayed and the machinery inside them has taken on the appearance of an enormous inventory of industrial relics. The status-ridden educational system has ignored the changing needs of the industrial community, with the result that those decaying factories have faced the additional problems of a starvation of skills. This skills famine has taken on a new dimension in the age of microprocessors and laser beams; in this second industrial revolution Britain will be condemned to the role of helpless observer, unable

to take advantage of a whole universe of technological opportunities, new products and better working methods. For a hundred
years, Britain's industrial workforce has lagged behind, caught in
the habits that made the country 'the workshop of the world'.
Now, starved of the electronics skills, lacking the highly trained
population essential for survival in this new industrial era, Britain
seems condemned to remain exactly that. Several generations of
Britons saw the term 'workshop' as an accolade from those who
envied the country's factory lifestyle. Now, the accolade has
turned to condescending pity. A workshop is, after all, a pre-
industrial concept, a long way from the Coca Cola global metropolis trumpeted by the high priests of post-industrial society. And
the Britain of the 1980s will see even its workshops offering fewer
and fewer jobs to a working population confronted by the prospect
of a twenty-first-century serfdom.

After greening, America greys[4]

Britain, however, is only the pioneer. Just as it led the revolution
into industry, so it has been the first to encounter the complex
issues of post-industry. In the United States, Holland, Germany
and Belgium, the countries that followed Britain's lead in the
nineteenth century, the first signs of trouble are already visible.
There is but one difference: the collapse of industry in Britain, and
the growing crisis in the rest of the economy, will take the country
back to its old habits of social organisation, based on the power of
land and a traditional leisure class. Elsewhere, the demise of
industry will give way to more 'modern' forms of politics, where
the centres of power will be determined by new technologies, not
by ancient privilege.

As much has been recognised by those same gurus of the post-
industrial church. After a generation of teaching the wonders of
their Utopian future, they were forced by sheer weight of facts to
recant. How could they, after all, witness the decline of the US
motor industry, with its mammoth bankruptcies, and the collapse
of city finances in such places as New York, Detroit, Brussels and
a long string of other urban centres, without asking themselves
whether their optimistic theories have stood the test of time?[5]

Daniel Bell has now reversed his Utopian forecasts. He admits
that those visions of an ever-prospering America, which lay at the
heart of the post-industrial preachings of the 1960s, have now been
exposed as nothing more than mirages thrown up by the imperial
climate that overtook American intellectuals during the post-war
years. In *The Cultural Contradictions of Capitalism*,[6] Bell now
argues that the prospect of Utopia is slipping away:

> The reverse remains, that the period of American economic
> dominance in the world has crested and that, by the end of the
> century the United States, like any ageing *rentier*, will be living
> off the foreign earnings on the investments its corporations
> made in the halcyon quarter century after World War II.

One of the founders of the theory of economic evolution, W. W.
Rostow, has also seen the error of his earlier ways. In *The World
Economy*,[7] he writes: 'There is a danger not of a great depression
like that of 1929–1933 but of the advanced industrial nations being
caught in a protracted phase of chronically high unemployment
and low growth rates.' And for Britain, which Rostow once
regarded as the model of industrial success, he reserves a blunt
verdict: 'In a sense failure bred failure.'

The dream of post-industrial plenty is thus turning into a night-
mare of industrial stagnation and crisis, although complicated by
the emergence of destabilising surpluses in many areas of the
world economy, an additional crisis that is examined in Chapter 4.
The failing of America, the mounting problems in West Germany
and the rest of mature industrial Europe around the North Sea
basin, together conspire to magnify the shock waves as they wash
over ailing Britain in the 1980s. Many of the old industrial powers
will make the transition to another kind of economic framework,
with the help of planned strategies and the new technologies that
are already creating new forms of industry, new products, ultra-
efficient management systems. They will survive the decade of the
second industrial revolution; they may even reach the Utopia
promised in the 1960s by Rostow, Bell and their ideological
brethren, although it seems certain to carry the hallmarks of the
technological Hades of 1984. But Britain will not be among them.
That second revolution may take hold, but only in isolated sectors.
The bulk of Britain's tired economy has already had its day. As the

technological imperative creates a super-industrial constellation of
advanced economies – in Asia, parts of Europe, regions of the
United States – Britain itself will split into two. There will be a
small, closed world where knowledge is God and the altars are
tended by a monastic order of information brokers. And there will
be a vast backwater economy around it, where unemployment,
menial work, crafts, moonlighting, barter and brigandry are the
standard features of everyday life. For most people in Britain,
there will be no real life after industry. For them, post-industrial
society will be a replay of the Hundred Years War. And they will
find themselves on the losing side.

A NEW DARK AGES

4

A new Dark Ages

What is the nature of this new era of challenges that already over-shadows the frayed edges of Britain's disintegrating economy? Can it be any more serious than the disruption that came with the oil crisis of 1974, a threat that Britain's North Sea resources can now, we are told, so easily absorb? The new era is far more extensive in its impact and more dangerous than the world we have grown used to over the past five generations. It has been described by one writer as the Coming Cataclysm, by economists as the Fourth Kondratieff Cycle and by journalists as the Crisis of Capitalism. It is all those things and more. It is the revival of that brutal state of nature that preceded the rise of modern politics and economics. In this new order the law of the international jungle will prevail. The 1980s will be years of daunting change that will make the threat of future shock seem mild by comparison. And Britain could well be the first victim of its violent justice.

The new international order is no less than the old, primeval world of survival economics. After a generation of post-war peace and prosperity, underpinned by the international system set out at the Bretton Woods conference of 1944, the world economy has fallen prey once again to precarious instability. The habits of deference of the poor colonial countries to rich and exploitative masters have given way to assertive oil producers and aggressive nationalism. A strident Islamic revival has driven a wedge into comfortable Western expectations. A second industrial revolution of uncharted dimension offers technological marvels and the threat of overwhelming floods of information, new products, new industries and a clash of international competition as the struggle

Figure 4:1

INDUSTRIAL STRUCTURES

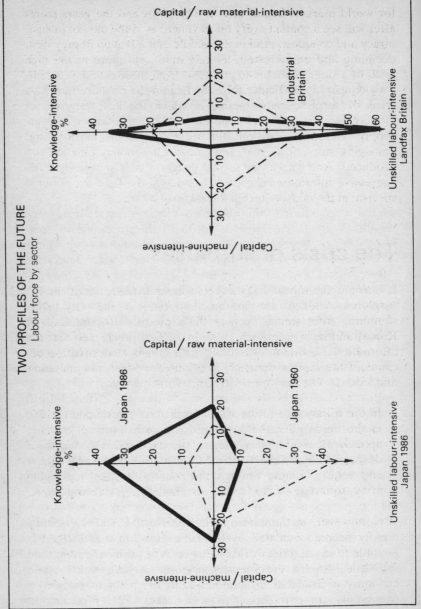

TWO PROFILES OF THE FUTURE
Labour force by sector

for world markets begins afresh. The 1980s and the years thereafter will see a conflict every bit as violent as in the days of pillage,
piracy and conquest. And in the middle of it a Britain ill-prepared,
declining and uninterested, looking more and more to the high
walls of a siege economy to protect it from these economic perils.
Two dangers in particular threaten Britain the offshore island. A
crisis of surpluses now looms, in which the key resources of
modern economic life will flood the world in an unexpected oversupply. Resource inflation will bring with it the tensions and
damaging side-effects that, until now, only money inflation has
produced. And with it, the second danger: a new mercantilism, an
aggressive international conflict caused by the fight for national
survival in the midst of technological revolution.

The crisis of surpluses

It is ironic that this new Dark Ages should be the result of chronic
surpluses. After all, the fashionable doctrine of the early 1970s,
stemming from studies such as those produced by the Club of
Rome, and by writers such as Alvin Toffler, proclaimed that the
international economy was faced with imminent destruction because of the rapidly diminishing resources of fuel, raw materials
and food. In *The Eco-Spasm Report*,[1] Toffler wrote:

> In the rolling green hills of Connecticut, in Dorset and Devon,
> in the fincas outside Bogota and the farms north of Sydney,
> apocalyptic nightmares plague the landowners – images of
> desperate city dwellers cut off from food, medical aid, energy
> and water, fanning through the countryside like a pillaging
> army, squatting on the farmsteads, stealing livestock and crops.

It is, however, in the nature of incontrovertible truths that they
rapidly become outdated by the facts. Now, in the 1980s, it is
possible to say that the world faces a crisis of too much rather than
too little. Almost every major resource needed by a modern
economy is available in abundance, to the point of dangerous
oversupply. In part this crisis was overlooked for ideological
reasons; it did not suit the members of the Club of Rome, or

like-minded economists elsewhere who called for an end to growth, to attract attention to evidence that contradicted their case. More especially, the coming crisis of surpluses escaped their notice because they were looking at the wrong resources. That oversight was to prove fatal to their carefully constructed arguments. For, instead of a world starved of key supplies, we now face a growing threat of being overwhelmed by excess.

Labour

World Watch of Washington have estimated that by the year 2000 we will need 1,000 million extra jobs to give work to the world's population. Put another way, we are confronted with a massive oversupply of labour. In the OECD area alone – that of the rich industrial countries – total unemployment is fast approaching 20 million. In the developing world, the unemployment level is many times greater.

Information

Knowledge is power; without it no modern economy can function. Yet, because of the micro-processor and the ancillary systems of the electronic revolution the industrial world will rapidly approach information overload. A little knowledge is a dangerous thing; too much information, like too much purchasing power, creates a risk of knowledge inflation. Business will be choked by excessive administrative detail; government will amass personal data to the detriment of liberty and privacy; individuals will be inundated by facts and figures. The new social disease of the twenty-first century will be Educated Incapacity – caused by an excess of dry, technical knowledge destroying the ability to take decisions on ordinary human grounds such as courage, imagination or even love.

Money

The 1970s will go down as the decade of too much money. In Chile the prices spiral touched 1,000 per cent, in Argentina and Brazil it soared to three-figure levels. And in the developed industrial world of Japan and the North Atlantic the decade was haunted by the spectre of prices gone mad. Milton Friedman was to be canonised as the patron saint of a new religion – monetarism.

Most people were content to point to the oil crisis of 1974 and 1975 as the cause of rocketing prices. The real reasons for the coming of permanent inflation are complex but can be summarised in outline terms. Since the beginning of the post-war era the spending power of millions has been steadily boosted by new forms of money. Easy credit, plastic cards, large-scale bank-borrowing to buy houses or cars – all have added uncounted spending power to the earnings of households. In addition, the financial system became more efficient in the way it moved that spending power around. New technologies such as electronic funds transfer – the use of computer networks to register purchases, credit or debit bank balances or settle bills – bring a further dimension to this pattern of increasing efficiency. The result is that spending power now moves so quickly it can be in two or more places at once. The same amount of money can be used several times over at the blink of an electronic eye.

In the late Middle Ages the discoveries of distant lands yielded untold riches: spices, silks and incense. But eventually they brought a vast influx of purchasing power in the form of silver from the Americas. Prices across Europe went through the roof. The governments of the day played with interest rates to protect themselves. The price of gold rose constantly. Cities and even governments reneged on their growing debts. And taxes went up; in Florence, so long considered a model of good administration, the tax burden became so great that the population began to leave. The parallels with life in the 1980s are too close for comfort.

Technology

Industry thrives on inventions. The first industrial revolution was triggered off by an escalating supply of better machines, in cotton spinning, brewing, agriculture, mining. But the process of absorbing these new techniques was slow, spread over more than a century. In the second industrial revolution the rate of flow of high technologies has begun to reach destabilising proportions. Too much technology could produce a 'technological crisis' totally unforeseen by the researchers who have produced the new ideas. The coming of the motor car, for instance, was hailed as an unmatched contribution to the quality of civilised life. In the 1890s it was possible to write:

The improvement in city conditions by the general adoption of the motor car can hardly be overestimated. Streets clean, dust-less, and odorless, with light rubber-tyred vehicles moving swiftly and noiselessly over their smooth expanse would elimin-ate a greater part of the nervousness, distraction and strain of modern metropolitan life.[2]

Who would have told him then what mechanical hell would eventu-ally overtake those same metropolitan streets?

At least the technological threats of old industry seem tangible, visible dangers. A 1986 technological crisis will be quite a different matter. Information technology already poses a dire challenge to the quality of individual life. Through the 1980s the access to and control of such information systems will take on increasingly feudal form, with knowledge power concentrated in fewer and fewer hands to the detriment of a growing mass left outside the walls of the computer demesne.

Other high-technology enterprises are fraught with risk. Herman Kahn has identified almost seventy separate problems under the heading 'technological crises'. They range from the un-expected side-effects of intrinsically dangerous technological experimentation in molecular biology, genetics and chemical research to bizarre possibilities such as generational changes, interplanetary contamination, super-cosmetology, and new forms of humanity including 'live' computers.[3] The New Dark Ages will have more than their fair share of torture.

Food

Throughout the post-medieval period food supply has been a perpetual source of panic. The writings of the Reverend Malthus at the turn of the nineteenth century dwelt sombrely on the prospect of global famine and mass starvation as the population grew beyond the level of the world food supply. The new pessi-mists of the early 1970s returned to the same theme. In the words of the economist Leonard Silk: 'The crisis stems not from a de-ficiency of demand but of supply, the most dramatic manifes-tations of which have been shortages of food.'

The new pessimists were wrong, as they were on the entire range of issues they addressed. The world is not short of food and shows itself capable of maintaining a food production *surplus* until well into the twenty-first century. Research recently completed by specialists at the Organisation for Economic Co-operation and Development in Paris provided the following conclusions:

1   Agricultural production doubled in the twenty-five years to 1975; in the developing world it grew by more than 130 per cent.

2   This level of production has been sufficient to exceed average per capita requirements across the world. Global agriculture today produces enough to give every individual a daily intake of 3,000 calories – better than many in Europe already enjoy.

3   'World food demand in the year 2000 will not be pressing against physical limits' to production; world supplies of arable land could be increased by 50 per cent by 2000.

4   Grain yields in Asian and African developing areas are only one-third of the level in advanced neighbours like Japan; new technologies could produce an agricultural boom across these vast acreages.

5   The world supply of usable land is easily sufficient for future needs.

6   World agriculture generally is on the brink of a technological revolution that will raise output substantially: *high-yielding grasses* will improve pastoral conditions; *improved feed conversion ratios* in the livestock sector will lead to increased meat production; *new cereal varieties* capable of producing their own nitrogen requirements will transform existing notions regarding fertiliser usage; *new possibilities for multicropping* will add to acreage yields.[4]

By the beginning of the next century the world farming industry could be encountering a problem of surpluses every bit as damaging to specific countries as has been the surplus in world steel in the 1970s. The causes of that food surplus would be the same – the entry of new producing countries into the framework of world food production. And, as with steel, the consequences for the

British farming sector could be very damaging. British steel found itself too inefficient and too expensive to face the challenge of price-cutting that world surplus brought with it. British farming could meet the same fate. Against European farmers the fight to maintain supremacy has already been lost. Now, with the competition to come from rapidly improving third world producers, the crisis of surpluses could strike right at the heart of the most ancient of Britain's industries.

Energy

The 1970s became dominated by an energy paranoia; if resources were fast running out, said the theory, then energy would be the first to reach crisis-point. The anxiety was misplaced. World resources of energy are easily sufficient for the needs of mankind over the foreseeable future. Certainly, energy supply will not be a constraint on economic growth in the twentieth century and will even run into surplus if a technological breakthrough suddenly transforms the cost pattern of currently expensive fuels. Such has been the experience of the developed world since the birth of industry. A glance at the statistics of energy resources in Table 4:1 will illustrate the falsity of the energy doom-mongering that became such a profitable industry in its own right after the oil crisis of 1974–5.

The statistics are clear; on current projections of world consumption, even existing fossil fuel resources are more than adequate for several centuries. If new technology options are included, there is a possibility of an energy glut before the year 2000. Here are some examples:

1   Using *breeder reactors*, the fission method of utilising uranium and thorium could yield the equivalent of 125,000,000,000,000,000 tonnes of oil in terms of energy – or, to be scientific about it, 125×10^6 MMTOE (billion tonnes oil equivalent).

2   Some estimates suggest that resources available for *D–T (lithium) and D–D reactors* are such that energy yielded through fusion processes could be as much as 250×10^6 MMTOE, a figure so great as to make reference to it irrelevant.

3   Solar energy is, of course, an open-ended resource; each year the earth's surface receives solar energy equivalent to 100,000 MMTOE.

PRINCIPAL FOSSIL FUELS AND WORLD CONSUMPTION

Table 4:1

	World Reserves ($Q = 10^{18}$ BTU*)	Potential World Reserves ($Q = 10^{18}$ BTU*)
Oil	3·7	14·4
Natural gas	1·0	15·8
Coal (incl. lignite)	95·0	170·0
Shale oil	19·0	2000·0
Tar sands	1·8	1·8
Total	120·0 Q	2200·0 Q
Years of world consumption at current projections	102	500

*British Thermal Units

Sources: *Exploring Energy Sources: A Preliminary Report*, Washington DC 1974; *US Mineral Resources*, US Government Office, Washington DC 1973; *Resources and Man*, National Research Council, Committee on Resources and Man, W. H. Freeman, San Francisco 1969

Such figures are difficult to grasp in terms that make sense of current problems. Compared with current world consumption of energy they are limitless: in 1974, as the oil crisis struck, the world consumed energy equivalent to 5·6 MMTOE. By the beginning of the next century it will have reached roughly 15 MMTOE. Nuclear and solar resources represent but two of the vast energy stores that exist in untapped form, awaiting a technological leap that will bring them into everyday use. Political resistance has played its part in restraining the exploitation of nuclear sources. Such resistance will not stand in the path of other, renewable, energy forms (listed in Table 4:2) that could themselves transform the politics of power. Thus, energy surplus is guaranteed in the long term by technological imperative. In the medium term the

POTENTIAL ANNUAL PRODUCTION OF SOME RENEWABLE ENERGY SOURCES (MMTOE)

Table 4:2

	Technical Potential	Achievable Potential
Forests/fuel farms	5·7	1·9
Organic wastes	0·1	0·1
Hydro-electricity	2·3	1·1
Glaciers	0·1	–
Winds	2·3	0·7
Geothermal	0·3	0·2
Thermal from sea	0·7	0–0·7
Tides	0·03	–
Total	11·53	4–4·7

Source: International Institute for Applied Systems Analysis, Laxenburg, Austria 1978

different suppliers of energy – from the oil sheikhs to the coal companies and the national power generating utilities – will be confronted with a growing problem of price competition. To use the words of an authoritative OECD study:

> World production of energy will not be limited in any way by the volume of resources; future energy systems may be mainly based on nuclear energy and on solar energy. Once these systems are established energy costs should not tend to increase.[5]

New technology products are bound to create stiff competition, and the resultant new mercantilism will be dangerously extended by the crisis of energy surpluses. Energy mercantilism will manifest itself through a bitter struggle for safe supplies; it is no coincidence that in 1980 the multinational oil companies invested more than $1,000 million in the search for coal alone. The emergence of massive surpluses in energy supply will also mean an even more bitter rivalry of cost-cutting and cartelisation as profit margins shrink in the face of excess energy capacity.

Minerals

Despite the forebodings of the 1970s, world supplies of basic ores and other raw materials seem assured until well into the twenty-first century. As new techniques and new materials reduce the need for traditional metals the existing abundance of known reserves will turn into oversupply. In the words of analysts at OECD: 'Physical scarcity of industrial raw materials through natural depletion of resources and reserves is not a likely eventuality.'[6]

These cautious words, however, disguise the true picture. World reserves of key raw materials are now large enough to lead to serious oversupply if a trade war erupts between the raw material producing areas. As Figure 4:2 shows, known reserves of all the

Figure 4:2

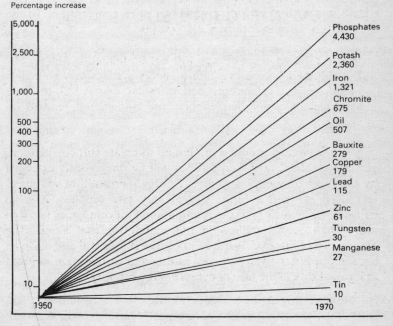

THE RISE AND RISE OF 'KNOWN RESERVES'

Percentage increase

important raw materials rose dramatically after 1950 as new exploration unfolded the immense wealth of the earth's crust. And then again, such huge percentage increases in reserves figures give only the vaguest guide to the magnitudes involved. At the start of the 1970s 'known reserves' of phosphates, for example, stood at 1178,000,000,000 metric tons, iron ore at 251,000,000,000 metric tons. Oil reserves are adjusted upwards almost by the month. In 1970 world reserves were estimated at 553 billion barrels. According to the International Energy Agency, this rising path of discovery runs parallel to a falling rate of extra use. In 1980 oil represented 52 per cent of total primary energy. By 1990 the figure will have fallen to 40 per cent. The consensus view within the oil industry is that total world oil reserves may be well in excess of 2,000 billion barrels – enough to supply the non-communist world for more than a century. And more than enough to draw a very large question mark over the economic viability of Britain's high-priced North Sea barrels.

The new mercantilism

Antonio Serra, a Neapolitan writer of the sixteenth century, made a reputation for himself by remarking that the kingdom of Naples had run out of precious metals because imports were greater than exports. A simple observation, but at the time akin to the discovery of DNA or the splitting of the atom. The mercantilist precept had been launched: wealth came through winning the battle of trade. But while the precept might have been newly defined, the mercantilist urge was as old as trade itself. Long before Serra, governments had used their powers to protect local merchants at the expense of foreign rivals. It was, for instance, as common six hundred years ago for politicians to impose a Buy English policy on the population as it is today for Ministers to encourage a Buy British campaign to prop up an ailing motor company.

All through the centuries the mercantilist tradition has persisted. The English woollen industry was ruled by the protectionist institution known as the Staple. The Merchant Adventurers and the Baltic Hanseatic League were typical features in the age-old system of jealously guarded national or local markets. Indeed, the picture of pre-industrial Europe as a free-ranging anarchistic economic community open to any merchant is a blatant myth. To repeat the historian R. H. Tawney:[7]

> The medieval consumer is like a traveller condemned to spend his life at a station hotel. He occupies a tied house and is at the mercy of the local baker and brewer. Monopoly is inevitable. Indeed, a great part of medieval industry is a system of organised monopolies which must be watched with jealous eyes to see that they do not abuse their powers.

Now, after a century of experimenting in free trade politics, this old pattern of monopoly and national protection is on the way back.

In this new age of mercantilism the technologies are more complex and the products more sophisticated. But markets are still markets and rivals still fight for their growing share. From the days of Adam Smith, the first modern economist, to the mid-1970s the world flirted with a different way of doing business. It was called 'free trade', and from the nineteenth century onwards the industrial countries paid lip-service to the idea of one vast world market. The United States, Benelux, the European Economic Community, the General Agreement on Tariffs and Trade were all trumpeted as first steps towards ever-larger free trade areas. They were meant to put an end to the monopolies and trade restrictions that had always limited the free exchange of goods. It was an ambitious experiment; but it has failed.

The world of trade is returning to its old habits of aggressive competition – a new mercantilism in which the prime aim is to protect the kingdom against the ravages of too assertive foreign merchants. OPEC, or more especially its inner sanctum of Arab oil producers, is merely the modern counterpart of the English Wool Staple of the fourteenth century. The EEC is a vast Hanseatic League, closed to outsiders and organised around jealous units of national economic power. And in Britain the growing crisis is pushing the country inexorably towards a state of economic siege, with the enemy once again to be found in Continental Europe. Is there any real difference between those medieval guilds – the Drapers, Haberdashers and Merchant

Tailors – whose monopolistic ways made the life of the high street consumer every bit as restricted as that of Tawney's traveller, and their twentieth-century heirs, the trade unions? In the troubled years of Britain's economic decline it is these unions, with their demands for import controls and withdrawal from Common Market links, that are leading the way to the siege. Nothing changes in the mercantile world. Only the names are different.

Now, with the coming of the second industrial revolution, with its C3 society (examined in Chapter 9) and the growing crisis of surpluses, a new age of trade rivalry has arrived. The sheer explosive force of high-technology production and of twenty-first century products flooding into the market-place at ever-falling prices – such is the effect of computerised production processes and the vast capacities of modern logic circuits – makes a battle amongst the trading nations inevitable. The price war in electronic gadgetry will be just one part of this new age of commerce. The latest data processors can offer capabilities that once needed 30 tons of valve-driven computer; and these modern tools can be produced at almost zero cost and packed into a minute space. The price war in office equipment, in home devices, in games and educational tools, will be a fight to the death. The spoils of victory will be immense: the chance to dominate a world market worth billions. The losers could include the household names of the post-war era: Hoover, IBM, ITT. In the new mercantilist world of the 1980s and after, the huge bulk of these corporations could prove their greatest handicap as they face a challenge of high-speed change. And if they go under, what happens to ageing America as it lives out its dotage on the income that derives from, as Daniel Bell has put it, 'the investments its corporations made in the halcyon quarter century after World War II'? In the maelstrom that would follow, Britain would be the first to succumb.

Impossible? Who would have predicted ten years ago that mighty Chrysler would, by 1980, be in dire financial trouble, bailed out by government-guaranteed loans of $1,500 million? In the fast-moving new game of corporate survival, big is very definitely ugly and dangerous. In the same month that Washington officials announced their rescue plan for Chrysler, another US multinational celebrated the attainment of the magic figure of $1,000 million in sales. The little-known Norton Company had joined the brotherhood of commercial giants. But in the sudden death atmosphere of the new mercantilism the company board was far from overjoyed at its achievement. The chairman, Robert Cushman, wrote in *Business Week*:

> The simple fact is that we are not doing as well as our figures suggest. No company is. And the future is far from rosy. I think the public should join the real world. The health and future of American corporations are not what they appear to be and people should understand this. It will take a truly enlightened society to rebuild our industrial plant, to compete in world markets, to create jobs for coming generations . . .[8]

Chairman Cushman had put his finger on the problem for America. For many of his US colleagues, the advice is still worth taking. In Britain, however, the process of ageing has already gone too far. The enlightened people never came; the industrial plant was not to be rebuilt on sufficient scale. The rest of the story is academic; those world markets are steadily slipping from the grasp of Britain's exporters, those 'coming generations' will grow up in a society where work is a luxury for the privileged few. The first industrial revolution was dominated by a small group of countries; so will the second be – but this time the domination will centre on distant places such as Bangkok, Taiwan and Tokyo.

Already, the crisis of surpluses is threatening the old order of industrial geriatrics, although the threat is posed by the products of traditional factory culture. Overproduction by the world motor industry has brought chaos to the giant corporations. Chrysler has succumbed. Ford in America is forced to hold back on new models in an effort to offload hundreds of thousands of unwanted old-model cars. The deserts of the south-western states have been turned into mammoth car parks to take the vehicles belching out from the production lines of US motor companies. Their sales are lower than at any time in the last twenty-two years. In May 1980, while Norton's Robert Cushman was writing his pessimistic contribution to *Business Week*, the US motor industry hit rock bottom. For every ten cars sold twelve months earlier, it was now selling six. As Japanese and European rivals pour their own vehicles on to the world market, this crisis will take a turn for the worse.

In Europe, meanwhile, the surplus in cars was setting off a chain reaction of bitter commercial conflict. The threat from Japan has produced a protectionist outcry against Datsun, Honda and the other Japanese manufacturers. Over the 1980s the next phase will open up: Europe's car makers will turn against each other in a battle for survival. By 1985 a massive world surplus of more than half a million vehicles will have overwhelmed the marketing strategies of the world's car companies. One cause is the well-publicised super-efficiency of Japanese producers; by 1985 they could be selling nearly one million cars in Europe, excluding the further 100,000 Honda cars that by then should be rolling off the production lines at British Leyland. In this sense, Leyland has already succumbed to the Japanese challenge. The real cut-throat fight is on Europe's mainland. As Volkswagen, Renault, Fiat, Peugeot and others compete inside a vicious spiral of competitive confrontation, invasion from non-European producers adds to the rising temperature. US car producers, struck by stagnation and decline at home, are planning to offload some 200,000 compact cars a year on the European market by the mid-1980s. Brazilian and Korean factories are spewing out cheaply made vehicles for the export market in an ever-growing flood. Even East European producers, having built their motor industry with the help of European companies such as Fiat, are preparing for an onslaught on the consumers of the Common Market. By 1985, they have planned, some 300,000 East European cars will be shipped to the EEC market each year.

Thus, an unparalleled crisis of surplus already confronts Europe's car makers. It is now being magnified by a second front in this commercial war. As the world car industry fights amongst itself for market share, the battle of car components is escalating alongside. As with vehicles themselves, components have created a vast market; by 1985 it will be worth some $15,000 million in Western Europe alone. The fight for this market will hot up as company after company hits trouble in the sale of finished vehicles. General Motors, Ford and Peugeot have adopted aggressive tactics to expand their footholds in the car parts business. Unipart, the offshoot of British Leyland, has managed to maintain a lead in the British market even as its parent company struggles against demise. But the campaign for domination of the parts market has only just begun. The production of motor vehicles is still the keystone industry in the developed world. Its job market is immense, its supporting role for other industries indispensable. As the world economy moves over to high-technology production and to a new range of consumer products, the motor industry will be used to hold the national economies steady during the period of change. The oversupply of vehicles and the battle for the market in components are pushing governments to look afresh at their weapons of self-protection.

Some governments have already decided on a strategy, in keeping with their own motor giants. They see salvation in the design and production of a 'world car' that they can build on a vast scale through a multinational network of factories. The new models would rely on a single world components system. And the placing of production lines inside the enemy territory of a competing country would protect the parent company from local acts of self-protection. It would seem an ideal formula for victory in the age of new mercantilism, with its permanent threat of import controls, anti-dumping suits in the courts and the emergence of a siege mentality, in countries, like Britain, where the national motor industry is disintegrating. More significantly, the coming of the 'world car' would put at risk those vehicle companies who are not large enough or strong enough to maintain a multinational presence around the world. These other vehicle companies, such as British Leyland, would be obliged to remain 'national-direct' exporters of the cars they produce. And in the cut-throat atmosphere that has now overtaken the world motor industry, such a handicap is likely to drive the last nails in the coffin lid of plans to resuscitate these local enterprises. In British Leyland the crisis of surplus could well have its first victim.

In the years to 1990 the market share of the 'national-direct' producers is set to fall. While worldwide car sales are expected to rise by 11 million units to 43 million by the end of the decade, the 'national-direct' exporters will see their share shrink by 500,000 or more. When British Leyland goes under, who will resist the call for a siege economy for Britain? The walls are already being built.

5

Don't shoot the economist

Economics has never been a serious science. Until the coming of statistics it floundered on the margins of literature and history as a polite pursuit for clergymen and noblemen. In recent years it has found its rightful place among the lower branches of show business. Indeed, the 1980s were to begin with a television extravaganza featuring the new superstar of economics, Professor Milton Friedman. In a series dealing with the sin of avarice and the money-printing powers of governments, this high-priest of the cult of 'monetarism' – a term Professor Friedman himself deplores – poured boiling oil on bureaucrats and punctured the most abiding myth of modern life, namely that money is good for you. It was a discovery that had already earned the econo-star a Nobel Prize, and around $200,000 worth of the very stuff he was condemning. Such is the debasement of the currency of the twentieth-century academic.

Nevertheless, the absurdity of a so-called science that takes two hundred years to discover that the production of too much of the commodity it has relentlessly praised – namely money – also leads to crisis and bankruptcy, escaped the attention of the masses who tuned in to watch *Free to Choose*. Economics has, indeed, far outlived its usefulness as a hobby for the leisured classes. There had, of course, been ample warning. In the view of the eighteenth-century English politician Edmund Burke: 'The age of chivalry has gone; that of sophisters, economists and calculators has succeeded.'

Mr Burke was right and in time the calculators were to become astonishing micro-processor brains that could all but dance and make tea. But the age of economists was coming to an end. The new world of industry that they were attempting to explain was elusive and fast-changing. It was a world with a hidden rhythm, a certain inexorable illogic. And it was not about to change its ways to suit the elegant equations spun by those latter-day sorcerers in their efforts to be liked.

It was only a matter of time before the promises made by economists turned to dust. Cherished notions about the coming of an age of prosperity have been exposed as hollow frauds. Governments and civil servants, so long regarded as the guardian angels of welfare in the cosmic process, are now attacked as overspending despots. Even money itself, so long the blessed host in the religion of plenty, is now rejected as inflation-producing poison. And all the ancient parables of the professors, about life in the prosperous kingdom of post-industrial society, are increasingly regarded as little more than a sham.

But don't shoot the economist. His only sin was in telling his political masters what he thought they wanted to hear. Politicians are in business for votes; economists crave the accolades of the intellectuals and the rulers. Meanwhile, the world changes. Now it has moved beyond the grasp of the social scientists. Economic truth is the first casualty.

Technology kills dreams

The greatest failure of economic theory was that it did not understand the impact of technology on business life. Now that the industrial world is in the midst of a sea-change in technologies, its basic weakness has been exposed. The second industrial revolution – of micro-processors, of advanced communications, of bio-technologies – has begun to overwhelm the shape of everyday life, from the factory to the farm. And no existing theories can offer a way of understanding or controlling it.

The developed world therefore faces a technological watershed. Old techniques, old processes have run their course, while the task of rebuilding the technological foundations of our economies – itself a complex and staggeringly expensive prospect – is being undertaken in a haphazard fashion. We have arrived at what

Professor Gerhard Mensch has termed the 'technological stale-
mate'. Throughout two hundred years of industry, we have moved
through great cycles of change as the result of sudden bursts of
new inventions. Each cycle has been marked by a technological
revolution – steam power in the 1800s, electricity and the rise of
mechanical transport in the 1880s, electronics and plastics in the
1950s. But each cycle has ended in a crisis of stagnation.

The 1980s are already marked by the onset of a fourth such
long-wave technology phase – a fourth Kondratieff cycle, to use
the name of the heretical Soviet economist who pioneered the
thesis during the reign of Josef Stalin, and paid for his prescience
by becoming one of the first victims of the Stalin purges. Kondratieff argued that the great upswings of production and invention
that had carried the industrial world into the prosperity of the
twentieth century had come in long sweeps of fifty or sixty years'
duration. War, he observed, had stimulated investment and
production. And the end of each cycle, he said, was marked by
technological crisis as a generation of productive capacity ran into
obsolescence.

Kondratieff was only half right. The developed world is rapidly
approaching a technology breakdown not because of a widespread
obsolescence but because the pace of innovation is too fast. We
are being throttled by an unstoppable tide of new inventions, new
products, a new universe of communicating and thinking systems.
To echo Jay W. Forrester, the specialist at Massachusetts Institute
of Technology who designed Whirlwind 1, one of the first high-
speed digital computers: 'We are unbalancing the system with too
much capital expansion and too much debt; enough capital now
exists to sustain consumption output for one or two decades with
little new additional investment.'

The rise of cybernetics, the flood of investment and research
money into the industry of 1984 – the information industry – has
confronted the world with a new kind of Kondratieff threat, the
threat of information surplus. The sheer scale of companies such
as IBM makes such excesses inevitable. The annual turnover of
IBM, at more than $22 billion, is greater than the entire national
output of Portugal. Cash reserves periodically mount up to above
$6 billion. The company's outlay on research and development
alone is greater than the total sales of Britain's biggest computer
manufacturer, ICL. Many other multinational giants, from Shell

to Philips to Mitsubishi, control the same level of financial power. Their dedication to the pursuit of technological supremacy for themselves is a guarantee that the overbalancing act of new investment will continue, all the way to technological overload.

But this technology overload is accompanied by a host of other economic problems and it is this convergence that makes the 1980s a period of unprecedented danger for Britain's weak and declining economy. To begin with, the Western industrial nations have collectively been locked into a synchronised recession of unexpected depth and severity. Through 1980 and 1981 they will have attained an overall growth rate of less than 1·5 per cent – for all practical purposes a zero performance that is insufficient to maintain the momentum of industrial rebuilding vital to the regeneration of the old manufacturing base. For the rest of the decade the prospects for major recovery are poor. Even in the collectivist economies of Eastern Europe and the Soviet Union the story of declining growth and industrial stagnation is very much the same. Soviet growth is running at the low levels of the 1930s. The onset of longer-term decline in Britain and other key economies such as the United States, Holland, Belgium and West Germany will ensure that this super-recession becomes a lasting feature of vast stretches of the industrialised trading world, certainly well into the 1990s – by which time a reversal may be impossible. In the words of Chrysler chairman Lee Iacocca, who began the 1980s with a $2 billion handout from government departments and banks to stave off bankruptcy: 'Free enterprise has gone to hell.'

If the traditional system of Western factory culture is breaking down, there is no revolutionary alternative to take its place. All the options suffer from the same technological crisis and pattern of decline. After the great decade of optimism, the 1960s, the world economy has slipped downhill. One principal cause has been the collapse of the old plutocratic system of colonies – in both the West and the East. Over the 1960s the developing world took off into a gigantic industrial surge. Their growth rate of industrial production is now twice as great as that of the old industrialised countries, and they seem set for continued high growth. The old industrial countries, in turn, have been struck by a crisis of profits. Well before the oil crisis carved huge slices out of Western money reserves in the mid-1970s, the rich societies had encountered a dwindling in their profit-earning power. In troubled economies such as that of Britain this profits crisis merely served to exaggerate the weakness of industry: in a typical year in the 1970s, the rate of return on capital in British industry was little more than a third of what it was in retailing. The result was a massive growth in Britain's high street retailing sector, and a further neglect of the needs of industry for new investment. Britain had confirmed Napoleon's apt description: Europe's offshore island was indeed a nation of shopkeepers.

'There is thus a choice. Remain as we are, reject the new technologies and we face unemployment of up to 5·5 million by the end of the century. Embrace the new technologies, accept the challenge and we end up with unemployment of about 5 million.'

Clive Jenkins and Barrie Sherman, *The Collapse of Work*, Eyre Methuen 1979

The rise of a second group of industrial economies, in the developing world, brought a direct challenge to the future of the old industrial nations, and the old world countered that challenge by abandoning industry in favour of a new technological Utopia. The future of Mr Iacocca's free enterprise system has been gambled on a computerised regeneration. But the transition to that new Utopia will take time, at least until the next century, and more than an average degree of luck. The developed world faces at least two decades of painful readjustment as it attempts to escape from its dying traditional industrial base into a data-dominated, automated, cybernetic, micro-processed twenty-first-century lifestyle. Not all countries in the Western world will make that transition succesfully. One of the candidates for failure is Britain.

One key problem is that of 'mismatch'. According to economists such as Dr Michael Beenstock of the London Business School, the shift from old industry to new super-industry is fraught with complex tensions. Dr Beenstock has observed that when a major structural shift is taking place – in this case from capital-intensive factory production to information-based activities – resources do not flow quickly enough from the outdated, unprofitable sectors to

the industries of the future. According to the 'mismatch hypo-
thesis' this creates a serious distortion in the pattern of modernisation, with bottlenecks in the supply of new skills, investment
and new locations. In the case of Britain this distortion has almost
reached breaking point. The jobs mismatch is now producing
massive unemployment in one half of the economy – with forecasts of 4 or 5 million jobless by the early 1990s – and a skills
famine in the other. It is almost certainly too late to fill this gap
before the end of the 1980s; the educational and training system is
just not geared to a sudden change in industrial needs. And the
products mismatch is opening up a yawning gap between what
consumers want and what British industry can provide. More and
more new products are therefore being supplied through imports,
and putting added pressure on Britain's already catastrophic trade
balance.

The way the world works[1]

It is not just in Britain that mismatch, overload and decline have
combined to create an overwhelming anxiety. Says Stanford
economist Tibor Scitovsky in surveying the crisis of Western industry: 'The joints of that once wonderfully flexible structure are
becoming more and more calcified and rigid.' To the question:
'Will the patient survive?' no two economists can agree an answer.
But then, neither can they agree on the question itself, so different
are their respective viewpoints about the way the world works.
Quite contrary to the prevailing ideology of the 1960s – that the
world had become one vast economy – the new Dark Ages have
shown how anarchistic, how dangerously diverse, the real world is.

Since the smooth progress of the Bretton Woods system, established in 1944, was interrupted in 1971 with the de facto devalu-
ation of the US dollar, a giant question mark has hung over the
future of the Western economic structure. Beneath the problems
of transition to super-industry, of jobs mismatch, falling profits
and stagnating growth, there has been a fundamental change in the
biology of industrial life. That change can be summed up in two
seemingly obscure phrases: the Laffer Curve rebellion and the
post-materialist counter-culture.

The post-war international economy created at Bretton Woods was doomed from the outset to enjoy only a relatively short span of life. It was by definition an artificial system, erected and sustained by carefully worded technical arrangements and policed by the rich countries for whose benefit it had been created, and it was bound to falter as those countries' wealth and strength waned. But throughout its thirty-year existence the system relied on a very precarious assumption, namely that taxation was totally free of political considerations. This assumption flew fully in the face of the basic message of the Laffer Curve.

'There are always two tax rates that yield the same revenues,' says Arthur Laffer, a professor of business at the University of Southern California. In simple terms the point is this: when the tax rate is 100 per cent, all production ceases in the money economy. Even at £1,000 a day in wages, working for money would become senseless. But if the tax rate is zero, production in the money economy is limited only by the taste of the working population for leisure, since the people grow rich on the untaxed wages that they can earn. However, and this is the obvious catch, at neither extreme can the money economy function. With zero taxes there will be no government, and therefore anarchy will overtake everyday life. With 100 per cent taxes the money economy will disappear; workers will operate a barter system.[2]

The Laffer Curve, as shown in Figure 5:1, was designed to describe this predicament. At both extremes, for different reasons, government revenue will be zero. As the tax rate rises to B or D government revenues still increase, but at a decelerating pace as taxpayers lose interest in producing. As the tax rate rises still further to C or A, production ceases altogether. And government revenues fall to zero. The optimum point for the tax rate is E. At this point people are still prepared to continue production; government tax revenues are at their maximum. A move in tax rates towards either D or C will reduce revenues. It should be noted, nevertheless, that E is not necessarily half way up the scale between 0 and 100. It is the tax rate point at which taxpayers are still producing and the government is enjoying its maximum taxing power. The art of politics is to discover where E lies for the community you are supposed to govern.

In the post-war period, as welfare politics became a normal part of industrial life, the E point moved steadily up the tax rate scale.

Figure 5:1

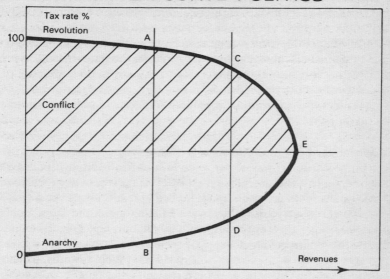

LAFFER CURVE POLITICS

Government spending rose as welfare programmes took over a growing proportion of national activity. By the mid-1970s British public spending – central and local government combined – accounted for some 60 per cent of national output. That trend had gathered force as all shades of political opinion accepted the welfare state; after all, it had been the product of initiatives from all three major political parties. The education system rested on the 1944 Act, created by the Conservative R. A. Butler. The health service was the result of work by Aneurin Bevan, a Labour politician, culminating in the National Health Service Act of 1946. And the social security system was built on foundations laid down by Liberals such as Asquith, helped by reforming civil servants such as William Beveridge. But this political consensus did not stop the E point rising along the Laffer Curve to the point of rebellion. Taxes reached a level of breakdown. In 1968 the British government collected some £8·5 billion from individuals and companies; ten years later the tax take had leapt to £33 billion. In both cases a Labour government was in power; in both cases the

burden fell on the mass of average wage-earners. The Laffer
Curve said: The welfare state is a con, giving money at one end
and taking it away at the other. The Laffer Curve was right. As J.
C. Kincaid notes in *Poverty and Equality in Britain*:[3]

> Widespread poverty is a direct consequence of the limited
> effectiveness of social security provision. Whatever may have
> been the case in the immediate post-war period, the social
> security schemes in Britain now fail to match the standard of
> those which operate in comparable industrial societies on the
> continent.

By the early 1970s the average British pension, at 17 per cent of
average earnings, was at the same level it had been in 1937. And
the taxpayers who were being asked to pay for this failing welfare
system were themselves being moved steadily along the Laffer
Curve to poverty; rising taxes were taking more and more from
wage-packets that were shrinking as inflation and low economic
growth ate into buying power.

By the 1980s the scene was set for a slide towards feudal
economics for Britain. The Laffer Curve effect had produced a
vicious circle that imprisoned millions. Taxes could only be
reduced at the cost of massive impoverishment as public services
were cut, welfare payments curtailed and government aids to limp-
ing industry were eliminated. The accelerating collapse of Britain's
industry had already depressed the wages of millions to below the
tax threshold, so the new regime of lower taxes would pass them
by. Those who would gain would be the big taxpayers; the tax-
cutting budget of 1979 took nearly half a million people out of the
higher tax bracket. The amount given back to big investors
through the relaxation of the investment income surcharge was
£780 million a year, more than ten times the benefit given to
one-parent families, nearly three times the gain to the elderly from
increased age allowances and seven times the improvement in
supplementary benefits, the primary guarantee of subsistence for
many poor families. As the Laffer Curve cuts more deeply, the
vicious circle will close. Britain will become, once again, the two
nations of the first decades of industrialisation.

Which way to the feudal economy, squire?

The politics of the Laffer Curve have remained a mystery even to the most enlightened rulers. When tax rates are high, government revenues are eroded by a mass exodus of the population from the official money economy. Put another way, punitive levels of taxation drive people into evading tax by working outside the tax system or by bartering instead of paying with notes and coin. This has been true all down the centuries. A chief cause of the collapse of the Roman empire was the change in tax policy introduced by Constantine. After a universal poll tax was brought in to replace a motley array of tithes, customs duties and levies, the people in the Roman provinces rebelled against Roman rule and supported the barbarians, whose tastes were less refined and who therefore needed far lower taxes.

The barbarians had more than their share of good sense; likewise the Mohammedans, who subjected their conquered populations to a simple tribute rather than to the comprehensive greed of the Greek administrators whom they replaced. But the hunger of modern governments for revenue knows no bounds, even to the point of admitting hitherto taboo activities into the money economy in order to exact taxes. Gambling, pornography and prostitution are now regarded as proper sources by the tax-gatherers. In Britain gambling alone produces an annual tax revenue of more than £300 million. And in the end such avarice ignites a quiet rebellion amongst the taxed. A sub-economy flourishes once again, as it did throughout medieval times.

British tax specialists estimate that there now exists a 'black economy' of more than £10 billion. It could well be closer to £15 billion, or roughly 10 per cent of the national economy. This black economy consists of work carried out and payment made with the intention of escaping tax. All manner of jobs, from plumbing to legal services, and all manner of payment, from used pound notes to complicated company perks, make up this hidden world. It represents a rebellion on the grand scale, and takes a growing sector of Britain's economy back into the commercial lifestyle of the Middle Ages. In the fifteenth century the money economy covered only a fraction of economic life. More primitive forms of doing business, chiefly barter, carried most of the burden of making a living. Cattle were a popular exchange currency in many European markets, where animals on the hoof were readily accepted in payment for ploughshares, nails, harnesses and string. The English ambassador in Constantinople concluded a deal in 1588 whereby English cloth was paid for in 'white cattle' shipped from Danzig. And now 'fiscal poaching', the symbol of the black economy of the 1980s, has emerged as a modern counterpart to the rabbit-stealing of yesteryear.

Beating the Laffer Curve is not a purely British sport, though in Britain it falls into a more recognisable pattern of a return to feudal ways. The Finance Office of New York City, the Soviet Politburo and the city authorities in Brussels have each in their turn laughed at Laffer and come unstuck. New York went bust in 1975 after thousands of citizens migrated into neighbouring states to escape city tax demands. The city fathers were left with a rising tide of salary and pension obligations to teachers, firemen, police and refuse collectors. In the Soviet Union the regulation of food prices is necessary because 34 million Soviet farmers are taxed at a rate of 90 per cent – which is the result of the government's policy of allowing farm workers to keep only 10 per cent of the food they grow. This high tax rate lowers the production of food, in classic illustration of the Laffer Curve. Low food production means high prices or, in the Soviet case, price controls and very long queues of urban consumers. The accumulated cost of this queuing is a primary cause of low – and falling – productivity in the manufacturing sector of the Soviet economy. And in Brussels, Detroit, Jersey City and Buffalo the Laffer Curve has struck just as hard, in different ways but with the same effect.

Beyond the Laffer Curve, however, another more pervasive force is at work. It can best be described as the emergent Post-materialist Culture, and as it gathers increasing support over the 1980s it will magnify the growing trend towards a feudal re-ordering of Britain's society.

Position comes first

The industrial economy that has existed since around 1750 was built on the production of what can be called democratic wealth – that is, consumer goods that were made available, at affordable prices, to the broad mass of the population. Now, as industrial societies reach an advanced stage of maturity, all the rules are being broken. Democratic wealth is now overshadowed by a new phenomenon: oligarchic wealth. Such wealth is destined only for the rich few, and its importance will grow as the crisis of surpluses takes hold.

The rise of oligarchic wealth can be attributed to the emergence of what the late Fred Hirsch described as 'the positional economy'.[4] In essence, the positional economy revolves around exactly what its description suggests, namely status and privileged position. As the number of consumers grows and ordinary consumer goods lose their scarcity value, the market-place will take on new shape. Value will be given to those goods that are scarce for other reasons: (a) because of a special status imposed socially, (b) because of rarity, and (c) because of the effects of overcrowding or congestion. Almost by definition, positional goods are in fixed supply. They include antiques, a title, space on the beach, deference from others and access to privileged information. In short, they are the goods that only a small influential group can acquire, whether through great wealth or special social status. The positional economy is a twenty-first-century variant on the feudal society of peasants and princes.

Satisfaction is derived from the use of positional goods precisely because they are scarce in the social, as opposed to the material, sense. Hirsch sets out three categories of such goods. There are those that have value because there is a physical limit to their supply, for instance a Tiepolo painting or a Bernini sculpture. There are goods that are given a false scarcity through the imposition of social value, invariably by the very class or group that has privileged access to them. Membership of London's private clubs, or the gilt-edged English foxhunts such as the Quorn, are typical examples. And finally, there are those things that are made scarce by the operation of a powerful social mafia across a much broader range of opportunities. The screening of candidates for top jobs, the granting of peerages and knighthoods, the closed-shop functioning of the financial institutions of the City of London – all work through the string-pulling machinery of privilege, social status and the magic PLU formula. PLU is the final accolade: it stands for that class set aside from the rest by accent, education, lifestyle and lineage: People Like Us.

In time the positional economy will steadily replace the old consumer society with its democratic wealth. The speed at which this is completed depends on how quickly the consumer economy disintegrates or dies of congestion. In Britain's case the rapid decline in living standards and the resurrection of ancient habits of status and division will accelerate the process. Jobs will become subjected to new forms of deference and rank, even at the most mundane levels of employment. The clamour for a new age of privilege – manifested in the talk of a return to the creation of hereditary peerages – will transform itself into a society of honours and patronage far more effective in its intent, far more feudal, than the comparatively harmless – though symbolic – system of patronage that has persisted into this industrial age. A peerage for a friendly raincoat manufacturer, knighthoods for businessmen who have helped with political funds, all these are descended from the medieval political process. But their symbolic significance has lain dormant, and they have been accepted by a wary populace as the harmless gifts of rulers. Now, with that populace steadily overwhelmed by the collapse of the economic vitality that gave them the spirit to laugh at this system of gifts, the patronage system takes on new meaning. In the positional economy titles come first.

Above all, the shift to the positional economy will return Britain to the very heart of its feudal pattern of influence: the land. Land is the ultimate positional asset. It is fixed in supply, in Britain at around 41 million acres. It grants its owners a quaint, inflated sense of social power precisely because of its reflection of the feudal norm. In short, land ownership conveys prestige, and in the emerging positional economy, where industrial values become meaningless, prestige will be regarded as a commodity far more precious than money.

But the prestige that comes with land ownership will incidentally carry with it a reinforcement of the very economic tendencies that conspire to create an unequal society. For the 'consumption' of scenic land – a highly prized luxury in the future oligarchy – will run hand in hand with a rapid increase in its value. The flight from overcrowding, the search for the ultimate badge of status, will push land prices through the roof. Says Hirsch: 'The sequence will involve a cumulative process of capital appreciation that will accrue to the benefit of the early rich and their heirs.' Thus, the positional economy will ensure that the upper ranks of the future will be filled, as in pre-industrial times, by that very same class that was given rank by the Conqueror himself, namely the owners of land. And the cycle of social power will have found its natural starting point.

Ironically, the demise of democratic wealth will be assisted by the broad consuming masses themselves. The economy of Britain's future will steadily divide into two: the oligarchs, accumulating their positional prizes, and a growing number who turn the other way, against the dictates of material satisfaction. This post-materialist culture has already set down its roots in the Western industrial economies. In the decades ahead it will give added impetus to the rise of feudal economics and its governing maxim: 'The rich man in his castle, the poor man at his gate.'

Recent research conducted by the Organisation for Economic Co-operation and Development, an official body financed by the twenty-four richest industrial nations, has reached startling conclusions about the future of the industrial ethic in developed countries.[5] Its researchers uncovered a 'silent revolution' amongst the young in their attitudes towards the consumer society. In their own words, they had catalogued the evidence of 'an indisputable socio-cultural change, ushered in by the youngest sections of the population'. This silent revolution is described as the post-materialist reaction (see Table 5:1).

Basing their conclusions on a number of surveys conducted over the 1970s, the OECD analysts identified a dramatic shift in attitudes. It stood for nothing less than the rejection of the values that had been the foundation of industrial economics and of the democratic wealth that came with it. And since this revolution was most strongly evident in the 20–29 age group, it seemed clear that it would gain more and more ground as this age group spread into the middle echelons of society over the next thirty years.

The post-materialist culture can be summed up in a single phrase, though it exhibits many differing components. It is

SILENT REVOLUTION: A CHECKLIST

Table 5:1

Post-materialism	Materialism
Town improvements	Powerful national defence
Nature conservation	Crime control
Society in which ideas more important than money	Law and order
	Stability of the economy
Protection of freedom of speech	Growth of national output
A less impersonal society	Control of rising prices
Increased participation in living and working environment	
Increased participation at political level	

'modern' in its aspirations, but feudal in its consequences. The 'silent revolution' is an abandonment of the industrial lifestyle at the precise point where that lifestyle is moving in the direction of breakdown, inequality and the resurrection of privileged power. The emergence of the positional economy means a return to the medieval pattern of status wealth. Because the young have lost interest in high politics, there will be no group strong enough to resist that return. As the OECD researchers point out, the revolution is centred on the middle classes, the classes that straddle the divide between the barons of economic power and those who toil. The withering away of middle class resistance and ambition will be the final step on the path to the feudal economy. In Britain the journey has already begun.

A NEW FEUDALISM

6

Death to industry

The Britain of the 1980s has abandoned industry. Its factory work-force is rejoining the world of crafts, or increasingly languishing in the throes of irregular employment and the dole queues. Some 15 million people form a vast service class which works for a tight-knit enclave of money-makers, who make their wealth grow as they always did, through an intricate network of commerce dominated by the City. There is, in other words, a sharp division in the economic system between two distinct groups: those who toil and those – a tiny elite – who make money. The distinction has existed since the Domesday Book itself.

Sharp-eyed observers have noted this ancient division of Britain into a small pecuniary class, which pursues ownership and acqui-sition, and an industrial class that sees its function as that of providing workmanship. As the sociologist Thorstein Veblen recorded in 1899: 'The economic interests of the leisure class lie in the pecuniary employments; those of the working classes lie in both classes of employments, but chiefly in the industrial. Entrance to the leisure class lies through the pecuniary employ-ments.'[1]

Yet what happens if the leisure class is closed to aspiring candi-dates by a mixture of taboos and social barriers, as it is in Britain? What happens to the industrial class if the factory infrastructure is starved of new investment, of skills, of educated management because the money-makers find better havens for their wealth in the commodity exchanges and financial markets? In Britain today the answer is clear: the money-makers continue to grow wealthy, the industrial classes lose faith in industry – and the result is de-industrialisation.

The statistics of Britain's industrial decline make familiar reading. But perhaps a better perspective is gained if these statistics are used to sketch a vision of Britain in 1990, by which time the facts of that decline will be glaring and irreversible. It will be the Britain that George Orwell imagined when he wrote, in *The Road to Wigan Pier*[2]: 'As prosperity declines, social anomalies grow commoner. You don't get more aitchless millionaires, but you do get more and more public-school men touting vacuum cleaners and more and more small shopkeepers driven into the workhouse.' But first, the facts.

The decline of Britain's industry can be traced to the watershed of 1870, when the pecuniary class, which has never been comfortable with a large, energetic factory culture and the troublesome factory worker who comes with it, encouraged a shift to a more genteel society. A string of social reforms, aimed at dampening the ardour of horny-handed sons of toil, were suddenly entered into the statute-book. The 1867 Reform Act extended the franchise, as did further laws in 1874 and 1884. In 1873 the bewildering mass of convention and legal form that passed for English law was codified, more or less, in a Judicature Act. The 1870 Education Act brought national elementary education. A local government board appeared. In 1871 a Trade Union Act and a consolidating Factory and Workshops Act appeared. A long list of other legislative changes added to this great reforming flood.

The significance of this sudden flurry of reform escaped the notice of the wider public. But its effect was shattering. It came at a time when British industry was already on a path to decline, thanks to a widespread lack of interest among the Victorian elite in the problems of the factory infrastructure. The result was a neglect of industry at exactly that point in its life cycle where it needed new impetus to carry it into the mass-production age along with the United States and Germany. Britain opted out of industry to pursue the virtues of gentlemanly life. And from 1870 onwards British industry slipped steadily downhill, to be temporarily rescued from time to time by some unexpected bonus: an influx of treasures from the colonies, $6 billion in Marshall Aid from the United States after the Second World War, the passing benefits of North Sea oil.

By the 1870s the demise of industry had passed the point of easy rescue. The other elements in the British economic armoury were

to follow the same declining trajectory over the century that
followed:

industrial leadership	peaking around 1870
naval dominance	peaked around 1914
world creditor	peaked in 1914
empire	declined after 1939
inventive energy	peaked around 1965
population	declining from 1980

The productive power of British industry deteriorated, improving
only with the prospect of war, in true Kondratieff fashion. In
broad terms Britain's rate of productivity growth was only 60 per
cent as good as that of major industrial rivals. After the Second
World War the neglect of British industry became even more
comprehensive. The billions of dollars in Marshall Aid were
squandered on propping up the financial strength of the City institutions rather than rebuilding decaying factories and towns. It is
doubly ironic that the act of squander was masterminded by a
young Minister at the Board of Trade, Harold Wilson, who was
later to place such great store on the white-hot technological
revival of the Britain he led as Prime Minister. It is triply ironic
that the same Harold Wilson, by this time a knight, was then given
the task of discovering exactly why those same City institutions
had failed so consistently to provide money for the regeneration of
British industry.[3]

Throughout the twenty-five-year period from the end of the
Second World War to the oil crisis of the early 1970s, the rate at
which output was ploughed back into investment in Britain was
only two-thirds the level seen in the rest of the developed world. In
the early post-war years it was as low as 10 per cent against an
OECD average of 25 per cent. The cumulative impact of this
neglect was fatal. It was to lead to the decimation of British industry and the creation of vast industrial deserts where once
thriving production lines had stood. Imports flooded in to take the
place of ships and cars once made in Sunderland and Birmingham.
In time no sector of Britain's manufacturing base was to be saved
from the onslaught of foreign goods made with better machines
and more efficient methods.

In the 1970s – in a repeat performance of that flurry of self-examination a century before – there was a rush of concern about Britain's economic crisis. The literature that resulted was both comprehensive and authoritative. The US-based Brookings Institution, in a gesture that reflected a fear that Britain's disease would infect the United States itself, had already charted the tragic course of decline. Their report, *Britain's Economic Prospects*, set off a chain reaction of studies, surveys and learned dissertations. But the sorcerers missed the point. An earlier report from the Brookings Institution had already given the answer.[4] In *Why Growth Rates Differ*, Edward Denison had concluded that beyond the elegant phrases of the 'sophisters, economists and calculators' the real reasons why an economy would slide downhill were hidden in the special characteristics of each individual country. These 'residual factors' were incapable of strict definition. In Britain's case they were buried deep in the peculiarities of the social structure, where a hatred of industry, best described as the Dirty Hands Disease, pervades everything. Translated into the actions of the practical world, it meant that manufacturing industry was under-financed, badly managed and regarded as less than second best in the social firmament.

'Many educators dislike to the point of contempt the activities and the values of the industrial sector. They see it as dependent for its success upon pandering to the baser human emotions of greed and envy.'

Sir Alex Smith, Chairman, Schools Council, in 1977

Thus, while the developed world is going through a vast technological revival, Britain is being left behind. Despite an innate genius for invention – a talent just as true of Britain in the Middle Ages – the country has consistently turned away from the practical possibilities of new ideas. In 1948 that same Harold Wilson had told the House of Commons: 'In the past we have sometimes been slow to put these ideas into full use, or even occasionally neglectful of them altogether, often with very grave results.' But nothing changed. Two decades later the chief economic adviser to the British government, Sir Alec Cairncross, returned to the same theme: 'It is indifference to the possibilities of technical progress far more than lack of capital that prevents a more rapid improvement in productivity and income.' And still nothing changed. The resistance to practical application in industry was a deep-rooted prejudice against which the explosion of energy around 1750, at the start of the first industrial revolution, can now be seen for what it really was: for Britain, a flash in the pan.

Despite an impressive array of post-war British inventions – the fuel cell, the hovercraft, the unravelling of the mysteries of DNA, the building of the first supersonic transport – the world of industry slowly died of technological anaemia. Right across the factory landscape production lines aged and output stagnated. A random selection of sectors would uncover the same problem of too little change, too late. The production of bricks, for example, was revolutionised by the British invention of the tunnel kiln back in 1902. But the invention did little to overhaul the production process in British companies. Fifty years later the same invention was introduced into German brickmaking, and spread rapidly through the industry. By 1966 German brickmakers – only seven years after they had seized the opportunity – had achieved four times the British level of use of the tunnel kiln method. In two other cases, the basic oxygen steel process and shuttleless looms, British industry did not have the advantage of first access to the new technology. British steelmakers were last to introduce the basic oxygen process amongst the major industrial countries and British textile firms the third slowest to bring in shuttleless looms. It is no accident that steel and textiles are the two parts of British industry closest to total annihilation. And it is of no more than nostalgic interest that British textile makers pioneered, by many years, the use of numerically controlled textile machinery, itself the precursor of the electronically supervised devices of the silicon chip revolution.

But it is in the critical area of machine tools that Britain's performance has been most lamentable. It is this failure, above all others, that has dealt the death blow to industry. The British factory has become a twenty-first century museum of old manufacturing culture. A recent survey of the country's stock of machine tools revealed it to be older and less efficient than that of any of the industrial countries that challenge British goods in world markets. More than 60 per cent of the British machine tool inventory was more than ten years old. In Germany the level was only 35 per cent, in Japan just 37 per cent.[5] Worse than that, the British machine tool industry, the actual engine-room of the industrial sector, had run down to a point of outmoded vulnerability. By the start of the 1980s Britain was relying on foreign suppliers for these vital tools; imports were already running at some $600 million annually. By 1984, the forecasts indicate, orders for British-made machine tools will have slumped by another fifth. Exports will deteriorate and imports will continue to climb. The machine tool industry itself has been savaged by the decline. In 1971 more than 81,000 people were employed in the machine tool companies; now they employ fewer than 50,000 and the number is contracting by the year. And to the popular cry 'But surely old tools are best, their familiarity is their strength?' there is the answer drawn up by Sir Steuart Mitchell, a specialist on the machine tool industry. He calculates that Britain's old machinery gives a competitive lead to rivals such as Germany and Japan of the order of 20 per cent – the equivalent of a cut in their selling prices of one-fifth.

Thus, Britain seems doomed to a bizarre fate in the super-industrial world of the next century. From being the workshop of the world the country will become an archaeological site from the Western industrial past, full of entrancing and mysterious survivals. But there will be no industry. When the seeds of renewal were being planted by other industrial nations, during the 1960s and 1970s, Britain continued on its neglectful way.

In the crucial decade to 1975, when other countries were laying the foundations of the new high-technology infrastructure of the next hundred years, the British reaction was dominated by an immense lethargy. When the first investments in twenty-first-century techniques were being made elsewhere, Britain's research budgets fell consistently, from a national total of £1,365 million in 1964 to £1,293 million in 1975. In the vital electronics sector the spending stagnated; in aerospace it fell by one-third. Britain was the only example among the major industrial nations of a declining investment in the future. In Germany, for instance, spending on research and development leapt by nearly 50 per cent; in Japan it nearly doubled.[6]

And in the very building blocks of industry, the factories and capital equipment that will produce tomorrow's goods, the story has been much the same. In a typical year, 1977, the level of

British spending on fixed capital was actually lower by £250 million than it had been ten years earlier. The pattern for the 1980s is for more of the same fatal neglect. It is the official decision that the Britain of 1984 will be investing roughly £820 million of taxpayers' money in future industry through government-funded research and development schemes. Ten years earlier the figure had stood at £2,000 million.[7] In every leading industrial country assistance from government is regarded as essential if fledgling industries are to survive and flourish in the 1980s and beyond. In Britain the latent prejudice against industry dictates a very different view. In the 1980s the once-thriving industrial zones of Clydeside, South Wales, the Midlands and Belfast will slowly die. (The impact on employment in these regions will be catastrophic, as shown in Table 6:1.) To echo the words of EEC Commissioner for Industry Viscount Étienne Davignon: 'On present trends in a few years the UK will be overtaken by other future Community countries, particularly Spain.'

THE JOBS HOLOCAUST: NORTH VERSUS SOUTH

Table 6:1
Unemployment in the mid-1980s: a forecast

	% of workforce
South East	9·0
East Midlands	9·5
East Anglia	10·5
Yorks. and Humberside	12·0
South West	13·0
Scotland	13·5
North	14·0
North West	14·5
West Midlands	15·0
Wales	15·5
N. Ireland	20·0
Total in 1984	3 million plus
Total in 1985	4 million plus
Total in 1986	5 million plus

The first industries to die will be motor vehicles, shipbuilding and aerospace construction. Others will be increasingly threatened with extinction: textiles, instrument engineering, machine tool

production, electrical consumer goods, steel. As the profits of failing British companies drop into losses, capital programmes will be
squeezed and research budgets, considered a luxury in many
British boardrooms, will be axed. That vicious circle was described
in vivid terms in mid-1980 by writers in the business section of the
Sunday Times, as they surveyed the scrapyard of Britain's industrial landscape at the start of the new decade:

> British business faces an unprecedented collapse of profits.
> Battered by inflation, the soaring pound and astronomical in-
> terest rates, industrial and commercial firms can expect to make
> only £17 trading profit next year for every £100 made in 1979.
> As the crisis accelerates with the force of a tropical hurricane,
> the consequences for employment and the capital investment
> which lies at the heart of Britain's trading prospects for the
> 1980s, are dire.[8]

But then, the collapse of industry's profits is only the next logical
step in the unwitting destruction of Britain's factory base. The
more favoured financial sector, where investment has steadily
risen while industry went without, has seen its profits climb to
dazzling heights. To give a true perspective the writers from the
Sunday Times could have added that Britain's big four high street
banks had just announced, between them, combined profits for
the year totalling £1,000 million, much of it generated by those
same astronomical interest rates that were killing industry.

A more soberly worded comment came from the *Financial
Times*, where the writ of Lord Cowdray, the power behind the
pink pages of this City institution, insists on more measured tones.
Here the concern had shifted to the Stock Exchange, where real
profits can still be made, even in the middle of a tropical hurricane.
Said the newspaper's financial editor:

> Beneath an apparently unruffled surface an invisible crash is
> taking place in share prices on the London Stock Exchange. In
> reality the stock market has split itself into two. While share
> prices of financial, service and oil companies have been moving
> ahead breezily, the valuation of Britain's manufacturing in-
> dustry has been knocked down.[9]

This low-key assessment stood for nothing less than the final irreversible symptom of the death of British industry. The City institutions, for so long uncomfortable in the presence of factory chimney and shop steward politics, had signalled their desire to hive off the industrial sector into a quiet backwater of the world of money, where it would dwindle harmlessly, unobserved. The motto of the City operator is 'Sell in May and go away'; the better resorts, the country retreats offer peaceful respite from the rigours of jobbing, broking and dealing. The verdict of the City in May 1980 was a telling one. The shares of fifty major industrial companies were being sold on the London Stock Market for less than half their asset value. As news of the profits collapse spread through the dealing rooms and offices of the square mile (reliable forecasts pointed to a profit figure for British industry in 1980 of £2,500 million, less than one-third its level in 1975), the abandonment of industrial shares became a stampede.

'The North Sea oil problem or opportunity is the old story of the peasant who found gold in his back garden. It was the main economic issue in 16th Century Spain. In the case of Netherlands natural gas it gave rise to the misleading label of the "Dutch disease". It has arisen in Australia in relation to mineral resources where it led to the famous "Gregory Report". But it needs the British to make the discovery of black gold into a tragedy instead of a piece of good fortune.

'There seems no alternative but to abandon the spurious moralising which regards manufacturing as superior to other activities . . . '

Financial Times, 3 July 1980

The result was a confirmation of everything that had happened to Britain's factory framework over the preceding thirty years. Industry and the City were not of the same stuff. The City was founded on the manipulation of money, not on manufacture. The job of funding the factories of industrial Britain came as an unwanted intrusion on the City's self-governing lifestyle. The Temple of Mithras lies beneath its streets; like the worshippers of Mithras, the institutions of the City prefer the sunshine of distant climes to the dark satanic mills of Lancashire and Ebbw Vale. And now, after two centuries of temporary aberration in that lifestyle, industry has gone away again. The manipulation of money can now enjoy its rightful pride of place, unfettered by the claims of the makers of things. The splitting of the stock market into two rammed home the disdain for the industry of Britain's 1980s. The *Financial Times* summed it up:

> The 45 companies in the property sector, which between them employ rather fewer people than one of the smaller divisions of Guest, Keen and Nettlefold, are now valued at something like £3,250 million. This is comparable with the figure for the whole of the mechanical engineering and metals and metal forming sectors. London and Scottish Marine Oil Company, which has a grand total of 40 employees in the UK and which only a few years ago was no more than a gleam in its promoters' eyes, is now valued at more than the combined capitalisation of Tube Investments, Vickers, Dunlop, Tootal and Bridon.[10]

The City had, indeed, sold out in May. And for Britain's industry the message seemed clear: Rest in Peace.

7

Domesday 1986

When William the Conqueror ordered a comprehensive survey of the wealth and patterns of ownership in his newly acquired kingdom, the result was a snapshot of the country in 1086: who was rich, who was poor, who pulled the strings in politics. And it was completed without the dubious contribution of those modern-day sorcerers, the economists and the statisticians, who strive so frantically to give an air of scientific credibility to projects which are otherwise little different from that exercise nine centuries ago. There is one significant difference, however: the England of the eleventh century was an expanding, optimistic economy with its future before it. The Britain of 1986 will be but a shadow of that promised land.

Already the signs are there. The Organisation for Economic Co-operation and Development, basing its assessment of Britain's prospects on official government figures, reached the following conclusion in February 1980: 'The growth of investment, and thus productive potential, has been disappointing, entailing a process of gradual de-industrialisation.' Those cold, calculated words stand for social holocaust. De-industrialisation is a formal, academic word for the destruction of jobs, living standards and future prospects. It means rising imports, with a consequent crisis in trade; it means the disintegration of industrial communities where for so long family life thrived on the wages and employment of the factory; it means a dependence on foreign enterprises for the design, quality and operating characteristics of everyday products; it means the steady abandonment of those manufacturing skills that are the very cornerstone of a balanced economy. In the end it spells disaster for the vast service sector with its banking, insurance and other financial activities, since these services only exist to assist and support the work of industry. This service sector, with the money machine of the City at its core, will be forced to work exclusively for foreign industry; the City of London will be turned into an offshore state.

The trade crisis has already hit Britain. The decline of industry has thrown the weight of consumer spending on to imports. In the decade up to the beginning of 1980 the import content of home spending rose by 125 per cent for finished manufactures.[1] Over the same period exports, other than North Sea oil, rose by only 40 per cent in terms of the foreign exchange that they earned, since the decline of industry meant that even Britain's exports were now made up increasingly of imported parts. The balance of payments deteriorated over this period by some £4,000 million, its impact only blunted by the passing financial blessing of offshore oil.

The prospects for the mid-1980s are daunting. With Britain trapped in the middle of an illogical spiral of rising costs and rising currency – the latter produced by the insane mechanisms of the world money market, which sees no further than the supported wealth of North Sea oil – the level of exports is set to fall as British goods are priced out of the international market-place. By 1985 British exports are likely to be some 12½ per cent lower in volume than they were at the start of the decade. Imports, in the meantime, will be flooding in to fill the gaps left by the collapse of British production.

The consequences of this trade crisis will be an unparalleled drift towards national insolvency. Forecasters with the Cambridge Economic Policy Group estimate that by 1985 Britain could face a deficit on trade of some £8,000 million – equivalent to an entire month of national output. And thereafter the outlook would become steadily worse; as North Sea oil production levels out and even falls, oil imports will begin to rise, adding further to this staggering deficit.

The collapse of industry will, in turn, destroy millions of jobs. Entire regional populations, once prosperous on manufacturing, will be ravaged by the slow death of unemployment. On current trends of de-industrialisation there will be nearly 4,500,000 adults without work in the Britain of 1986. Apart from the social disruption that this would cause, yet another financial burden will fall on that shrinking fraction of the economy which still has work. The cost of supporting such an immense army of jobless would add some £2,000 million a year to government spending, a massive increase that would put an end to government plans to cut back sharply on public spending. The result would be higher taxes on individual wage-packets and dramatically higher levels of inflation – or a fall in wages. This time, however, the cost of living will not fall in sympathy, as it did during the years of the inter-war depression. In the Britain of 1986 prices will be determined in large part by what the outside world dictates.

To put this point in the technical phraseology of the economists, the long-term trend means that Britain's gross domestic product – the country's yearly output – will contract from £114,000 million in 1979 to just over £100,000 million in 1985. In crude terms this would mean that each individual would suffer a loss of income of roughly £230 a year. And there is no prospect that this frightening trend would change for the better in the years thereafter; on the contrary, this decade of poverty for Britain could well be only the beginning of a permanent slide to pauperdom. But then, such a curve of impoverishment is only a continuation of a well-established pattern. While Europe experienced a boom of growth and prosperity over three post-war decades, Britain missed the boat. In the twenty years up to 1980 Britain's national output grew at a pace that would, in an ideal world of equality, give an extra £1,100 a year to every Briton. A creditable performance – but well behind others in Europe. Ireland and Italy, two countries long regarded in Britain as poor European cousins, easily surpassed the British achievement. In Ireland per capita income rose by £1,300 over the same period: in Italy the rise was £1,400. Over the rest of the developed world the rate of income growth was nearly double that of Britain, at £2,000 per head.

Such comparisons of income can be dismissed as empty, materialist exercises. But in the harsh world of money such differences count, more and more as the law of compound interest pushes the income gap wider with each passing year. In 1980 Britain's national income per unit of population was only 50 per cent of the level of countries such as West Germany, Sweden, Denmark and Holland, and only 60 per cent of the level in France, or Japan. Indeed, the income levels in Greece, Spain and Ireland were closer to that of Britain than was Britain's to those of her richer

European partners. In practical life such comparisons translate
into brutal economic fact. The wealthy society can compete in
world markets for costly raw materials, minerals and consumer
products. Its citizens can travel more easily, and buy property and
business assets in foreign parts. At home, such differences in
wealth are the differences of which the quality of everyday life is
made. Surplus national wealth builds hospitals, schools and roads.
It makes feasible the redistribution of income in favour of the
low-paid, although such an outcome is not guaranteed. Without
such a surplus a redistribution is practically impossible, since not
even the economists have devised a means of making four beans
count as five. In short, the failure of Britain's economy to generate
adequate surplus wealth is a key factor in the drift to neo-
feudalism.

The new paupers

The 1980s are to be the decade of poverty for growing millions in
Britain. At the start of this ten-year period there were already
some 6 million working adults whose weekly pay rate was below
the poverty level of £60. Put another way, one wage-earner in
four amongst the adult labour force was on the borderline of
pauperdom – a twentieth-century version of the work-house
beggar. Of the 2 million part-time workers on the fringe of the
labour market, it has been estimated that one-fifth had earnings
that were 30 per cent or more below the level at which supplementary benefits became available. Is this very different from the
flavour of life in the Britain of the early nineteenth century, when
the Poor Law and the Speenhamland system were the outward
signs of a society that was divided between landowners and industrialists who demanded cheap labour on the one hand, and a
mass of underpaid labourers on the other? Then, as now, it was
the labourers who were castigated by polite observers for their
indolence and vice-ridden ways. The figures, set out in Table 7:1,
are instructive. In 1979 the earnings of the poorest tenth of male
manual workers stood at 68·3 per cent of the average; in 1886 they
stood higher, at 68·6 per cent.

But this picture of British poverty only touches the surface. The
stark figures stand for millions more people, mainly children, who

are increasingly caught in the trap of family poverty. For 6 million adults earning poverty-line wages there will be as many as 18 million family members steeped in poor-house ways. By 1986 this huge number will be added to considerably as millions of wage-earners join the ranks of unemployed, and see savings and household capital dwindle as loss of work turns into a permanent state of jobless serfdom.

'In 1795 the Berkshire magistrates, sitting at Speenhamland, philanthropically authorised the supplementation of agricultural workers' wages from the Poor Law Funds. These allowances, to bring the workers' money up to a living wage, were based on the price of bread and the size of families. The immediate result -- human nature being what it is -- was that all the local farmers lowered the wages they paid their workers.

'Substitute "rate of inflation" or "retail price index" for "price of bread" and "government collected taxes" for "poor law funds" and the Speenhamland system can be seen at work today.'

Michael O'Connor, freelance journalist, in 1980

This crisis of family poverty will add a new and disastrous dimension to the perspective of Britain's economic decline. Research published in the summer of 1980 revealed an already critical condition overwhelming family life. The social disease of low pay, from which Britain has traditionally suffered, has made it essential for millions of families to have both parents working if any kind of subsistence wage is to be attained. Even this has not prevented a dramatic slide into widespread family poverty. In 1977 some 1,260,000 families received an income which put them below the officially defined level for supplementary benefits – below what can be termed a subsistence wage. This 1977 figure represented a rise of 40 per cent in the number of pauper families in just four years. Just as striking was the discovery that this growing mass of people being paid less than subsistence wages was now as great as the number who were poor because they lived on retirement pensions. In terms of economics, apart from any social comment, this is absurd; British employers pay millions of people less for working than they would receive for not working at all, either through retirement or through drawing their money from social security funds. The mentality of poverty which afflicts so many British companies could, in the end, defeat them as millions stop work in order to raise their standard of living.

LOW PAY: LITTLE CHANGE OUT OF A CENTURY

Table 7:1

Year	Median Earnings (£ per week)	Lowest Decile %	Highest Decile %
1886	1·2	68·6	143·1
1938	3·8	67·7	139·9
1979	88·2	68·3	148·5

Source: *Poverty and Inequality in Common Market Countries*, edited by Vic George and Roger Lawson, Routledge and Kegan Paul, 1980; and New Earnings Survey, 1979

POVERTY: ON THE RISE

Table 7:2

Social Category	1968	1976	1976 as % of 1968
Total population	55,049,000	56,000,000	102
Pensioners	7,133,000	8,617,000	121
People aged 75 or over	2,491,000	2,847,000	114
Families receiving family allowances	4,257,000	4,592,000	108
Supplementary benefit recipients	2,736,000	3,050,000	111
Unemployed	560,000	1,359,000	243
Unemployed receiving suppl. benefits	235,000	684,000	291
Unemployed receiving no benefits	110,000	200,000	182

Source: Peter Townsend, *Poverty in the United Kingdom*, Allen Lane, London 1979

But the hidden crisis of 1986 will come through the collapse of work for women. Through the years of industrialisation Britain's factory population was swelled by the growing employment of women. At the start of the 1980s more than 10 million women formed a large proportion of Britain's labour force. Many of them have taken jobs to lessen the effects of low incomes. And many more will join them in the search for work as the economic crisis deepens and family budgets shrink. By 1986 another million women will have added to this number – but most of them will find the world of work a depressing prospect. Industrial decline has meant fewer jobs in production; in the twenty years to 1980 about one million women were forced out of industry as jobs disappeared. This decline will continue, biting deep into the availability of work. But the hidden crisis will come in the service sector – offices, banks and other administrative centres – where high technologies will destroy millions of jobs by replacing woman-power with thinking machines.

The service sector produced a revolution for women workers. The typewriter and the filing cabinet created a gigantic market for their skills. It may have been a refined prison, but it offered a earning power that before had not existed. In the post-war years this market was to open up on the grand scale. In the quarter-century to 1976 the employment of women in service activities rose by more than 2 million to 6·7 million. It accounted for practically the entire increase in service employment during that period. Most of the growth was in part-time jobs. Now that age of growth is over. The age of C3, the electronic century, has begun; it will eliminate the routine functions of the office, the factory and the high street shop. It will give the task of filing, copying and calculating to the garnet crystal universe with its infinite capacities for work. And the refined prison of services that helped support millions of British families through the employment of mothers will prove to have been a subtle trap indeed.

Over the 1980s millions of women will wake up to find themselves condemned to the dictates of what economists call 'the secondary labour market'. The rapid expansion of service work came largely through the growth of part-time work. Employers preferred the flexibility that was given by a twenty-hour working week. They could cover the periods of high commercial pressure, without the burden of paying full-time wages. And millions of women saw such part-time employment as a means of maintaining a semblance of family life. But this secondary labour market had its inevitable drawbacks: no career structure or prospect for promotion, no learning of skills, no protection through union involvement. In short, the secondary labour market is little better than the boonwork of eleventh-century feudal England – spasmodic employment in the service of the lord of the manor, its timing dictated by the seasons, its pay dictated by the whim of the landowner. And as technology reduces the number of jobs available to the twentieth-century service worker, employment will be given to the lowest bidder. The inevitable consequence of the collapse of work in the secondary labour market will be pay scales even lower than the ones already creating a crisis of family poverty for millions.

Much of this crisis will go unnoticed; women have traditionally been the victims of statistical error. A vast group of 'missing workers' – of unregistered unemployed – has long existed beneath the official figures of jobless. Thus, even the forecasts of 4 million unemployed for the mid-1980s are in need of upward revision. More important, the majority of these missing workers are women. Thus, it has been estimated that every time 100 more people are added to the register of unemployed, the true figure for unemployment rises by 214. Of these extra 114 missing workers, two-thirds are women. Most significant of all, a growing number of them are young mothers, attempting to raise family income to a subsistence level. Mothers of children under five years old were the most job-hungry seekers of work in the Britain of the swinging 1960s and thereafter. Unfortunately, they formed part of the secondary labour market, that pool of 'disposable labour' that gets work when times are good for business, and gets discarded when the curve turns downwards. It is no accident that the Royal Commission on the Distribution of Income and Wealth found that:

Those families where the youngest child was under five years old were on average worse off than others, no doubt because such families' wives, whose earnings are of crucial importance to a family's level of income, were less likely to be employed.

This is family life in the Britain of the 1980s: a growing number of households trapped by the labour market and by the spread of

GOVERNMENT ESTIMATES OF THOSE IN POVERTY: ON THE RISE

Table 7:3

(Figures in thousands)

	1960	1976
Under supplementary benefit standard	1,260	2,280
At or not more than 10 per cent above standard	710	1,630
Receiving supplementary benefit	2,670	4,090
Total	4,640	8,000

BRITISH POVERTY: NORTH VERSUS SOUTH

Table 7:4

Region	% of people in income units in or near poverty
Northern Ireland	50
Scotland	37
North West	36
South West and Wales	34
Northern, Yorks and Humberside	33
West Midlands	30
Anglia and East Midlands	29
South East	27
Greater London	27
All regions	32

Source for Tables 7:3 and 7:4: Peter Townsend, *Poverty in the United Kingdom*, Allen Lane, London 1979

low pay policies; the prospect of literally millions living below the officially designated poverty line by 1986, and millions more joining them by the end of the decade as the withering away of industry produces a jobs holocaust of unparalleled scale. Such a trend is perhaps in keeping with the doctrine of inequality preached by leading advocates of free market economics, the doctrine that has come to represent the spirit of this new age of realism. It is also an ingredient in Britain's drift to eleventh-century politics; inequality of wealth is the primary characteristic of feudal life. The rest is a matter of social habit, an area in which Britain is well provided, with the etiquette of the pre-industrial manor so close to the hearts of modern Britons.

It seems the greatest irony that this Britain of 1986 should be such a depressing place. After all, the year marks the centenary of the birth of one of the great symbols of democratic wealth, Sunlight Soap. In 1886 William Lever, the son of a Bolton grocer, started the mass production of soap in his Lancashire factory. He also launched into a massive campaign of advertising that was to make Sunlight Soap the trademark of the popular consumer society that mass-producing industry could make possible. Now, a century later, that industry is withering fast and the right to democratic wealth is falling under growing strain. All the more ironic that the wealth that soap gave to William Lever now pays for work which reveals the sad facts of Britain's crisis of poverty. The Leverhulme Trust, dispenser of the Lever family fortunes, was to fund the work of the Study Commission on the Family, which published a survey in the summer of 1980. The daunting statistics of Britain's new paupers, which form the basis of this chapter, are drawn very largely from their work. One hundred years; a country moves from clogs to clogs in three generations.

8

The siege of 1990

Inequality may bring national economic revival to the Britain of the twenty-first century, at least in the crude measures of national wealth that give no impression of everyday social conditions. But that pattern of inequality will be attained only at the cost of widespread social deprivation and the real possibility of political disintegration. As the country rediscovers the flavour of pre-industrial life it will encounter, too, the violent instability that is its most notable quality. Consider, for instance, the violent rebellions that marked the clashes of rich and poor in each century prior to the coming of factory culture. Chaucer's century was typical: between the Black Death in 1348 and the Peasants' Rising of 1381 the country was racked with strikes, riots and violent demonstrations as unions protested against the wage controls imposed by Parliament. Union leaders were sent to prison for their over-exuberance on the medieval picket lines. Pre-industrial Britain was a volatile fast-breeder reactor of social discontent.

Only the serious shortage of labour kept Chaucer's England from outright revolution. The deaths brought by plague caused wages to rise sharply; the strikes and wage claims lost their relevance. Right through the centuries the same cycle of riot and appeasement ran its course. Even the England of new industry, in the eighteenth century, was shaken by uprisings of what the historian George Rudé has called the 'pre-industrial crowd'. London was constantly the centre of massive dislocation as workers took to the streets: against non-conformists in 1709, 1715 and 1716, against Walpole's taxes in 1733, against the Gin Bill and the Irish in 1736, against the Jews in 1753. From then onwards rioting became a normal part of daily life; it was an inevitable result of the immense social changes that were being generated by the growth of industry.

But Britain did not erupt into full-blooded revolution as did France in 1789. In Britain a palliative arrived to stave off the holocaust that had overwhelmed the landed classes across the Channel. The coming of industry brought democratic wealth in the form of mass-produced consumer goods. Wages slowly rose to points beyond the wildest dreams of pre-industrial labourers. Through the nineteenth century this democratic wealth, with its soap powders, household gadgets and great Exhibitions, poured oil on the troubled waters so long stirred by the 'pre-industrial crowd'.

Now British industry is dying, and with it the prospects for peaceful transition to the second age of industry, that of micro-electronics and optical fibres. This second industrial revolution is taking hold only haphazardly across Britain's economy. Enormous tracts of the factory landscape of the West Midlands, South Wales and Clydeside are being left to decay. Some parts of industry will make the move into the new technologies, but even here the place of the individual worker will be threatened with overwhelming change. For in those factories where the Gollies and Robbies of the C3 society are brought in to run the production lines the impact of future shock will be even greater. While the dole queues lengthen, those left to work in the electronic factories will be surrounded by faceless versions of the workshops of traditional industry. The very rhythm of factory work will be revolutionised in favour of intelligent machines with TV eyes. The electronic factory will run for ever and a day: no meal breaks or personal problems to interrupt the flow of output. And its coming marks the end of an era for industrial working man and woman. In the C3 society of the future the one-eyed robot will be king on the factory floor. The human hand will take second place.

Hence, industry has turned full circle in its use of human work-power. The rise of the factory produced a massive population of industrial workers. Industrial trade unions grew up to complement the established groups of the pre-industrial economy, groups of craftsmen who had for centuries worked with metals, yarns and timber in their own homes, to form a cottage industry economy. During the nineteenth century this cottage industry infrastructure was replaced by mass-producing factories and mass trade unions. Through forming the Trades Union Congress and the Labour Party these new mass unions were to gain considerable size and political power: 2 million union members in 1901, 4 million in 1914, 12 million in 1980. Now the cycle is turning back. As high technology changes the face of industry, mass-production factories of the old kind are becoming outmoded relics. The rise of electronic cottage industry is taking the modern economy in the direction of the medieval household factory. The small technology-based firm is becoming the favoured unit for the computer-organised, technology-orientated industrial framework of the next century. And the role of manual labour will be reallocated to intelligent machinery. Knowledge labour will be the prized commodity of the twenty-first century, not the human hand.

The economy of the electronic cottage will offer a totally changed lifestyle to the average worker. In Britain, however, the prospect will be distorted by the poor national performance in shifting over to the technologies of the C3 society. While in countries such as France or Japan the change to new technologies will be more even and widespread, in Britain it will be patchy. Some industries will be revolutionised; most will continue on their path to decay. Thus, in Britain the social system will divide into two distinct parts, separated by a chasm of knowledge. It is this chasm that will lead to the siege of 1990.

There will be the tiny fraction that is modernised, with its optical fibre conduits, its word processors and its mini-computers, its facsimile machines and its teletext. The workforce of this sector will be educated and skilled in the arts of *compunications* – the buzzword of the C3 society. They will converse in a version of Orwell's Newspeak, a language he himself had imagined for the later years of the society of 1984 but which seems to have arrived already in the computer programmes of the information industry: 'byte-parallel 1/0', 'hexadecimal', 'ultraviolet erasable PROM', 'scratchpad RAM' are just a taste of the vocabulary of the closed world of compunications. This closed world will have its own monastic orders of specialists, steeped in the rituals of the computer. They will guard the secrets of their work jealously: millions in company' profits will hinge on the control of key data about markets, products or corporate plans for the future. They will shelter behind the protective walls of corporate security, and the vital computer store will be defended by the sophisticated weapons of electronic warfare: voice recognition devices to supervise passwords, decoding apparatus to prevent access to sensitive files by unwanted intruders, heat sensors to detect the presence of unauthorised personnel. They will in every sense reproduce the siege conditions of those troubled times all those centuries ago.

Outside the city walls there will be the other, forgotten side of the divided economy of the 1990s. The mass of unemployed, under-employed and the de-skilled will, by then, have fallen prey to the accelerating collapse of British industry. They will be the men and women who cannot find haven inside the domain of the information industry, because they lack specialised training or privileged access to the small job market offered by the compunications sector. This mass of unwanted labour will come to regard the information economy as a closed world to which they cannot be admitted. They will blame the destruction of their own wage-earner lifestyle, rightly or wrongly, on the privileged high priests of information with their magic electronic systems. And in the end their reactions could be as violent as those of their angered predecessors in the 'pre-industrial crowd'. For those early mobs the standard weapons were arson, the pulling down of buildings, the smashing of the offending machines. In the C3 society the response may be no different. Already, the computer strike[1] has demonstrated how effective the paralysis of information systems can be. How much more damaging to the computerised economy of the future would be the outright destruction of those heavily guarded data-bases through explosion or hijack? Thus, the scene is set for social confrontation – between information power and those left behind by the pace of technical change.

But the scenario of two nations at war between themselves is only part of the siege mentality of Britain's future. The crisis in the national economy, due principally to the disintegration of the manufacturing base, is pushing the country inexorably in the direction of a state of national siege, too. The mounting deficits on trade, the emergence of a new age of mercantilism in the international economy as countries compete aggressively for markets, raw materials and new technologies, the prospect of 3 and 4 million people without jobs, all point that way. It is no coincidence that the Confederation of British Industry began the decade of the 1980s by calling for selective import controls to protect hard-pressed British companies. The change of heart by the CBI is entirely in keeping with the siege climate that is rapidly overtaking the industrial sector.

Britain's economic problem is the result of failing industrial production. And where industry fails to produce, foreign manufacturers fill the gap through imports. In the short term, the result is a growing deficit on trade, as imports exceed exports on a steadily increasing scale. In the longer term the result is economic disaster; the eventual collapse of industry makes it impossible to pay for imports at all. Thus, the range of goods in high street shops runs downhill as home industry stops producing and imports become too expensive. The average household sees its range of choice steadily narrowing as the flow of democratic wealth, the consumer goods of the industrial age, dries up.

For decades Britain has sheltered behind a bizarre set of myths about its ability to pay its way in the world. Britain's perennial deficit on trade, ran the argument, was of minor importance; the great earning power of the City of London, through banking and insurance, would always save the day. Writers such as W. A. P. Manser were to make a literary career out of dispelling the myth of Britain's failure.[2] The trade figures, they argued, were a misleading anachronism caused by ignorance of the invisible exports of the City institutions: 'Throughout her history Britain's invisible earnings have generously exceeded her deficiency in visible incomes.' And indeed the dense statistics support the contention that Britain's invisible economy has been in strong surplus since the birth of statistics themselves. From 1826 onwards the figure for invisibles rose steadily. By the end of the 1960s the money machine of London's square mile was pulling in a surplus of £1,000 million a year. By the mid-1970s it was running at £2,500 million. All would be safe even if Britain's declining industrial performance created a growing threat of imports. Or would it? The drift of Britain's fortunes suggests otherwise.

The siege economy of 1990 will result from the unexpected failure of Britain's invisible strength. For the first time since the industrial revolution turned Britain into a first-rank manufacturing workshop – with the single exception of the abnormal years of the Second World War – the miracle of invisible earnings is turning to dust. The impossible is happening: the earning power of the City of London is losing its impetus. Invisible imports are now slowly overtaking the export earnings of the financial institutions. The last defence against national penury is in danger of being swept away.

A careful eye could have spotted this drift to invisible deficit. From an invisible surplus of £2,400 million in 1978 the figure dropped to £875 million in 1979. In 1980 the slide continued. By 1986 the basic balance of payments, with long-term capital movements added in, could well be the wrong side of £10,000 million. In the time-honoured British tradition this mounting financial haemorrhage is dismissed as a passing problem caused by foreigners. The British contribution to the EEC budget, we are told, has been the prime cause of this loss of invisible strength. Certainly, the £1,000 million that flowed into Brussels each year was a cause for concern at the beginning of the 1980s. And the reductions agreed with EEC governments in the summer of 1980 may stem the flow. But those EEC contributions were not the root cause of the decline; they merely disguised the pattern of deterioration in Britain's ability to pay its invisible way.

The failure of the invisible economy cannot be blamed on Common Market budgets or the iniquitous demands of French farmers. It is due to factors inside Britain itself, above all to changes in the position of the British economy in the world, many of them the result of deep-rooted industrial decline. For decades, the country reaped a rich harvest in interest, profits and dividends brought back by companies operating overseas. As recently as 1978 this repatriation was running at around £1,000 million a year. But the tide was already changing; in the space of twelve months that colossal surplus had dropped to £200 million. And as the 1980s began, the trend to massive outflow commenced in earnest. At the centre of the trend was a group of immense foreign-owned oil companies that were now gathering their own rich harvest in the North Sea. Hundreds of millions of pounds began moving back to their overseas headquarters as offshore profits climbed. As North Sea production rises through the mid-1980s this outflow will mount dramatically. By 1985 a figure of £4,000 million would knock a very large hole in Britain's invisible balance sheet.

Then, too, the much-vaunted banking sector is losing its position in the international market-place. The onslaught of US banks and the rapid growth of German and French rivals have squeezed the British banking fraternity hard. Earnings by British banks on Eurocurrency business, for example, have been declining sharply. Fittingly, the new decade began with Britain's banks registering their first deficit on operations in foreign currency since the first years of the Eurocurrency market in the 1960s. The outflow was already greater than £300 million a year. Even the key institutions of the City – the insurance syndicates of Lloyd's, the commodity houses and brokerage firms – seem destined to hit financial trouble in the 1980s. World insurance is moving into one of its most difficult periods: 1979 was the worst year on record for the aviation market and analysts are predicting that marine insurers will face a decade of mammoth claims as the ageing world supertanker fleet throws up a growing index of collisions and explosions.

Add to this long list of financial negatives the impact of Britain's high inflation and oil-inflated sterling rate, which together have a marked effect on local costs, and the prospect seems clear. The invisible economy can no longer be regarded as the ever-present guardian angel of Britain's declining industry. The decline is becoming total. And by 1990 it will have reached a point where siege policies will seem inevitable.

Of course, the 1980s are destined to be a decade of mercantilism. The imperative of this new dark age of economics guarantees a rash of trade protectionism and aggressive international competition in the war for world markets. The crisis of surpluses, the rise of a global industry of high-technology products that can be carried cheaply to distant markets, the crisis of old industries and the accompanying cries for protection of jobs – all these make it inevitable that governments throughout the industrialised world will adopt measures for their own protection. But nowhere will the clamour for a national state of siege be as vociferous, as total and as successful as in Britain.

Imagine a country, once prosperous and bustling with industry and empire, that is struck by dangerous decline. Unemployment stands at 5 million and is set to rise even further. Entire regions are being laid bare by mounting bankruptcy and corporate collapse. A crisis in trade overwhelms the balance sheet of the economy. And imagine the attraction to a desperate government, and to a seething electorate, of a siege strategy that is designed to shut out the merchants of a too-competitive world. The thought evokes images of the England of the Middle Ages, with its Staple ports and its strict controls on the imports of wool, designed to protect the fledgling woollen industry. Citizens were obliged by government instruction to assist local industry on the path to prosperity through buying English woollens, and wearing woollen garments ostentatiously on prescribed days. Now, with the crisis in trade mounting, such a vision has growing attractions.

The siege of 1990 would involve a drastic curtailment of the individual right to buy. The first victims could be the exotic goods that Britain does not produce. The banana, after all, was little known in the high street shops of the Second World War, when imports were precious luxuries. But the siege would be directed, too, against the consumer goods of Asian, South American and European manufacturers with their lower production costs and more sophisticated design. In short, the real price of siege would be a steady limitation on consumer choice, an observable greying of the market-place to a point where the average supermarket and department store looked as enticing as its counterpart in Smolensk or Novgorod. So while the British market-place of labour in 1990 could be split into two warring camps, with a mass of unemployed and menial workers confronting the monks of information shuttered behind the closed doors of the computer world, the economy itself could well have taken the last resort by retreating behind high walls of protectionism.

Economists working at the Department of Applied Economics in Cambridge have employed the advanced technology of the information society to produce simulated pictures of Britain's economic future. In the early months of 1980 they used their computer model to chart a route to the siege economy of 1990. Up to 1985, they concluded, Britain's rapidly deteriorating condition would require restrictions on imports of manufactured goods. By then oil production from the North Sea may have levelled off or even fallen, posing the additional threat of a mounting oil bill for Britain in the years to 1990. And in this second half of the decade the crisis would approach a point of total breakdown. As unemployment passes the 5 million mark, as imports flood in and the trade deficit becomes unsupportable, the options for the British government will narrow. By 1990 it could be necessary to impose a tariff wall against imports of manufactures as high as 70 per cent of their value. Such a Draconian measure would be essential if the economy was to be pulled back from the brink of insolvency. The levies imposed on foreign goods would raise the money needed by the 1990 government to meet the cost of mass unemployment. It would give protection to British industry which could grow at a rate of 4 per cent a year behind the castle walls, a rate of growth undreamed of for decades. The industrial base may even begin to recover, giving work to some small fraction of that vast jobless throng.

That is the computer verdict on the drift of Britain's economic future. The siege of 1990 may be, in the end, the dictate of the very same high priests of electronic information who are building the fortress of social siege inside the computerised economy itself. At the international level, Britain would encounter explosive reaction from trading associates. After all, the weakness of Britain's economy has made it a soft target for European and Japanese rivals. The EEC has enjoyed commercial pillage on the grand scale in Britain, every bit as profitable as the original Conquest. In the twenty years to 1980, the EEC countries poured manufactured goods into the British market, exceeding their imports from Britain by some £7,500 million. Over the 1980s this trend will continue. As the Paris-based analysts of the OECD put it as they looked ahead to Britain in the 1980s: 'The marked loss of cost competitiveness in manufacturing since late 1976 points to a continuing strong import penetration over the forecast period.' They stayed quiet on the future of Britain's politics as this trade crisis heaped more financial troubles on a government machine already borne down by the inexorable slide of the home economy.

Crisis, nevertheless, makes for strange alliances. And in siege Britain many long-standing rivalries will be forgotten in the battle to survive. Britain's employers share the same goals as their erstwhile opponents, the unions, as both drift towards widespread protectionism to defend British industry. The Confederation of British Industry now calls for a system of import controls, as have the unions for some years. According to research conducted for the International Labour Organisation, British employers and unions are now co-operating to put heavy pressure on government officials to secure protective trade deals. The progress of the negotiations on the Multifibres Agreement, which governs international trade in textiles, exposed a strategy of siege on the part of British industry. Similar attitudes have overtaken British footwear, leather goods, machine tools, electronics and a long list of endangered industries. The siege of 1990 has already entered its first phase.

9

Castles to the power three

The commuting citizens of Prutopia take steam trains to return home to their low-tech villages after a day of work at the data-base complex. They spend their leisure hours restoring relics from the industrial past, such as textile looms and old steam engines, or baking bread. Their lives are monitored at every turn: their health, their social life, driving habits, cooking, central heating, as well as every functioning detail of their workplace. Paper is rarely seen on their twenty-first century daily round. Their non-commuting neighbours earn a living as craftsmen, working with leather, fine metals, porcelain or plastics. This is one of the lucky communities in the employment belt of Britain 2010.

To the north stretch millions of acres of economic desolation, with only the data-base complexes standing out as high-technology fortresses. The factories stand in ruins, their machines rusting slowly to dust. There is still the land, farmed in differing degrees of efficiency. There are the agri-centres, with their bio-technological process plants. And there are the isolated zones of the information economy, a small closed world where esoteric knowledge, manufactured by computers of the utmost sophistication, reigns supreme. The vista is that of high-technology feudalism; for the people of Prutopia, knowledge is power and work is a four-letter word meaning never. Outside the privileged villages and the centres of real economic influence, unemployment is of epidemic proportions, ravaging the illiterate population in true Black Death style. Britain has drawn apart into two nations and the risk of violent confrontation has given the castle a new lease of life.

The typical community in the Middle Ages was run on ignor-

ance. The broad mass of the population, tied to the land, was
unschooled and illiterate. The law was the law of the Church; the
friars, with their privileged access to the sacred information of the
Gospels, interpreted it. In time the great universities of Oxford
and Cambridge were built on these religious foundations. And
they were to become the symbols of a society governed by ritual
and esoteric knowledge. To this day, Britain is ruled by the same
clerical mysteries, with one small difference. In medieval times
that esoteric knowledge was drawn from the scriptures; its very
obscurity gave it power over an ignorant community. In the
Britain of Prutopia, the knowledge will be stored in data-bases and
defended with fury. But Oxbridge will still be Oxbridge.

Figure 9:1

VILLAGE LIFE 2000

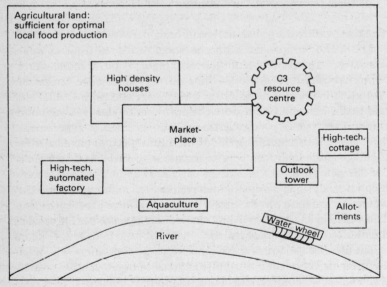

A conceptual model for a self-supporting community of the future,
developed by Andrew Page for The Dartington Hall Trust in collaboration with Tetra Design, London.
The community, of roughly 2,000 people, would be organised to meet
the economic and social challenges of the twenty-first century. Significant characteristics would be intensive use of land and heavy reliance
on the high-technology information resource centre.
A more elaborate outline is to be found in *The Protopian Manuscripts*,
Document 1 of the appendix.

Already the high priests of this new religious order have adopted the vocabulary of the high-technology Church. It is as mystical as the code-words of the Catechism, with the scientific blackness of Newspeak. Take this typical paragraph from an article written for a computer magazine by the founder of, believe it or not, the 'Petsoft micro-softwarehouse':

> There are four technologies that are being drawn together to produce a single product which will change our lives. That product is the Complete Communications Centre, or C3 in industry jargon. C3 is a microcomputer with embedded modem, video screen, printer, solid state RAM memory and video-disc storage unit combined. With it you will be able to conduct almost all normal business functions from home. It will transmit and receive electronic mail, voice, computer data and video pictures over an integrated communications network.[1]

The electronic cottage has arrived.

The 1970s were filled with the superlatives of the computer specialists. The coming of the silicon chip made possible miniature computers which revolutionised the world of knowledge. From the 30-ton, 20,000-valve monsters of the 1950s, the computer industry had pushed an equivalent store of data on to a wafer that was but a fraction the size of a postage stamp. But those 1970s superlatives were little more than whispers of the future pace of change; over the 1980s and 1990s the very foundations of social and economic conduct will be turned upside down by an irreversible flood of new technologies, new products and systems of communication that will make the forecasts of the 1970s seem primitive by comparison. The world of C3 will be as different from today as we are from the lifestyle of pre-Hispanic Mexico.

The Pandora's Box of the high-technology revolution will affect civilised life far beyond the limited impact of micro-processors and video screens. The very basis of agriculture is being overtaken by giant steps towards self-reproducing feedstuffs. Simple cell protein, for example, could eventually replace traditional animal foods. It is made through the farming of bacteria, yeasts and algae and offers an open-ended supply of high value diet for livestock, even a protein supplement for human food.

The economic ramifications of the growth of bio-technology

alone are all-embracing, literally revolutionary. A genetic
engineer at the Cetus laboratories in California has recently raised
the protein productivity of a microbe by 12,500 per cent. The most
simple cells can synthesise chemicals that are too complex for
existing man-made technology. Research scientists at Unilever
have developed a method for cloning palm oil trees. After cloning,
the trees form plantations of identically-twinned palms for the
production of soap. Their regular size will make the task of
harvesting a matter of pre-programming an army of computerised
machines. Much the same scientific research is making it feasible
to produce alcohol from sugar cane, cassava and palm nuts. In
Brazil a budget of some $1,300 million is being devoted to this
process. In time, say the scientists, plant-based alcohol could
replace petroleum as the power-source of the everyday car. In Japan
thousands of microbe applications have already been patented.

'Prudential Assurance, Britain's largest investor in shares,
yesterday announced that it is setting up a new subsidy,
backed by £20 million, to invest in technology.
  'The new company is to be called PRUTECH.'

Guardian, 20 June 1980

'More than half the companies receiving government aid to
apply micro-electronics to their manufacturing are located in
South East England. Of the 271 applications for grant, 164 are
located in South East England. Wales is bottom of the list with
only three applications. The North West received 16. Even the
second highest – the South West – received only 23 appro-
vals.'

Industry Department, 20 June 1980

The list is endless. Some ideas may end up on the scrapheap of
research, as did much of the grain experimentation that promised
so well for Asia and Africa in the 1960s. Many will succeed,
housed in laboratories-cum-factories where controlled conditions
will guarantee the survival of a gigantic agri-industry. Thus, bio-
technology will bring a future shock to agriculture as dramatic as
that brought to white-collar work by the video-electronic age. It
could ensure, for example, that the prospect of world food
shortage will disappear. It could bring a collapse of food prices

comparable to that of ever-cheapening micro-processors. What are the implications, for instance, of a science that can produce as much as 1 million pounds of extra daily protein from a 1,000-pound mass of microbes, when the average farmer can produce only one pound of extra protein daily from a 1,000-pound cow, at the cost of expensive field-grown grain feedstuffs? This is the nature of the new farming. It will bring about a deep social crisis in the agricultural communities, as jobs on the land are replaced by science. Britain's own industrial revolution began in farming, with improved cultivation methods, better tools, more effective seeds and fertilisers. It drove millions from the farms into the towns; the world of work was turned upside down. In 1700 more than 90 per cent of Britain's population lived in the countryside through tilling the fields. Today less than 3 per cent work the same fields, producing infinitely more. Now another revolution approaches.

This time, however, there is a complicated catch. The first industrial revolution was able to answer the questions that it posed, even if the new lifestyles that came with those answers were shadowed by the greyness of factory conditions. As science overwhelmed the land, the technology at work in industry created a second hinterland for the labourer. He moved over to earn a living on the production line, down the coal mines, in the shipyards. This second industrial revolution is, once again, born of massive technological revolution. But there is no vast cushion of new employment to absorb the people displaced by science. Bio-technology will change the face of food production; the tools of the C3 society will build a new industrial framework in which only the skills of high-knowledge are needed. Even these skills will be called upon under a strange form of computer tyranny of the jobs market. In short, the economy of the future will evolve into an unplanned-for super-industrial feudalism.

The C3 revolution has been described as creating an exciting office of the future, the electronic cottage that can perform all the functions of the highrise corporate headquarters in but a fraction of the space. The description is misleading: the C3 revolution will change the face of all work – in the office, the factory, the home, even in the fields. In the words of one prophet:

Come the revolution there will be: more pictures and less print; more talking and less walking, more electronic signals and less

paper and more private communication, if no less mass broadcasting . . . the old definitions will have to be discarded, and so
will the old rules for making separate jurisdiction of communications, transport, publishing and banking.[2]

But even this prediction only touches the surface. The revolution
will affect the production line, the design studio, even the cow-
shed, where feeding and milking patterns will be carefully supervised by micro-processor.

The reaction to this prospect has all the hallmarks of the misleading praise for post-industrial society that filled the bookshelves
of the universities in the 1960s. Now the optimism is showered on
the micro-chip and the optical fibre. According to the editors of
the *Futurist*: 'Automation has already revolutionized the factory.
Now it is about to revolutionize the office – freeing workers from
rigid schedules, busy work and the aggravations of commuting.'
And in the view of Alvin Toffler, whose book *The Third Wave*[3]
appeared in the first year of this decade of revolution with a
message of awe-inspiring faith in man's technological future: 'A
new civilisation is emerging in our lives and blind men everywhere
are striving to suppress it.' The message seems clear: civilised man
is entering his third generation. After agriculture and industry,
now comes the third wave of electronic magic, and only the foolish
should resist.

Such professional optimism misses the point. All new technology carries with it the promise of great benefits. The word
processor will take away the tedium of the typing pool. The vehicle
production line is already being taken over by robots: at Volkswagen the giant Goliath welders work alongside smaller robots on
body shell construction. The coming of Gollies and Robbies has
meant great flexibility in the production of more than 3,000
variations of a standard Volkswagen van. In farming, a more
scientific approach to seed cultivation, fertilisation and crop
rotation through computer programmes can only enhance the
productivity of the land. But a revolution only succeeds if it is
total. If the C3 revolution is unfinished it creates two economies:
one is modernised to twenty-first century standards, the other is
left behind as a second-class hinterland, to be dominated by the
secret, super-efficiency of the information lords. Prutopia is not a
fantasy world; it is Britain after the revolution fails.

As we shall see in later chapters, the mature industrial economy has reached a point of dialectic – of division into two distinct parts that now confront each other in a state of growing friction. The rise of the positional economy against the so-called economy of democratic wealth, which came with the mass production of industry, is a feature of this same trend. But in no sphere is the split more divisive and potentially more corrosive of established social patterns than in the area where C3 technologies are changing the face of work. It is even more corrosive where, as in Britain's case, the technological revolution is incomplete and affects only a fraction of the overall economy.

The high-technology era, from bio-tech agri-business complexes to the Complete Communications Centre of video-electronic wonders, brings to an end the contribution of the skilled artisan to the production of democratic wealth. Put more simply, the first industrial revolution replaced muscle with machine, thus liberating the artisan for work of imagination. The second industrial revolution kills imagination. And the highly skilled artisan, whether designer, chemist, production engineer or metallurgist, becomes nothing more than a machine-minder in twenty-first-century guise. Take, for example, the fate of the draughtsman trained in the design of complex structures. In the case of architectural design, each building or structure has to be drawn up in a three-dimensional framework. In other words, a 'real' model of the proposed building has to be constructed before approval of the project. The earliest architects and designers would have built working models to examine in detail. The new technologies offer a computerised substitute for this process which breaks the design down into mathematical functions and stores it in binary form. Through computer graphics systems the design can be constructed as a model and displayed on a screen for professional inspection; every angle of the design can be examined as the computer turns the display through a three-dimensional cycle.

Until now such facilities have represented a major tool for the skilled designer, bringing a supporting test-bed for his ideas. But with the acceleration of technical achievement in the computer world his role has lost its purpose. The development of manned computer graphics in the area of structural analysis now means that equations for the analysis of the structure under design are set up automatically and then solved automatically upon request of the analytical output. All is driven by micro-processor intelligence, from the questions to the answers. Displacements, loads, shear and moments are all worked out by artificial brainpower and thrown up on the VDU screen for examination. The computer has all but usurped the task of human curiosity. The result is a widespread process of de-skilling in which the work of supervision of such problem-solving exercises passes to less trained operators who know only the techniques of monitoring the hardware and software activities. The experienced structural engineer, with his 'real-world' knowledge, becomes redundant.

The C3 revolution with its intelligent systems has put an end to the central axiom of the computer world. For decades it was argued that a data-processing system was only as good as the human brain that programmed it. Hence the governing philosophy of a generation of computer specialists – GIGO, or garbage in– garbage out. That phase of human superiority is over. From now on the science of cybernetics brings a new world of machine intelligence where artificial brains can even provide that most precious of human commodities, namely imagination. At least, that is the prospect offered by the onward rush of information technology. In the end, as specialists are eliminated by thinking machines, there could be no source of imaginative design to turn to other than the friendly IBM with its seeing eye but no heart. Within the remaining decades of the twentieth century, the computer industry will have developed a device with an IQ of more than 120. It would be capable of seeing through a minute televisual eye. It would be able to act on what it sees through complex commands to its high-technology electronic brain. Through its sophisticated mechanical limbs it could weld, draw, stir tea or thread a needle. Each act it performs would be registered and remembered in an effort of self-programming. It would be learning how to function as a human being, with each new step filed away for future use, far more effectively than would a child with its fallible human memory. And conversation by voice synthesiser would allow the most erudite discussion of the price of corn on the Chicago futures market – courtesy of satellite. According to Professor Heath of the Heriot-Watt College in Scotland, we are rapidly approaching the point where robots could be regarded as people with their own civil rights: 'If they are people, the secular consequences are obvious. They must have the

vote; switching them off would be classed as an assault and the
erasure of memory as murder.'

The technological prospect is therefore double-edged. On the
one hand a breathtaking range of achievements that seems
destined to overwhelm the factory and the office of the future, and
bring a revolution to agriculture. But on the other, a destruction of
the professional function with the vital role of imaginative thinking
taken over by cybernetic systems. In the 1970s, as the silicon chip
age dawned, and was welcomed by the pundits and the professors,
we comforted ourselves with the thought that the human mind
would always be superior. After all, was it not the case that while
even the most advanced 1970s systems could handle just 10^3 units
of intelligence, the human brain could cope with 10^{14}, including
the extra bonuses of imagination, aspirations, political judgment
and humour? Now even this margin of superiority is being whittled
away. The HAL computer in Kubrick's fantasy film *2001*, with its
emotional involvements and temperamental interventions, was
not far off the mark. If anything, it will be with us sooner.

'About forty men, leaning on crowbars, picks and shovels,
smoking, talking, milling about something in the middle of the
pavement . . . an air of sheepishness, as though there were
nothing but time in the world . . . These were members of the
Reconstruction and Reclamation Corps, in their own estimate
the "Reeks and Wrecks." Those who couldn't compete economically with machines had their choice, if they had no
source of income, of the Army or the Reconstruction and
Reclamation Corps . . . Around the bar were old men, pensioners, too old for the Army or the Reeks and Wrecks. Each
had before him a headless beer in a glass whose rim was
opaqued by hours of thoughtful sipping. These oldsters . . .
arrived early and left late, and any other business had to be
done over their head.'

Kurt Vonnegut, *Player Piano*, Avon Books, New York 1969

In the workplace this destruction of the role of imagination is
the high-skill counterpart of unemployment. There is the intervention of the computer to take over the cross-checking and fault-
finding skills of the trained human eye and brain. The resultant
design is refined by programmed inputs and outputs. There is the

destruction of the knowledge base of educated professionals by the accelerated pace at which obsolescence overtakes their accumulated skills and experience. It is now recognised that in many fields of high technology the knowledge of the skilled specialist is out of date even before she has been fully trained. A pure mathematician reaches peak performance at twenty-four, a theoretical physicist at about twenty-six. Many companies will not recruit an electronics engineer over twenty-three and will specify very precisely the area of knowledge required. His days are already numbered by the march of C3 technology. Thus, what the cybernetic systems fail to do in de-skilling the highly trained technical expert by taking away his work, the simple process of ageing will do instead. And it will all be over by the time he or she reaches thirty.

' "Herr Momus dispatches any clerical work of Klamm's which may become necessary in the village and as Klamm's deputy receives any petitions to Klamm which may be sent by the village." As, still quite unimpressed by these facts, K. looked at the landlady with vacant eyes, she added in a half-embarrassed tone: "That's how it's arranged; all the gentlemen in the Castle have their village secretaries." '

Franz Kafka, *The Castle*, Munich 1926, translation published by Secker and Warburg, 1930

This is the world of Prutopia. A mass of unemployed have been thrown on to the scrapheap of post-industrial society by the demise of industry. And the meritocrats, offered glittering prizes in the liberal years of the 1950s and 1960s for their specialised skills, are being displaced by the same technologies that they were educated to create. In this sense the rise of popular education with its accent on the working class scientist seems little more than a confidence trick played on a generation in order to provide the thinking machines of the future, machines that could be controlled more easily than the rising tide of white-collar, articulate, union power that grew on the back of that secondary technical training. It seems ironic that their most prominent British spokesman, Clive Jenkins of the Association of Scientific, Technical and Managerial Staffs, should advocate in a book on the crisis of professional de-skilling that the displaced worker should learn to throw away his spanner in favour of the tennis racket.[4] In Prutopia, the tennis rackets will come from Taiwan and the grass to play on will be part of the new landed wealth of the Prudential Assurance Corporation. Even if the unemployed technician of the future can afford the entrance fee to the tennis club, he will find himself trapped in a feudal time-warp.

This Prutopian doom is not inevitable; other countries may find a way to controlled and beneficial use of the powerful weapons of high technology. But in Britain such a fate seems guaranteed by the lack of a concerted programme for such controls and, more dangerously, by the failure of British industry to invest sufficiently in a balanced structure for its high-technology future. The education system has ignored the need for a popular awareness of the lifestyle of the 1990s, and industry has repeated its abysmal failure to invest in modernisation (see Table 9:1). Hence, the country has to suffer the worst of both worlds. Only small parts of the economy will be carried into the new world of information. They will become adjuncts to a global village of esoteric knowledge in which powerful information is stored, processed and communicated by

KNOWLEDGE FOR THE FEW

Table 9:1

Micro-computers in Britain and the United States

Total sold	US	500,000
	UK	55,000
Used in business	US	250,000
	UK	40,000
In education	US	75,000
	UK	6,000
In schools	US	30,000
	UK	1,500
In private homes	US	175,000
	UK	10,000

In the state of Minnesota, with a population of 4 million, there are 1,300 micro-computers in schools – about as many as in schools in the whole of Britain.

Source: *Guardian*, 10 July 1980

INFORMATION MOVES MONEY

Table 9:2

Investments of European banks in computer-related equipment

| | US dollars | | |
	1979	1985	1990
Investment per employee	3,430	5,738	8,168
Investment per branch	45,000	73,429	101,634
Total installed equipment (millions)	6,860	10,900	14,700
Computer terminals (units)	175,000	340,000	600,000

HIDDEN BRAINS: BRITAIN LEADS

Table 9:3

Ratio of front office computer workstations to back office workstations in European banks

UK	1:6·2
Germany	1:1·2
France	1:1
Sweden	1:0·1
Total Europe	1:1

Source for Tables 9:2 and 9:3 PACTEL

invisible electronic hands. Banking will become an invisible, international fraternity (see Tables 9:2 and 9:3). Already through SWIFT, a transnational network of computers and transmission networks, the international banking system is evolving into a tight-knit cybernetic community. The same process is overtaking the other components of the international money machine; commodity trading, insurance and currencies are supervised by the very best C3 brain-power that high profits will buy. Britain's service sector has taken full advantage of these systems. The rest of the economy, not least the long-neglected industrial base, has been passed over.

Open the pink pages of the *Financial Times* on any typical day. There, in the dense columns of sober news and comment, is the mounting evidence of a country dividing into two. On 10 June 1980, a day of joy for the pillars of the financial community, British Steel announced that 1,500 jobs in Scotland were to go; a footwear group in Northamptonshire announced the closure of six manufacturing units with a loss of 400 jobs; Cadbury the chocolate maker published details of 700 redundancies and plans for short-time working for another 2,600; the UK construction industry forecast 'a widespread and continuing decline' in their workload for at least the next three years. It was a typical day in the journey to Prutopia.

'Life assurance operations of the home service insurance industry last year generated more than £900 million worth of new savings in the UK . . . with premium income advancing 25 per cent to £1,146 million and investment income 23 per cent to £923 million.'

'The spread of computer technology in Britain during the next decade will be severely constrained by shortages of skilled manpower . . . the National Economic Development Office argues that this problem will prove a far more serious obstacle to development than the much discussed social consequences of the widespread application of the technology.'

'The problems financial institutions have in vetting investments in high technology projects are to be studied by Sir Keith Joseph, Industry Secretary . . . Sir Keith acknowledged that such funds are not available in the UK.'

'For the first time in seven years big foreign companies are queuing up to apply for London Stock Exchange listings . . . The removal of exchange controls, the growth of London's bond markets, the increasing interest of UK investment funds in foreign shares – these are the reasons cited for the surge.'

'British imports of electronic products increase by 54 per cent.'

Financial Times, 10 June 1980

   This polarisation into two distinct social groups of knowledge has in fact been a feature of British society since the early Middle Ages. As Thorstein Veblen pointed out, learning was a by-product of the priestly vicarious leisure class. As the body of knowledge expanded, there arose a distinction between esoteric and exoteric knowledge. Esoteric knowledge comprises spiritual learning and other learning of no economic or industrial effect. Exoteric knowledge, in contrast, describes skills in industrial processes and knowledge of such natural practical terms. This division of knowledge separated the leisured governing class of priests, academics and aristocrats from the artisans and farm workers. The distinction has survived through to the late twentieth century. It is reinforced by the rise of the new information technologies, which favour those with privileged access to the closed world of higher 'electronic' learning dominated by the giants of the financial and service sector. The basis of that privileged system is the leisure class in all its forms.

This division of knowledge lies at the very core of the British disease. It represents the victory of the abstract over the practical. It creates in the centre of the British education system a peculiar status cult that puts the academic brain, with its priestly qualities, above the technician with his exoteric outlook. As Veblen put it:

> There are such things in the usage of the learning community as the cap and gown, matriculation, initiation and graduation ceremonies, and the conferring of scholastic degrees, dignities and prerogatives in a way which suggests some sort of scholarly apostolic succession.[5]

This dominance of the priestly mind helps explain why the British engineer is paid only half what is paid to a university professor, while in Germany – where priestly knowledge carries less weight – the engineer is paid more than his scholarly rival. It may also explain why a British graduate engineer has a lower level of basic pay than a skilled manual worker with no higher education at all. It may even be the reason why skilled fitters in industry have been caught by the same fate: between 1914 and 1975 the differential in pay rates between skilled fitters and labourers roughly halved in favour of labourers. One reaction is to welcome the democratic notion of equal pay rates for all types of work The other is to observe that there is a noticeable bias against skills derived from exoteric knowledge. And British industry is the casualty, caught by a bizarre system of social ordering that spreads downwards from the altars of Oxbridge.

The extent of this socially ordered bias against technical skills is

summed up graphically in the evidence of Britain's Electronic
Engineering Association to a Committee of Inquiry:

> The serious shortage of engineers will get worse and will spread
> further to other sectors of the economy and the reasons for stark
> inadequacies in both the quantity and quality of engineers avail-
> able to industry lie primarily in deep-rooted and mostly ill-
> informed social attitudes towards the engineer and industry.[6]

Such a damaging practical outcome is the eventual result of an
education system that places greater value on abstract thought, on
the articulate expression of philosophical ideas and on the capacity
to argue sophistically about such things as the basic truths of life. It
is an education system that is dominated by the literally dreaming
spires of Oxford and Cambridge, whose power filters down through
the monastic system of the British governing elite. The Inns of Court
in London reflect the same closed shop lifestyle. The upper levels
of the Civil Service are still monopolised by Oxbridge graduates and
will be even in the early twenty-first century: in the mid-1970s
almost two-thirds of the external candidates who passed the Final
Selection Board came from Oxbridge. This phalanx of 'priestly'
administrators will form the leadership of the British Civil Service in
2010.

In short, the continuing power of the ancient English universities,
with their ecclesiastical flavour, stands for the triumph of esoteric
knowledge over the practical mind that is necessary for the growth
and prospering of industry. It supports the long-held view of the
historian R. H. Tawney: 'The hereditary curse upon English education is its organisation upon lines of social class.'[7] But now, as
Britain makes a half-hearted effort to adapt to the challenge of C3,
this triumph of the esoteric brain is nothing less than the building of
a tyranny of truly medieval proportions.

In *The Uses of Literacy*,[8] Richard Hoggart told the Britain of the
1950s that it was moving towards the creation of a mass culture. The
growth of popular entertainment, a widespread readership of
newspapers and journals, the impact of radio and television on the
ordinary household, all pushed in the same direction of a democratic network of information. Hoggart's book was, in effect, an
examination of the political power of the printed word and of the
mass readership that goes with it. The same point was made in

Marshall McLuhan's survey of mass communications *The Gutenberg Galaxy*.[9] He says:

> In the electric age the very instantaneous nature of co-existence among our technological instruments has created a crisis quite new in human history. Our extended faculties and senses now constitute a simple field of experience which demands that they become collectively conscious.

The style of presentation differs, but the writers' message, to use a McLuhan term, is the same. Modern technology has made information democratic; it has broken down the ancient barriers of learning that gave rise to the mystical strength of the Oxbridge priesthood. Alas, in Britain's case nothing could be further from the truth. After

Figure 9:2

A CASTLE TO THE POWER THREE

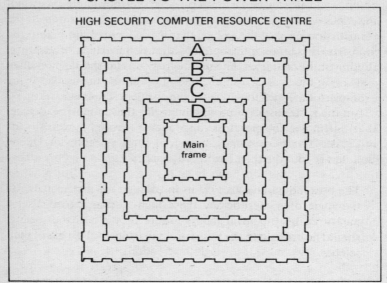

HIGH SECURITY COMPUTER RESOURCE CENTRE

A
B
C
D

Main frame

A   Outer limits: physical barriers to entry
B   Inner limits: access controls through voice signatures etc.
C   Outer sanctum: access through 'least privileged' system
D   Inner sanctum: software protection – files, operating system

Main frame computer: internal defence mechanisms such as division of operating system through partitions

a brief flirtation with democratic information, during the years of the Hoggart generation, the country has reverted to its old ways. Once again, the castles of knowledge are being built, this time with the help of the computer.

The other key book of the age of democratic information was Michael Young's *The Rise of the Meritocracy*,[10] which appeared in the wake of Hoggart's essay on mass culture. Young examined a different facet of the same drift towards democratic education. His conclusion was that educating on the basis of free access to schools and universities would produce a new meritocracy where the order of value would be based on IQ. Thus, in the meritocracy of the future, said Young, the governing formula would be IQ + Effort. But the thesis, like that of Hoggart, could only survive so long as education and technology continued to spread through the Britain of the 1960s. They did not. The decade of the 1960s was to mark the high point in Britain's drift to a mass culture society. Having started the decade as the third largest economic unit in the world, the country had already begun its inexorable slide downhill. The swinging 1960s were years when the pendulum swung backwards, to the resurrection of all those values that had governed life before the industrial revolution interrupted, with such impertinence, the rural rhythm of the centuries. The meritocracy was to be little more than a gleam in the eyes of a small band of optimists, themselves living examples of the meritocratic idea they were describing.

But then, Michael Young was only reflecting a widespread belief that technological progress also meant giving power to the brightest. The guru of post-industrial society, Professor Daniel Bell, has set out the theme with great clarity:

> The post industrial society in its initial logic is a meritocracy. By the logic of a meritocracy these high-scoring individuals (as measured by I.Q.), no matter where they are in the society, should be brought to the top in order to make the best use of their talents.[11]

On the surface such a tendency towards 'government by IQ' carries a vaguely democratic flavour. But in Britain's case it does little more than set the scene for an inevitable return to the despotism of controlled information.

A lesser-known study on education, published during the early

1960s, came far closer to the longer-term truth. Sir John Newsom, in a report on average and below-average pupils, warned that Britain could be moving towards a feudal system of education, with the country divided into 'Egg-heads and Serfs'. Newsom was concerned at the British obsession with a small highly educated elite, even if that elite sprang from a more egalitarian approach to education. But his conclusions, like those of his contemporaries, were soon to be overtaken by technology. In the short term there was, indeed, a prospect of domination by an elite selected through the operation of the Intelligence Quotient. By the 1980s, however, the power of the IQ elite was already waning; the rise of C3 technologies was putting machines in its place.

Already we are on the brink of artificial intelligence with an IQ level of 120. As the technology of the computer industry moves on, there will be machinery with the brain power of a genius. It was no accident that the 1980s began with an unprecedented breakthrough in the development of artificial intelligence. In Monte Carlo the world backgammon champion, Luigi Villa of Italy, was beaten 7–1 by computer programme BKG 9.8. It was the first time a computer programme had beaten a world champion at any board or card game. Experts agreed that BKG 9.8 'played with great accuracy and imagination and clearly emerged the victor'.[12] Certainly, the victory was not a matter of the methodical search capabilities that it takes to win in chess. The branching factor for chess – the average number of predictable legal moves that can be made beyond a given position – is about 35. The branching factor for backgammon is more than 400. A foolproof computer programme for backgammon will need to contain an element of personality, in order to evaluate each future move in terms of safety, longer-term tactics and so on. It will need to exercise judgment at the very highest human-type level. BKG 9.8 reached that level.

The backgammon episode may appear a frivolous event of no real relevance to the future of education. But its implications are far-reaching. High technology is now down-grading the role of human intelligence. For a generation it was thought that IQ power would change the social order by giving status to those with advanced education, irrespective of social origins. The long-standing monopoly of the Oxbridge system, with its belief in the power of higher learning and priestly leanings, would be broken and replaced by a broad-based meritocracy in which the skills of practical science and inquiry would be given greater value. The hope was short-lived. Across the entire spectrum of the economy the meritocracy is being overturned by the artificial intelligence systems of the information industry. Architects and designers are being de-skilled or replaced by manned computer graphics. Complicated transactions in the financial world are entrusted to vast cybernetic networks which work at levels of complexity and speed far beyond the limited talents of the accountant and the clerk. Across British industry, already ravaged by the slow death of degeneration, the jobs that remain will fall prey to the best and brightest robots. In other words, the twenty-first century economy will be able to exist without that exoteric knowledge that was essential for the growth of traditional industry and which gave work, ambition and a modest prosperity to the industrial worker. That exoteric knowledge will, by then, be provided by the same kind of artificial intelligence that triumphed at the tables in Monte Carlo.

Thus, Prutopian Britain will be a feudal system of knowledge. Exoteric learning will have been relegated to a lowly position in the ranking of expertise. The engineer, designer, architect and surveyor will become, once again, part of an artisan class of lesser status. Their functions will have been usurped by the artificial professionals of the C3 society. Meanwhile, the esoteric knowledge of the Oxbridge kind will enjoy a new age of privilege, giving a refined, articulate gloss to the humdrum lifestyle of a ruling plutocracy whose administrative burden has been lifted from them by the Complete Communications Centre.

It is therefore not difficult to sketch out the social order in this post-industrial feudal world. There will be the landed and powerful class, with its hold over the information sector. Through their monopoly over stored knowledge – in itself the high-technology equivalent of land – they enjoy almost total influence over the manipulation of the key components of the economy, from the electronic transfer of funds to the organisation of the future markets for essential commodities. There will be the priestly arbiters of learning of the old kind, pursuing their traditional task of providing the human factor in the arts, the law and the senior reaches of policy-making. There will be a mass of unemployed, many millions strong, unwanted by industry and an irrelevance on the land. There will be a second body of de-skilled, demoted and alienated technicians, the old guardians of exoteric knowledge – now surplus to requirements in the global village of electronic substitutes. And a small group of post-industrial clerks, employed to run the machinery of the computer domain but knowing very little of the larger constellation of power that they serve. This last group is made up of the people who catch the commuter trains from high-tech zone to low-tech village. And each evening, when they leave for home, they close behind them the great doors of castles to the power three. Nothing has changed since the days of Domesday. Knowledge is still power.

THE LANDFAX ARISTOCRACY

Landfax: an economic system run by the owners of land and information

10

The new land hunger

The collapse of Britain's industrial economy is creating a new power structure – the landfax aristocracy. As industry fades away two areas of stability and profits will remain: land and the technologies of information. As more and more wealth is pushed into these two areas, Britain's economy will take on new shape. In outward appearance it will seem like a disparate mixture of old landed wealth and the prospering world of banking, insurance and the City institutions. But the underlying pattern of ownership will be simpler. Old landed wealth is taking over the information world, as well. The result is a new aristocracy with its feet planted firmly on both sides of Britain's declining industrial base. One foot will stay with the land, the other will grow with the explosion of the information technologies. This is the landfax aristocracy that will run Britain in the twenty-first century.

Land, of course, is the ultimate resource. It was there before the coming of industry and will be there, still, in the not too distant future when Britain's industry has died away. Since the Conquest of 1066 land has remained the constant factor in Britain's power politics. As Mark Twain said: 'Nobody's making it anymore.' And nowhere is this more true than within the strict confines of Britain's island boundaries. As a result, all the institutions, the social habits, the economic lifestyle have evolved within strict physical limits, with stultifying effects. Thus, land was the cornerstone of the power system created by William the Conqueror. And land is the cornerstone of power today, with the added dimension of that other ultimate resource, information.

Land and information ruled England in the years after the

Conquest. Land acted as the prize for loyal service to the Crown. The key to information was literacy; in those days knowledge was confined to the clerics who surrounded the king, offering advice, interpreting the law, preaching the gospels. In a typical charter of 1077 the old alliance of land and information of the priestly kind is displayed. The charter records the foundation of Monks Kirby Priory, a place-name redolent of churchly influence. It is built on land given to Geoffrey de Wirce, a Breton lord of the first post-Conquest generation, 'which he has earned by service from William the illustrious king of the English'. Land was distributed on a feudal basis, to loyal servants in return for support. Knowledge was controlled within the Church, a twin pillar of royal power. This was the old landfax system. Today it exists in high-technology form.

A political system dominated by landfax principles cannot escape the dead weight of feudal habits. The feudal estate perpetuates the rule of rank, chivalry and service – all the social mechanisms that give Britain its essentially pre-industrial flavour. In practical terms it means a permanent nostalgia, a hankering for the green and pleasant land that existed before the vulgar intervention of dirty factory culture. It means that the successful manufacturer thinks it correct and natural for him to aspire to the mannerisms and lifestyle of the lordly domain. Thus Lord Leverhulme, maker of soap for the masses, builds castles and buys the Western Isles to mark his ascendancy. Today, his heir is Lord Lieutenant of the City and County of Chester, Steward at Royal Ascot, a product of Eton and Trinity College, Cambridge, who dines at Boodle's and lists as his chief recreations the aristocratic pursuits of hunting and shooting. Meanwhile, the making of real things – the things that brought him those accolades – is somehow abandoned along the gravelled driveway to nobility. And the feudal ideal of military service pervades all. Lord Leverhulme has the official duty, as Lord Lieutenant of his county, of raising the citizen army for the Crown on the way to the third world war.

The new landfax aristocracy works in the same way as its eleventh-century counterpart, through monopolising the vital resources of land and knowledge. Land is finite; information is infinite. The first finds value because it is fixed in quantity. The second finds value because it is the ultimate perishable commodity. Information is out of date the moment it is made available, all the more so in the fast-moving world of C3 technologies. Yet without the hard facts of the moment no business, no decision-making centre, can survive against aggressive rivals. Thus, the conquest of land and the control of information continue to be the two pillars of landfax power.

There are 43 million acres of usable land in Britain, excluding the urban areas with their eccentric price structures. Ever since the Conquest, the history of the ownership of Britain's land has been the history of Britain's social climate. Nine hundred years later, the ownership of that land reflects the same order established by that first illustrious king of modern Britain. True, that order has been modified by the manual workers and technicians who came with industry, and the outward appearance of Britain over the past two hundred years even 'suggests a country hell-bent on creating an egalitarian lifestyle. The appearance, however, is an illusion.

'There is an old Chinese tale concerning the man in Hell about to be reincarnated who said to the King of Reincarnation: "If you want me to return to Earth as a human being I will go only on my own conditions." "And what are they?" asked the King. The man replied: "I must be born the son of a Cabinet minister and father of a future scholar of the First Class in the examinations, I must have 10,000 acres of land surrounding my home and fish ponds and fruits of every kind and a beautiful wife and pretty concubines, all good and loving to me, and rooms stocked to the ceiling with gold and pearls and cellars stocked full of grain and trunks chockful of money and I myself must be a Grand Councillor or a Duke of the First Rank and enjoy honour and prosperity and live until I am a hundred years old."'

C. L. Wayper, *Teach Yourself Political Thought*, English Universities Press, 1954

In 1873 a second Domesday Survey was conducted to prove to the world that a century of industry and eight centuries of post-Conquest history had destroyed the feudal past. It proved the opposite; it proved that the ownership of land was still concentrated in a very small number of wealthy hands. And while incomes might have grown with the rise of factory production, the subtle distinction was rarely made: income is merely a temporary reward for work that will one day cease; wealth, however, is permanent.

Wealth is stored in the assets of land and other fixed resources that continue to produce income even after the sun has set. Today, land and the resources of information gathering and processing are the key factors in economic power. And both are being conquered by a small and determined group. While the feudal dream has seduced the people who built the superstructure of British industry in the nineteenth century, and thereby condemned it to atrophy and decline, the landfax system is designed to support the pastoral lifestyle of traditional aristocracy.

The economic reasoning behind the landfax strategy is very sound. It reflects the precarious state of Britain's decaying industrial economy. Security lies in the stable prospects of land and information-based services, where value is maintained against the ravages of inflation and where the double bluff system can work to maximum efficiency. Thus, the ownership of land, after a period of broader distribution, is now reverting back to the clannish monopoly by the few that characterised pre-industrial Britain.

It is not surprising, given the awesome political and economic power that goes with land ownership, that the details of its distribution are shrouded in secrecy. It is, of course, a breathtaking contradiction that the landfax aristocracy – so wedded to the ordering and distribution of facts and figures through its growing control of C3 resources – should nevertheless be so reticent about disclosing the facts about its own holdings of land. But that reticence is understandable; land, like knowledge, is only powerful while it is shrouded in mystery and esoteric privilege. Nevertheless, fragments of the real pattern of ownership of Britain's land can be pieced together (see Table 10:1).

To begin with, the predominant share of Britain's land has never been given up by the landed families. At the last survey, made by John McEwan in the late 1970s, 12 million of Scotland's 19 million acres were owned by a small group of landlords with estates above 1,000 acres. The top ten landowners held more than 1,500,000 acres between them; almost a quarter of a million of those acres were owned by two members of the Cowdray family, the Duke of Atholl and Lord Cowdray himself. At the 1980 price of roughly £1,500 an acre for good Scottish land – as long ago as 1975 the financier Edward Reeves paid £1,000 an acre for a 17,000-acre estate in the Strath of Kildoran – these top ten landowners can value their collective holdings at some £2,250,000,000.

WHO OWNS THE LAND: A SELECTION

Table 10:1

	Acres
Government departments	1,142,000
Local authorities	902,000
Statutory agencies/nationalised industries	556,000
The Crown	404,000
Oxford and Cambridge colleges	200,000
The Church	165,000
Financial institutions	750,000
Individuals	
Duke of Buccleuch	275,000
Wills family	260,000
Seafield family	185,000
Sutherland family	158,000
Duke of Atholl (Pearson family)	130,000
Lord Cowdray (Pearson family)	88,000
Lord Leverhulme	99,000
Duke of Westminster	
Scotland	60,000
Cheshire	18,000
Central London	300

Sources: Northfield Report, Cmnd 7599, HMSO, 1979; John McEwan, *Who Owns Scotland*, Edinburgh University Student Publication Board, Edinburgh 1977

In England the situation is more obscure, not least because of the stout resistance put up by the landowning groups to any suggestion that land ownership be made an openly recorded fact. The Report of the Northfield Committee on land, the most recent effort to catalogue the trends in land distribution and acquisition, is punctuated with admissions of failure in the face of this resistance:

Throughout our work we were hampered by the lack of detailed information on many of the topics we studied. It is disturbing that so little is known about the pattern of acquisition, ownership and occupancy of agricultural land and that Governments should have to take decisions, which may have far-reaching effects on agricultural structure, on the basis of incomplete or non-existent data.[1]

The recommendation of the Northfield Committee was that a full system of land registration should be set as a final goal and that the Agricultural Departments should take action to fill the gaps in public knowledge. The recommendation was to be lost in the election campaign of 1979 and has disappeared from sight.

It is certain, in any case, that any attempt at a full-blown Domesday Survey of late-twentieth-century Britain would be resisted to the point of rebellion by the landowners themselves. The Country Landowners Association, for example, has traditionally rejected the idea of a table of land ownership, although a 1976 report concedes:

> At one end of the spectrum the small working farmer attracts sympathy . . . the closer the owner of land, whether owner-occupier or resident landlord, is identified with the smaller working farmer, the less the likelihood that he will have to bear the brunt of political attack arising from envy.

And the possibility of help from the Agricultural Departments in producing a more open record on land is very remote. Because of the massive weight of the land lobby these departments seem destined to support the land against the public wish to know the facts. At the time of writing, in the summer of 1980, all four ministerial posts in Agriculture are held by farmers.

Nevertheless, there is sufficient evidence to piece together a picture of Britain's land in the late twentieth century. The picture is a telling one: a new land hunger has taken hold. As the economy runs into a downward spiral of disintegration, money is moving fast into the last safe haven. And an alliance has sprung up between the money-making institutions of the City of London and the rolling countryside beyond. This alliance is the underpinning of the landfax system.

To begin with, the redistribution of land in this century has not greatly altered the old wealth pattern. On the centenary of the Domesday Survey of 1873, statistics published by the Inland Revenue showed that 95 per cent of total personal wealth in land was held by individuals with estates worth more than £10,000; in

1973, before the onset of double-digit inflation, this threshold separated the better-off minority from the rest. Second, the pressure on land ownership has been increased by the rapid growth of state holdings. Roughly one-fifth of Britain's acreage is held by agencies of the state, including the Forestry Commission, the Ministry of Defence and other departments of central government. In this sense, a large part of Britain can now be said to fall under the control of Britain's senior civil servants, the group some have described as the new ruling class.[2]

Figure 10:1

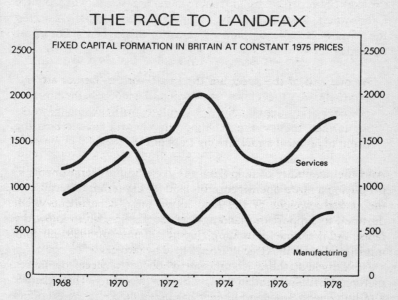

THE RACE TO LANDFAX

FIXED CAPITAL FORMATION IN BRITAIN AT CONSTANT 1975 PRICES

But a more significant discovery is that the new land hunger is sweeping away the tenant farmer. In 1873 about 90 per cent of British farmland was worked by tenants. By the early 1970s this figure had fallen to below 50 per cent. Fewer landowners, bigger estates. In 1908 the owners of farmland actively worked just 12 per cent of Britain's acreage; tenant farmers worked 88 per cent. By the late 1970s the picture had been reversed. Tenants farmed 43 per cent of total acreage; owners farmed 57 per cent. And the trend is moving inexorably towards concentration of ownership. At the turn of the twentieth century there were some 500,000 farm holdings in

Britain. Now that number has been cut by more than half. According to the Northfield Report, by the early twenty-first century the tenant farmer will be a disappearing species, today's numbers cut by another 50 per cent. The real outcome could be even more extreme, as the land hunger takes hold. By 2086 British land could be back to the pattern of total aristocracy set up by William the Conqueror nine centuries ago.

'Although I may be accused, if not by my Honourable Friend then by some of my other Honourable Friends outside, of trying to convert pragmatism into a new philosophy, I must confess that having been in Caithness and Sutherland a few months ago, and having come down the Strath of Kildoran on a lovely evening – travelling at such a leisurely rate one has time to admire the scenery – I thought: "What the hell would we want to do with these acres of land in any case?"'

Hugh Brown, Under-Secretary of State for Scotland, 1974–9

This land hunger has its parallel in the world of high finance. As the manufacturing sector loses its attraction, more and more funds are being pushed into farmland and into urban property. This surge into land is creating a second British economy, quite separate from the factory culture that came with the industrial revolution. And by its sheer size it now overshadows that factory sector, taking first place in the race for new money. In the brief period between 1972 and 1974 the rush into land and property added £50,000,000,000 to the paper value of British acreage; the increase was almost equivalent to the entire national output for a year. And while that speculative boom ended in financial chaos as secondary banks and property companies went under, the hunger for land grew more voracious as industry continued to decline. Within two years the surge into land had recovered its momentum and has become a permanent feature of Britain's landfax economy.

Where the speculators left off the great institutions of the City took over, ironically with the help of funds given to them by the same industrial workers whose jobs were slowly disappearing in the wake of the landfax revolution. This gigantic fraud, the so-called 'double bluff' system, is the most damning characteristic of the 1980s.

11

The double bluff

The rise of British industry, which though temporary was to replenish the wealth of the tired landed aristocracy, was founded on a monumental deception. The loyalty of the vast, toiling labour force that poured into the factories during the nineteenth century could only be maintained if the workers could somehow be convinced that they had a growing stake in the wealth they were producing – even though they did not. The operation of this double bluff was put succinctly by the man who was to be the father of twentieth-century British economics, John Maynard Keynes. His description is so clear that little extra has to be added by way of modern embellishment:

> On the one hand the labouring classes accepted from ignorance or powerlessness, or were compelled, persuaded, or cajoled by custom, convention, authority and the well established order of Society into accepting, a situation in which they could call their own very little of the cake, that they and Nature and the capitalists were co-operating to produce. And on the other hand the capitalist classes were allowed to call the best part of the cake theirs and were theoretically free to consume it, on the tacit underlying condition that they consumed very little of it in practice. The duty of 'saving' became nine-tenths of virtue and the growth of the cake the object of true religion. There grew round the non-consumption of the cake all those instincts of puritanism which in other ages has withdrawn itself from the world and has neglected the arts of production as well as those of enjoyment. And so the cake increased; but to what end was not clearly contemplated.[1]

The Britain of the 1980s stands as a perfect monument to the success of the double bluff system. If it acted effectively during the high point of Victorian expansion, it was nevertheless threatened by the changing political climate of the years after 1945. The rise of consensus politics, with its welfare ideals, threatened to spread too widely the wealth produced by industry. And as industry faltered and began to fail after 1960, the contracting cake of national wealth would have placed in jeopardy the smooth operation of this mechanism of sophisticated fraud. In the event, the double bluff system was salvaged by the emergence of a new structure of national finance: the massive financial institutions. They worked under the guise of insurance company or pension fund, but their impact was no different from the subtle financial machinery that had under-pinned the first age of double bluff at the end of the nineteenth century. These institutions were based on the same appeal to the 'duty of saving'; non-consumption of the cake was preached as the true religion. And while a growing number of Britain's population did, indeed, neglect the arts of production and drifted into service work, the savings of the same 'labouring classes' of Keynes's description were poured into the rapidly filling coffers of City-controlled institutions. Industry and offices together produced a savings boom quite out of keeping with Britain's overall economic distress.

The growth of these double bluff institutions was to be literally explosive. In 1957 the British pension funds held assets of some £200 million. By the start of the 1980s these assets had climbed to around £40,000 million. The insurance companies were to grow at a rate almost as fast, from assets of £4,800 million in 1957 to more than £50,000 million in 1980. Together, these two massive blocks of corporate wealth form an unchallengeable colossus that is now growing at the rate of £10,000 million a year.

In true landfax style these newly rich financial giants were to turn away from industry to push their money into the twin pillars of the landfax economy – into land and into the financial infrastructure of the invisible money-machine of the City of London. The rate of investment in land and property was to take off spectacularly from the late 1950s. In 1957 the pension funds had just £44 million invested in property. By the end of the 1970s this figure had leapt to around £6,000 million. From representing just 2 per cent of the pension funds' investment portfolio it now approaches 20 per cent.

And much of the rest of their growing wealth has been stuffed into the paper pyramid that supports the intricate workings of the City.

Already, half the stocks and shares listed on the London Stock Exchange are owned by the financial institutions. Well over a third are owned by the life assurance companies and pension funds, the new agents of the double bluff system. According to forecasts provided to the Wilson Committee, which reported on the financial institutions in the summer of 1980 after three and a half years of intensive study, by the year 2000 the financial institutions will own two-thirds of the equities listed on the stock market. Every year nearly £10,000 million in new savings from Britain's wage packets flow into these same institutions. They seem set to become the dominant force in the money system of landfax Britain.

Figure 11:1

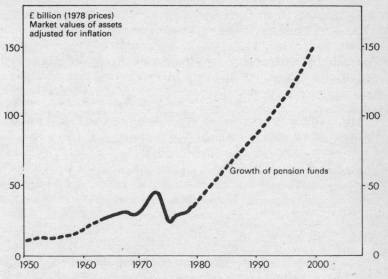

WHO OWNS BRITAIN IN A.D. 2000 ?

The impregnable asset-base of these post-war giants stands in stark contrast to the ailing industrial sector. As billions in savings have been channelled into the landfax economy, industry has gone without. While investment in manufacturing stagnated and fell between 1958 and 1980, capital formation in the financial sector rose five-fold.[2] It is not surprising, given the better rate of renewal of capital assets in the world of finance, that profit levels were much higher compared to profits in industry. British banks, which started the 1980s with an unprecedented boom in profits – in 1979 the four major London clearing banks earned profits before tax totalling some £1,500 million – have recently enjoyed real rates of return on capital of around 8 per cent, twice the level in industry.

As if to magnify the growing ascendancy of the landfax system, the financial sector is acting as a growing drain on the talents of Britain's best-trained people. Instead of going into industry, where skilled and innovative minds could help restructure the industrial base to meet the test of high technologies, graduates are moving into the high-profit world of finance. In 1965, for example, 229 first-degree university graduates went into banking and insurance. By 1978 the total had reached 1,070. And as prospects and earnings in the financial sector increasingly outstrip those in industry this internal British brain drain will accelerate.

BLUE BLOOD BANKS

Table 11:1
Social background of directors of Britain's big four banks: August 1980

	Barclays	Lloyds	Midland	Nat. West	Totals
Number of directors	29	21	25	30	105
Average age	59	62	61	58	60
Public school-educated	25	12	10	19	66
Eton-educated	12	4	–	9	25
University-educated	18	14	14	10	56
Oxbridge-educated	15	13	6	9	43
Titled	8	16	13	11	48
Hereditary titled	4	5	2	6	17

Source: *Investors Chronicle*; figures are actual, not percentages

The greatest irony lies in the pattern of control of the institutions that have grown up on the influx of wage-packet savings since the beginning of the 1960s. A glance at the boardroom membership of the largest institutions will confirm that they are run by the people who take decisions on the basis of what is good for the traditional world of money, the world of the livery companies, City guilds, and merchant banks that is so far removed from the factory culture that lit the first flame in the rise of pension power. It is only to be expected, therefore, that these newly emerged institutions should run their investment policies along lines which accord with the best interests of the old City hierarchy, a hierarchy not noted in the past for its devotion to the cause of common industry or the troublesome trade union workforce that it has spawned.

The report of the Wilson Committee was short on criticism of the great money machine of the City of London. Indeed, its greatest invective was reserved for the building societies, which by virtue of their provincial, small-saver roots do not belong to the City Establishment.[3] The building societies are, above all, children of the non-conformist, Chapel strain of British social development, the same non-conformism that created the trade unions, the labour movement and, of course, Harold Wilson. The episode illustrates a theme of British social politics: the upstart, having reached his point of success, is absorbed into the social framework he once so vehemently railed against, and given the reward of status. Sir Harold Wilson, latterly scourge of the savings banks of the un-banked factory population – 'labouring class' money has been poured into building societies in preference to the orthodox high street banks with their City connections – takes his knighthood and then turns on the economic background that gave him political life. It is, perhaps, only coincidental that the largest of Britain's building societies, the Halifax, has its origin in that same Yorkshire soil that Sir Harold claims as his own.

The immense and growing power of the pension funds and insurance companies, the financial supports of the landfax economy, attracted only minor criticism. The pension funds were chided for a certain lack of accountability, but otherwise their contribution to the economy was strongly praised. Indeed, the main burden of the Wilson report was towards giving the pension funds even greater power: 'The framework within which they operate has grown piecemeal and now needs to be systematised and strengthened.'

An attack on the pension funds colossus could have been devastatingly revealing, if the Wilson Committee had taken a more inquisitive approach. To begin with, the rapid growth of the pension funds has left British law hopelessly out of date on the requirements it makes of them. If an ordinary commercial company acted as do pension funds on the subject of releasing operational information to the public they could be in breach of the Companies Act. Mention was made of this in the recommendations of the committee, but another, more frightening, issue was neatly side-stepped. There is now the possibility that the British pension fund system could face financial collapse by the 1990s. And if this happened millions of pensioners would become the victims of the biggest rip-off in the history of money. More than £100,000,000,000 would have flowed into the pension fund accounts from the savings of Britain's working population.[4] By the 1990s all they might be receiving by way of pension payments would be handfuls of paper money better suited to a vast game of Monopoly.

Tucked away in an appendix to the report is a paper prepared by the Government Actuary's Department. Reading between its lines the conclusion is a staggering one: if Britain's economy continues to decline at the rate experienced since the mid-1970s, the pension fund system will face a monumental collapse. To begin with, the age profile of the British population points to a rapidly growing number of pensioners. In 1955 there were one million people receiving pensions. By the beginning of the twenty-first century there will be nearly 5½ million. The amount of money needed to pay these people the pensions to which they are entitled is therefore rising rapidly. In 1955 total pension payments amounted to £900 million in constant 1978 terms. By the year 2000 the figure will have increased to £9,400 million – more than twice as much as the funds receive each year from contributors.

The ability of the pension funds to pay these future entitlements depends on how well the British economy performs over the remaining years of this century, as the funds are invested in British activities. And it is here that the double bluff faces its greatest test. In the words of the Government Actuary: 'Many of the figures given in this paper are highly sensitive to the assumptions about the level of expenditure on benefits, the valuation basis adopted for the year 2000 and the yields on investments until that time.' In other words, the future viability of the pension funds system depends on the progress of Britain's economy over the next fifteen years. And it is here that much wishful thinking has taken over.

To start with, it is assumed that Britain's working population will increase by some 2 million up to the end of this century. This much larger working group would support the pension load as it increased. But what happens if Britain's accelerating industrial decline pushes unemployment past 3 million, 5 million and beyond? In this case a diminishing workforce will carry an ever-growing burden of debt to the rapidly growing body of retired. Second, it is assumed that pension fund investments will yield sufficient to cover the rising commitments to future pensioners. How can they reach such yields if the economy itself is contracting – on some forecasts diminishing in real terms by some £13,000 million between 1979 and 1985? And finally, what will be the consequences of continuing high inflation over the years to the end of this century? The Government Actuary assumed a rate of inflation of 6 per cent, on average, up to the year 2000. The assumption seems wildly optimistic, not least as rising unemployment pushes up the spending of the government on extra benefits, thus punching a very large hole in the strategy of reducing the supply of money in the economy. In crude terms, high unemployment can act to push inflation through the roof through generating government credit for the dole queues. What prospects then for the pensioners?

Figure 11:2

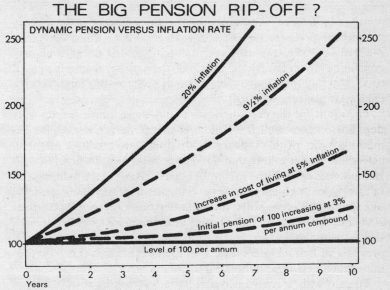

The Government Actuary takes a cautious line on what is, after all, a problem of potentially explosive force.

A reduction by 1 per cent in the yield on investments assumed for the valuation of the liabilities in 2000 . . . would increase the liabilities at that time by about 30 per cent in respect of active members [i.e., people still contributing] and 5 per cent in respect of pensioners, i.e. by about £33,000 million.

The cold phrases disguise a brutal message: the pension fund system is based upon the assumption of a future economy that stays on the rails. What if the rails give way on the route to 2000?

THE RURAL DREAM

Table 11:2
Drift to the land 1959–75

British manufacturing employment: changes in urban and rural areas, 1959–75

	Employment change (thousands)	% of 1959 manufacturing employment
London	−586	−40·8
Conurbations	−434	−6·3
Larger cities	+62	+9·1
Industrial towns	+255	+21·9
Non-industrial towns	+184	+32·8
Rural areas	+73	+84·1

Source: *Cambridge Economic Policy Review*

Thus, the double bluff approaches its acid test. It has been founded on the belief of millions in the virtue of savings and in the sanctity of the value of the money that they have saved. The collapse of that belief could usher in an era of true revolution. And if that era comes, the hunger for land and the control of information would turn into the primeval forces of a social holocaust. All of this is for the future. But not the future that never comes; this future is happening already.

The landfax revolution has its more bizarre side-effects, too. While billions are being pushed into land and information by the vast financial institutions, the hunger for land is spreading to the very bottom of the social hierarchy. In the past ten years or so there has been a growing clamour for allotments on which to grow vegetables, a clamour triggered off by the rising price of food. In England and Wales the waiting list for allotments rose more than 1,600 per cent during the 1970s. But, in keeping with the new mood of holding and preserving the power of ownership, no land was made available to meet this increasing demand. While the waiting list rose dramatically to above 130,000 by the late 1970s, the number of land plots available for cultivation actually fell by 62,000. The answer from the authorities was simple: there is no land for the giving.

There are, of course, two types of land in Britain and the dividing line has the flavour of class distinctions. There is land of the landfax type: it is valuable in terms of hard cash or for reasons of positional lifestyle essential to a leisure class. This is the land that sells at upwards of £1,500 an acre to adorn the estates of the landfax aristocracy, or upwards of £1,500,000 an acre for the urban investments that form the bedrock of their portfolio wealth. And then there is land left on the scrapheap by urban decay and industrial decline. This second class acreage is of little interest to the landfax investors.

Recent estimates indicate that there are now more than 250,000 acres of dormant land in Britain. Of this total, some 150,000 acres have been left derelict by industrial abuse and decay. Most of this land is of good potential and could be used for house building. If it were, in fact, reclaimed this derelict acreage could accommodate, at normal density, more than one million homes. Much of the rest is in degenerating urban areas or in awkward sites that would nevertheless be highly suitable for market garden cultivation on an allotment basis. Significantly, just 15,000 of these unused acres would be sufficient to eliminate totally the waiting list for small plots. However, the landfax economy is not concerned with marginal lands of no hard cash value. Indeed, the phenomenon of dormant land is actually growing as the country is divided more clearly into good land and bad. One survey in the London Borough of Tower Hamlets in 1974 revealed that the acreage of waste land there had quadrupled in a decade. More than 31 square kilometres of land lay idle in London at the last count. What is more significant, more than one-third of the dormant sites have been that way for over twenty years. Some of them have been out of use since the turn of the century.

The economists will tell us that this hunger for the land, with its elimination of the tenant farmer, the rise of the big landlord and the emergence of a City squirearchy, all makes sound economic sense. It also re-establishes the basic characteristics of pre-industrial life.

And in the end there is no real gain in terms of efficiency; indeed, the hunger for land is just as likely to lead to the falls in productivity that have plagued Britain's manufacturing sector since the mid-nineteenth century. New research by Professor Britton and Dr Hill at Wye College, London, points to a 'plateau of efficiency' in farm sizes of between 100 and 300 acres.[5] As farm sizes move beyond this limit efficiency often begins to drop. Yet it was in this type of land holding, above 300 acres, that the biggest growth has been seen as tenants have been pushed from the land and farm sizes increased.

This suggestion of a crisis of efficiency overtaking the landfax system has now been confirmed by researches completed at the Centre for Agricultural Strategy at the University of Reading. It now seems clear that the widely held assumption, promoted by the civil servants and their political spokesmen in Parliament, that British agriculture is of world class efficiency is no more than a facet of the national habit of wishful thinking. The land hunger that has pumped the wealth of the landfax aristocracy into the country-side is producing a farming industry choked by a surplus of money. Far from being held back by financial constraints, as are the investment-starved companies in the industrial regions, British farming is being overwhelmed by a surfeit of capital equipment, the greater part of it bought in profitable years to offset tax liabilities. 'The time has come to reassess the nature of and reasons for capital assistance by the state, especially in light of the observation that the long-term efficiency of the industry may not be well served by promoting investment at the current rate.'[6] The time has come indeed; as it did for manufacturing industry in the early 1970s. Nothing happened then, even though industry was dying from a blatant lack of new money. Too much money, or not enough: in the world of practical action, surplus is just as dangerous as scarcity.

Meanwhile, the drift to a landfax economy moves inexorably onwards. Money is flowing into the land and into its parallel sector of information-based services. Ageing industry is increasingly ignored when the spending decisions are made. A look at the creation of new capital over the 1970s illustrates the point. In 1968, net fixed capital in manufacturing increased by a total of £715 million; in the service sector it increased by just £704 million. Ten years later the flow of funds had shifted dramatically. Net fixed capital formation in industry was now running at £1,856 million; in services it had reached nearly twice this level, at £3,201 million. The spending in services – seen from this standpoint of real additions to the capital stock – had become the highest single category and stood at nearly one-third of the national total. In the 1960s services had ranked fourth in the capital formation league, representing less than one-sixth of the overall figure. It is worth noting, too, that capital for the service sector consists in large part of information technology – computer systems, point-of-sale terminals, word processors – which is going through a price revolution at ever-increasing speed. In terms of data-processing hardware this rapidly growing capital budget is buying even more technical power as the price per unit of number-crunching and fax-producing equipment falls with each passing month.

The rise of the landfax system, with its tiny group of landowners and financial institutions in control, does not figure in a typical assessment of modern Britain. The land is considered by most to be an insignificant part of the economic structure; about 2 per cent of the national working population works on the land. And the vital importance of the information sector, without which nothing practical can be done, is overlooked chiefly because it is an invisible domain. Yet in the twentieth-century economy of Britain these sectors represent the twin pillars of the economic system. Farming remains Britain's biggest industry in terms of assets. Its output each year is worth more than £4,000 million. Without the food that comes from the land Britain's balance of payments would plunge into unsustainable insolvency. And much the same can be said of the information sector. Roughly 60 per cent of the activity of Britain's economic system is taken up with the gathering, storage, processing and distribution of information. (In the United States the figure is between 65 and 70 per cent.) In an ideal world this vast sub-system of information would work for the betterment of all the sectors of the economy, including the manufacturing sector that has for so long supported the huge frame of Britain's 55 million population and given markets to the farmers and to the financial institutions. But the world of landfax works rather differently. Because of the discrimination of new investment in favour of land and services, and away from traditional manufacturing, the information technologies of the future will be concentrated in the landfax system, with industry left unmodernised and starved of the facts and figures essential for its efficient management. And as information replaces routine functions the entire shape of the working calendar will change. Jobs will disappear with the death of industry; for those in the service sector the revolution in information technologies will mean a change of workstyle as great as that posed by the industrial revolution, but with the time-frame for adaptation compressed from a hundred years to three or four. Britain is on its way to Prutopia – the land of double bluff.

12

Monks with expensive habits

The guardians of Britain's store of esoteric knowledge are still entrenched in the cloisters of Oxbridge, as they have been since England first began its creation of a governing elite. Despite the pressures for change that came from industrial revolution, despite the rapidly changing shape and needs of the technological community, despite the rise of 'lesser' colleges and technical schools and a demand for more popular education, the iron grip of Oxbridge has been maintained. From 1250 onwards the closed monastic worlds of Oxford and Cambridge have enjoyed a tyranny of knowledge unrivalled elsewhere in the developed industrial world, a tyranny with a vested interest in the destruction of Britain's industrial sector.

Thus, Oxbridge remains the breeding ground for Britain's land-fax aristocracy. Despite the pressures to modernise, the outlook of the Oxbridge graduate is still moulded by the rural ethos of the pre-industrial age. And despite the rise elsewhere of meritocracies educated by schools and universities that have kept pace with the approaching needs of the twenty-first century, Britain is still dominated by the heavy tradition of Oxbridge monastic thought. In June 1970, as Edward Heath fought Harold Wilson for the job of Prime Minister, *The Times* captured the sense of inevitability which that tradition gives to the membership of Britain's elites. 'The one thing that is certain is that either party will form a cabinet almost exclusively influenced by the values of 50-year-old Oxford men, advised by senior civil servants who were up at Oxford at the same time.'[1] Put more simply, Britain in the 1970s was to be governed by people educated and moulded in the distorted atmosphere of the 1930s, when crisis and external threat bred a strong brand of loyalty to the status quo.

Alas, Britain in the 1980s will be governed by the same Oxbridge products, despite the widespread belief that Britain was becoming a meritocracy in which the domination of those old monastic orders would be broken. A glance at the backgrounds of MPs, Ministers and civil servants will reveal the continuing power of the Oxbridge mafia. Labour Cabinets today are more dominated by Oxbridge graduates than ever before (see Chapter 14). The Cabinets of Harold Wilson and James Callaghan held twice as many Oxbridge Ministers as the post-1945 government of Clement Attlee and roughly double the number in the Labour Cabinets of the 1920s. Labour MPs as a whole are now more Oxbridge and university trained, and more middle class, than at any point in Labour's history.

It goes without saying that Conservative politics reflect a preference for the traditional elite-producing institutions, despite the impact of the educational reforms contained in the 1944 Education Act of the Conservative R. A. Butler. But even here there is no sign that Britain's experiment with popular education and more democratic access to positions of influence has eroded that preference for the public school/Oxbridge route to power. The Conservative Cabinet of Margaret Thatcher formed in May 1979 contained sixteen Oxbridge graduates out of twenty-one ministerial appointments; six of them had been educated at Eton before going to university, nineteen at public schools of one kind or another. In all respects these figures showed no real change from a typical Conservative Cabinet fifty years ago. Much the same observation could be made about the background characteristics of the several hundred Conservative MPs in the House of Commons.

Thus, the composition of elected members in Parliament suggests a House of Commons that is actually going backwards in terms of its class and educational outlook. Instead of reflecting Richard Hoggart's shift to mass culture, the bias of Britain's legislators seems more inclined towards the products of privileged education than it has been at any point since the creation of the Welfare State.

The upper echelons of the Civil Service, the permanent, non-elected bastion of the Oxbridge ruling class, have changed not at all. The results of entry tests into the top civil service grades still point in the direction of cloister power. The 1980 report of the Civil Service Commission showed that 58 per cent of candidates from Oxford and Cambridge passed the qualifying test against only 20 per cent of candidates from other educational institutions. In the selection competition as a whole the success rate was 20 per cent and 5 per cent respectively.

This Oxbridge bias is not surprising, given the mechanics of the selection procedure, which favour candidates with a public school education and a degree from Oxford or Cambridge. The result is the recruitment of a special kind of pre-industrial generalist, more at home in the combination rooms of an Oxbridge college than in the tough, practical world of modern business and industry. In the words of a recent House of Commons report – a minority report, of course – there is 'a bias of the Civil Service recruiting in its own image, a bias of the Civil Service paying too much attention to certain literary skills; a bias of the Civil Service in favour of the rounded individual of the sort created by the atmosphere of Oxford and Cambridge; and a bias of class, caste and cast of mind'.[2]

That bias will ensure Britain's Civil Service continues to be riddled with appalling indecision and a self-evident discomfort in the face of complex problems of technology. It is, in short, designed to perpetuate the values of Britain as they developed before the rise of industry. In other words, it is the instrument of the pre-industrial order which now is reasserting itself through the building of the landfax economy. It can come as no surprise, therefore, to discover that the wealth of the Oxbridge colleges is firmly rooted in that same non-industrial system, far from the threat of bankruptcy and poverty that will come to millions of others as industry disappears. In landfax Britain the power of Oxbridge will, as always, reign unchallenged.

Even though the Oxbridge colleges guard the details of their wealth as furiously as they protect their corporate privileges, an odd glimpse of their richly worked underskirts is a rare treat. On 11 December 1979, at Sotheby's auction rooms, Queens' College, Cambridge, sold a single-page, Anglo-Saxon document. It was an eleventh-century record of goods supplied by Ely Abbey to Thorney Abbey, both in Cambridgeshire, and was described as giving 'an exceptional insight into Anglo-Saxon rural life'. It fetched £57,200, upon which sum the college will pay no tax – and thus provided an exceptional insight into the sort of wealth the universities of Oxford and Cambridge presently enjoy.

The two universities have existed for around eight centuries, and from the very beginning they occupied a special place in British life.

They enjoyed the patronage of royalty, of the Church, indeed of all the most powerful elements in society. They had special political privileges (their own MPs, Statutes which can only be altered by the Sovereign's Order in Council). They had their own laws and systems of courts (as late as 1891, the Vice-Chancellor of Cambridge was trying and illegally imprisoning local residents). They also managed to stay a few steps behind any social changes taking place outside their walls: even today, some colleges refuse to open their doors to women, who make up less than a third of Oxbridge students. The Sex Discrimination Act is held not to apply to Oxbridge colleges, as a test case in July 1979 involving St John's College established. And in 1980, the majority of students who gained places at Oxbridge were still being educated at private schools. Despite the fact that 85 per cent of children are now educated in comprehensives, pupils from these schools make up less than a quarter of the universities' total intake.

'Riches, the dumb god that giv'st all men tongues,
That canst do nought, and yet mak'st men do all things;
The price of souls; even hell, with thee to boot,
Is made worth heaven! Thou art virtue, fame,
Honour, and all things else. Who can get thee,
He shall be noble, valiant, honest, wise.'

Ben Johnson, *Volpone*, Act One, Scene One

'I am a great believer in property developers. I believe British property developers are the finest in the world . . .'

Dr John Bradfield, Bursar, Trinity College, Cambridge

Oxford and Cambridge present an archaic front to the world. 'A sixteenth century member of the college,' wrote C. P. Snow in *The Masters*, 'dropped in the first court now, would be instantaneously at home.' Oxbridge's values and traditions have been preserved as carefully as its architecture. It has proved remarkably resistant to change, even in a Britain which, since 1945, has had seventeen years of Labour Governments supposedly committed to smoothing out inequalities in education.

One reason is probably that the majority of members of those governments were actually educated at Oxbridge. In fact, despite

the expansion of higher education, the two 'blue brick' universities
have actually *tightened* their hold on the top jobs. Oxford alone
accounted for ten members of Harold Wilson's 1966 Cabinet; fourteen members of Edward Heath's Cabinet were at either Oxford or
Cambridge; in Mrs Thatcher's Cabinet that figure rose to sixteen. In other words, 80 per cent of the 1979 Cabinet were
Oxbridge-educated. The domination by the two universities of the
'top jobs' is notorious and well-documented. In 1970, for example,
a study in *New Society* revealed that of 359 judges named in the Law
List, 273 went to Oxbridge. The number of articles, documentary
films and television series about Oxbridge is a testament to the
enduring fascination the media feel for the universities. The love-
affair is reciprocal. Both Fleet Street and the broadcasting world
recruit heavily from Oxbridge. In 1978, for instance, of the fifteen
graduates recruited by the BBC for their Research Assistant Training Scheme, thirteen had attended either Oxford or Cambridge.

The influence of the Oxbridge 'network' is infuriating to many
outside it. For hundreds of politicians, writers and academics –
radical in their views on most other subjects – Oxbridge is sacro-
sanct. The charge of hypocrisy is often heard. As John Cole put it in
the *Observer*:

Have you noticed how many social critics, however radical, forgo
any questioning of the role of Oxbridge? If they are graduates of
either university, they may assault the 11-plus, abolish grammar
schools, or be willing to do away with private education, but
when the talk turns to the two elder universities, their eyes glaze
over or their attention wanders.[3]

If there is an Establishment in Britain, Oxbridge is at the heart of
it, turning out the leaders, the 'captains of industry', 'the opinion-
formers' of today as confidently as it has ever done. Nor is this
assurance that an Oxbridge degree is essential for success confined
to Britain – the government is delighted to see Oxbridge export its
expertise. On 13 March 1980, Cambridge University announced
the establishment of a £90,000 a year endowment, financed by –
among others – the Bank of England and twenty-eight companies.
The fund was to last for seven years and provide twenty to thirty
students from southern Africa with the opportunity to study
at Cambridge. The project, which was called 'the Cambridge

Livingstone Trust', was open to applicants from Zambia, Malawi, Zimbabwe, Botswana, Namibia, Swaziland, Lesotho and South Africa. 'This is a major commitment,' remarked the university's Treasurer, Trevor Gardiner. 'We hope to help produce constructive leadership in southern Africa.'

Oxbridge seems to have a bottomless reservoir of cash, much of it on tap from the business community. Such generosity is perhaps not too surprising: according to the list of chairmen of Britain's top fifty companies, given in the *New Anatomy of Britain* by Anthony Sampson,[4] twelve went to Cambridge and eight to Oxford, and the two universities are studded with libraries, accommodation blocks and research facilities named after leading businessmen such as Wolfson, Cripps and Morris. Worcester College in Oxford has been given the money to build a three-storey block of student rooms by the Sainsbury supermarket chain (Sir John Sainsbury and Tim Sainsbury, Conservative MP for Hove, are both Worcester graduates). New College, Oxford, has raised over £1 million towards a new quadrangle. St Cross College, Oxford, was given £350,000 in 1979 by Blackwells bookshop. According to the *Daily Telegraph* (11 July 1979), Wadham College, Oxford, received 'a substantial grant towards its library from the Shah of Iran's twin sister, Princess Asraf Pahlavi', whilst nearby St Anthony's has been given £1·5 million by Ryuvo Yamazaki, executive managing director of the Nissan Motor Company (manufacturer of Datsun), to establish the 'Nissan Institute for Japanese studies'.

Two entirely new Oxbridge colleges are being built by businessmen. Dr Cecil H. Green, the British-born former chairman of the Texas Instruments electronics group has donated almost £2 million for the construction of a medical college to be named after him. Cambridge-born millionaire David Robinson, founder of one of the country's biggest television rental companies, also has a new college named after him. Founded in 1978 at a cost to Mr Robinson of £19 million, it will concentrate on science-related subjects.

This is just a sprinkling of the recent gifts and endowments. Most are never reported. Of those that are, nothing so crude as a figure is generally put on the size of the gift. (The recent donation by Fred Cleary, chairman of the property company Haselmere Estates, to Magdalene College, Cambridge, is a typical case. 'Quite simply,'

Denis Murphy, the Bursar of Magdalene, is reported as saying, 'Fred Cleary is the best thing that's happened to the college since Samuel Pepys.')

The willingness of the wealthy to come to the aid of Oxbridge ensures that the colleges seldom have to touch their assets – the example of Queens' College quoted at the top of this chapter was a revealing rarity. In addition to such treasures as manuscripts and works of art, the colleges have large assets in stocks and shares and property. Just how large those assets are is never disclosed. The Universities and Colleges of Oxford and Cambridge (along with Winchester, Eton and the British Museum) are specifically scheduled in the 1960 Charities Act as 'exempt' – in other words, they do not have to disclose the source of their income, nor pay any tax on it. The colleges keep their accounts as secret as the most secret Swiss bank accounts. Most of the time it is only possible to guess at the size of the holdings which generate their 'endowment income'. Some, such as Selwyn College in Cambridge, and Hertford in Oxford, are comparatively poor. Others, such as Trinity and Christ Church, are immensely rich. (This discrepancy in income was noted in the Franks Report of 1964, and following its recommendations a special university tax was introduced – to redistribute *income* within the universities. Thus in 1977 in Cambridge, when Trinity College's declared income was £1 million compared to Darwin's £1,067, the richer colleges paid £210,000 into a fund which was then shared among the poorer.) Some of the older colleges, generously endowed to begin with, have had six centuries in which to accumulate their assets. Above all, they have been able to use the generosity of the Charities Act to plough money back into extra investment.

Business and the academic life become strangely mixed, as history or science dons make decisions about investment running into millions of pounds. But there is nothing amateur about the size of the profit they create. One college don, who writes a regular column in the *Investors Chronicle* under the pseudonym 'Academic Investor', reveals that his college's portfolio is worth around £4 million, and that in twenty-six years it has risen in value three times as quickly as the Financial Times Index – £100 of the college's money, according to his reckoning, invested in 1953, is now worth £4,957! 'The College', he reported, 'manages its investment portfolio with a long-term objective: a satisfactory return in real terms

over the next century or two.' This leisurely aim frees the college
from the need to worry about short-term fluctuations in the stock
market. Not only that:

> . . . taxation does not remove any of the substantial divi-
> dends . . . For an *individual*, whose income is highly taxed, the
> position would be quite different, especially as his shorter time
> horizon makes him less tolerant of slow rises in share prices.[5]

The biggest college in Cambridge, and the wealthiest by far, is
Trinity. Its controversial ownership of Felixstowe Docks, the ag-
gression with which it has set about raising its revenue, and its
success in becoming the wealthiest of all Oxbridge institutions has
given it a concern with secrecy that amounts almost to an obsession.
How ironic, therefore, that it was the accidental misplacing of
confidential Trinity documents that enabled the first close inspection of what exactly is going on behind Oxbridge's ivy-coloured
walls. The set of Trinity accounts for the year 1972/3 allows a unique
opportunity for scrutiny.

In the ten years from 1970 to 1980, the average price of agricultural land rose roughly tenfold, from £200 an acre to £2,000 an acre.
It is the backbone of Oxbridge's wealth. The universities and
colleges of Oxford and Cambridge between them own – according
to the 1979 Northfield Committee on Land – 198,715 acres. This is
less than in the past but still puts them among the biggest landowning institutions in the country.

In 1973, Trinity's share of this was 16,096 acres, scattered across
thirteen counties and bringing in an annual revenue of £167,815.
Some of the land was given to the college by Henry VIII and has
been in its possession ever since. At 1980 prices it is worth over
£32,000,000 – if, that is, it was being sold according to the national
average price. Back in 1973, some of Trinity's land was being sold
for *£42,000 an acre*. Under the skilful control of its Bursar, a former
Zoology don called John Bradfield, Trinity was speculating in
land – with remarkable results.

In 1934/5, the college paid £59,519 for 3,277 acres at Trimley in
Suffolk. During the late 1960s and early 1970s, around 325 acres
were hived off and developed into Felixstowe Port. Over £400,000
was pumped into Trimley for industrial development and road
building, with the result that by 1973 the port was bringing in

£150,000 in rent. In 1972, having obtained planning permission, Trinity sold 65 acres of former allotment land to a company called Deblen Finances for £2,320,848. The deal, spread over four years, was designed to allow the building of 520 houses on the site. Deblen paid prices for the land ranging from £30,000 an acre to £42,000 an acre.

By 1973, Trinity was involved in a number of other lucrative ventures:

1   In 1939/41 the college bought 626 acres at Ilchester in Somerset for £33,578. In 1971 just 8 acres were sold for £33,796.

2   In 1967 the college bought 227 acres at Ashford in Kent for £72,670. In 1972, 10 acres were sold for £118,700. In 1973 'subject to the grant of outline planning permission for residential development' another 9 acres were sold to Ashford UDC for £229,325. Trinity retained full rights of access 'in case adjoining College land becomes developable'.

3   In 1954, the college bought 128–134 High Street, Sutton in Surrey for £26,215. In 1967, it purchased the land at the rear for a further £41,079. Two years later, part of that was sold for £25,000. Then, in 1973, the whole of the property was sold to Stead Investments Ltd, for £825,000.

These three deals alone, therefore, made almost £1·3 million for the college. On none of it did the college pay tax, neither was it made public. As it didn't have to be declared as endowment income, none of it was revealed to the university. Besides these speculative ventures which have been brought to fruition, other deals still in the pipeline in 1973 included:

1   140 acres of land bought at Ashingdon, near Southend in Essex. Cost: £195,000. 'Purchased', according to an internal memorandum from Dr Bradfield, 'in the hope of a modest amount of development in due course as a result of both natural demand and Maplin airport construction . . . should let well for farming and/or ponies while we are awaiting developments.'

2   384 acres of land at Lenham in Kent. Cost: £202,000. Classed

as 'potential development land' as the property will be 'crossed by the proposed M20 to the channel ports'.

By the early 1970s, Trinity's property empire extended over 53 towns and cities throughout the country. It ranged from Aberdeen to Brighton, from Norwich to Bristol. It embraced over 80 shops, 7 factories, 15 warehouses, almost 300 houses, office blocks and supermarkets. In London, Trinity owns the offices of the Ministry of Works in Tottenham Court Road, and the 34,000 square feet of studios and offices in Woodstock Grove used by BBC Television as its main training centre.

The range and complexity of its assets is breathtaking. According to a valuation of its investments carried out by the college's merchant bank, Barings, at the close of business on 15 December 1972, Trinity's various investment funds were worth over £12·3 million. The college's various portfolios covered everything: breweries, chemicals, shipping, property, mining . . . Trinity's total wealth in 1973 was, at a *conservative estimate* (Bradfield's own description of the figures in Table 12:1), £29,361,936.

Potentially the most profitable and most far-reaching of Trinity's many projects does not feature in this list: the Cambridge Science Park.

In July 1967, taking its cue from the 'Science Parks' which sprang up in the United States a decade earlier, Cambridge began to look at the possibility of making money out of the one asset of which it has most to offer – brains. As a special committee headed by Sir Neville Mott reported back to the university authorities:

The University already contains probably the largest concentration of physical, technological, biological, medical and agricultural research laboratories in any university in this country. If the Government research laboratories in Cambridge and its immediate neighbourhood are added to these the whole complex may be regarded as the largest non-industrial concentration in the country. The investment in scientific staff, equipment, and supporting facilities is therefore exceptionally high.[6]

A Nobel Prizewinner, the Cavendish Professor of Physics, and a former Master of Gonville and Caius College, Sir Neville Mott was a persuasive advocate. His opinion, that the growth of science-based industries 'would be in the interest of the County, City and the University', carried weight. The university approved his proposal, the City Council rubber-stamped it. All that was now needed was the land and the money. Enter Dr John Bradfield and Trinity College.

TRINITY COLLEGE, CAMBRIDGE: TOTAL HOLDINGS 1972/3

Table 12:1

Asset	Value (£)
Agricultural land (assessed at £550 per acre)	8,887,800
Urban property outside Cambridge	3,191,418
Trimley industrial	1,889,475
Other ground rents	142,500
Cambridge property (at rack rents)	2,932,660
Investment funds (excluding Staff Pension Fund)	12,318,083
Total	29,361,936

Trinity released thirty-two acres of derelict land on the northern edge of the city to be turned into the 'Cambridge Science Park'. The college made an initial investment of £1·5 million. The land was to be rented at £2·50 per square foot; it would not be sold, for, as the college's 1970 prospectus put it: 'It forms part of a larger property, all of which has belonged to the applicants for at least a century, and some of which they have owned since 1443; so continued retention would be a natural course for them to pursue.'

The first tenants moved in during 1973. They were Laser-Scan Laboratories, specialists in laser map-plotters for analysing atomic particle tracks; the company was created by scientists from the university's Cavendish Laboratory where the techniques had been pioneered. Six years later, under the headline 'Cambridge Goes Commercial', *The Economist* reported that Cambridge Consultants, a firm run by a Trinity graduate, founded in 1960, had just arrived on the Science Park. Their new laboratory was opened by another Trinity graduate, Prince Charles. The company was the thirteenth to establish itself on the site. By 1979, the Science Park was employing 400 people in a variety of high-technology companies.

Apart from Laser-Scan and Cambridge Consultants, the other

companies were: LKB Biochrom, Goodfellow Metals, Cambridge Communications Ltd, Intervet Laboratories, Optronic Fort Ltd, Lintech Instruments, Coherent (UK) Ltd, Cambridge Micro Computers, Ultra Violet Products, Well Log Services, and Cambridge Electronic Design. According to *The Economist* of 4 August 1979, at least one other company – the drug manufacturers Napp Laboratories – was on the way.

Thus, as the college moved into the 1980s, Trinity was capitalising on one of its few undeveloped (commercially, at any rate) assets – its scientific expertise. With more Nobel Prizewinners than the whole of France, it is potentially a very rich seam to exploit. How much revenue it is now bringing in to the college is, of course, confidential. Since the accidental disclosure of these figures, the wall of secrecy that surrounds Trinity's financial dealings has grown, if anything, even thicker. Even the 1973 figures seem to beg as many questions as they answer. Certainly, the overall valuation was deliberately underestimated. Given the rate of inflation and the impossibility of knowing just what Trinity has been up to during the 1970s, any speculation as to what the college might be worth ten years on is bound to be pure guesswork. Some 16,000 acres of agricultural land would by now be worth around £32,000,000. Given inflation, Trinity's urban properties must be worth at least that much. But who can tell what 'development' deals have been pulled off since then? Trinity's fortune, according to its own figures, was £4·5 million in 1960; by 1973 Dr Bradfield's 'conservative estimate' put it at £29 million. In just thirteen years, therefore, it had risen in value sixfold. Operating in secret, paying no tax, ploughing profits back into yet more investment . . . that trend can only be accelerating. If it isn't worth £100 million today, then it could be – very soon.

The dreaming spires of the Oxford and Cambridge colleges seem to the casual visitor quiet havens of peace, where great ideas are spun for the betterment of humankind. A peep behind the surface of those blue-brick façades reveals another world, a world that traces its ancestry back to the closed monastic orders of feudal times. Yet in spite of such ancient roots, no one could accuse the Oxbridge monks of failing to keep up with the times. In landfax Britain, where the lifestyle of those feudal times is being redis-covered, there is money to be made from land and information. And Oxbridge monks have very expensive habits.

13
The LeverPearson Effect

Two British families illustrate most vividly the nature of Britain's drift towards Prutopia. The Lever family and the Pearson family were made rich and powerful through revolution – the industrial revolution that built the towns and swelled the wage-packets of the factory population in nineteenth-century Britain. Both families were to rise to the zenith of the British aristocracy in the space of one generation. By the early 1920s Mr Lever and Mr Pearson had become viscounts. And, in true Buddenbrook fashion, both families turned to lives of 'music' as the inexorable logic of Britain's social framework carried later generations back into the lush pastures of the feudal era.

In their different ways these two families stand as living monuments to the rise and fall of democratic wealth. Both grew rich by capturing profits from the growing markets of household spending, and the transport and distribution systems needed to carry goods from the factories to the shopping basket. And in the space of one hundred years, both abandoned the industry that had given them an aristocratic lifestyle. Both Lever and Pearson today seem devoted to the landfax system and the ritualistic trappings that give that system its mystical hold over the rest of the country.[1] The Lever-Pearson Effect is the single most important factor in Britain's crisis. And carried to the logical conclusion of aristocratic growth, the two families will have merged through intermarriage by the early twenty-first century. Together they will form a union of two of the biggest fortunes in British economic history, though the industrial drive that created that wealth will have faded from the scene.

William Lever became rich on soap. His discovery that an industrial consumer class could be made clean by the mass production of household soaps, sold through widespread advertising, marks the beginning of the age of democratic wealth. The symbolism could not have been more appropriate. Soap, the enemy of factory grime, was the one commodity capable of returning the members of Keynes's 'labouring classes' to a pristine condition suited to the re-creation of the feudal dream. The discovery made William Lever rich beyond the wildest imagination of the inventors and builders who generated industrial revolution in the eighteenth century. By 1885 Lever had started his Buddenbrook voyage of discovery. Mass production processes were beginning to turn out bars of the magic material at a phenomenal rate. And Lever set off on the path to benevolent despotism, egocentric lunacy and a craving for the lordly powers of a Norman ruler.

Lever's career passed every landmark on the route to early Prutopia. His fortune was lavished on the accumulation of vast estates. Castles, manor houses and the baronial lifestyle became the characteristics of his contribution to Britain's industrial heritage. He worshipped king and country to the point of grasping with great eagerness the titles and honours extended to him. He was made a baronet in 1911, a baron in 1917 and a viscount in 1922. He raised a Leverhulme Battalion of 1,300 men from the factory estates in Port Sunlight and sent them to the Somme. About 100 of them returned in one piece. He pursued his own empire in Africa, and bought himself an entire community of 30,000 people in the Western Isles.[2] The islanders resisted his efforts to make them into a Hebridean wonderland for his own feudal gratification. Elsewhere, the resistance never came and William Lever, now Baron Leverhulme of Bolton-le-Moors, Viscount Leverhulme of the Western Isles, overwhelmed his subjects with a flood of monuments to his own greatness. Meanwhile, the soap production lines pumped out more millions in bars and pound notes. But the vital job of instilling a sense of change, a feeling for the future evolution of Britain's industry, was left behind in a welter of nostalgia.

Almost every brick laid by Lever in his years of construction carried the imprint of a man who had created industry only in order to condemn its filth, who took the wealth it produced for him only in order to re-create the lifestyle of the Middle Ages. At Port Sunlight in Cheshire he was to build the factory complex and village that stands today as a functioning testament to a feudal mind. Even today the residents refer to him as 'Uncle Bill', an avuncular ruler in frock-coat and top hat, waiting in the back of his massive limousine to catch late-comers on their way to the soap factory. They look back on the days of aristocratic luxury that he enjoyed as lost symbols of Britain's great industrial age, when nimble hands were paid five shillings a week to fold twenty-six pleats into the silver and gold wrappings that covered the fine soaps made for the Duke of Buccleuch, soaps that cost, for each bar, close to that five-shilling weekly wage.

Leverhulme's paternal style had its purpose: he aimed to create a security for his captive workforce that would in turn generate the sense of fear that would keep them subservient. He had realised, as his biographer W. P. Jolly has remarked, that fear could motivate as strongly as reward. He had concluded that the chief cause of the increased efficiency of Lever Brothers in the early 1920s was 'not the fact of any increased bonus, but the fact that we had begun to weed out inefficient men. We have been combing out inefficient men, and too highly paid men, elderly men and men past their work . . . I'm confident that this has produced a state of "fear" in the minds of the remainder . . . and it is this, in my opinion, which has been the cause of the improved efficiency results achieved today.'[3]

Above all, the riches that fell to the Lever family through the mass production of Vim, Sunlight and Knights Castile became the means by which a dynasty was established at the very heart of olde England, a dynasty blessed by monarchs and loved by the masses. Port Sunlight was but one small piece in the jigsaw of personal empire assembled by Uncle Bill. His efforts to carve out a kingdom for himself on the Western Isles of Scotland tell their own story. In the house magazine of Lever Brothers, the *Port Sunlight Magazine*, William Lever's project there is described in terms that reflect the contradictions that run through the very centre of the Leverhulme legend, in which industry and the feudal past pull in opposite directions: 'The Western Isles are the birth place of an industrial empire and the burial ground of a romantic idyll which cost nearly two million pounds.' The true story is somewhat more illustrative of the Leverhulme lust for lordly power. As the same *Port Sunlight Magazine* soberly recorded, 'He regarded the island as a living toy, having by then few fresh industrial worlds left to conquer.' Another source observes how the locals reacted bitterly to his imperial intervention:

It was to him that the disappointed and embittered islanders turned with renewed demands for land. The interchange between the anti-socialist, capitalist autocrat and his insistent tenants became a national issue and the matter was settled partly by state intervention.[4]

But then, in keeping with the feudal ethos that permeates down to the thinking processes of the 'labouring classes' that have perennially made Britain's rich men behave the way they do, Uncle Bill was forgiven his trespasses on the Western Isles. He was, after all, no different from the other lairds who have traditionally owned and governed Scotland, and still do. Said one local sage: 'If Billy Lever came back tomorrow, we'd carry him shoulder high to his castle.'[5]

If the Western Isles were a living toy for the soap king, Rivington Pike near Bolton was to be his Xanadu. He spent more than a million pounds on the building of a lavish folly on the high promontory overlooking a vast expanse of Lancashire countryside, from Blackpool to the mountains of North Wales. It was a high point that made him most assuredly king of the Lancashire castle. He even abandoned the old manor house of the estate he had acquired in order to build a more appropriate gilded perch a thousand feet above the factories and mills of the cotton towns below.

The house he built for himself was modestly called The Bungalow. But despite its name it reeked of splendour. It was given a second storey for servants' quarters, a ballroom with his own birth constellation set as decorative art into the ceiling and a range of potting sheds that resembled a small village. The bowling green he laid down ran forward from a long stone staircase carefully tapered towards the top in order to give Uncle Bill's contrived entrances a sense of added drama and an illusion of stature that his own diminutive height could not otherwise provide.

The Japanese gardens set out at Rivington Pike were of Babylonian extravagance, with a lake, waterfalls, oriental teahouses, pagodas, exotic ornaments and shrubs, even a long stretch of mock bamboo facings fashioned over many weeks out of concrete-filled drainage pipes. The gardens needed a hundred gardeners and landscape artists to keep them in trim. And, in typical style, Lever's passion for the Norman past carried him to the building of a replica of ruined Liverpool Castle in the grounds. To visit Rivington Pike today, with The Bungalow demolished, the ornamental lakes and landscape overrun and only the fractured tiles of the entrance halls and ballroom showing through the unkempt grass, is to pay homage to a bizarrely British phenomenon – a man who used the wealth produced by industry to go backwards in time.

But Lever knew, too, the guiding principles of Britain's double bluff system. The 'labouring classes' working in his factories were expected to entrust their savings to him for paternal safe-keeping. In a striking admission of his faith in double bluff economics, he explained his philosophy of village prosperity-sharing in simple phrases:

> If I were to follow the usual mode of profit sharing I would send my workmen and workgirls to the cash office at the end of the year and say . . . 'You are going to receive £8 each; you have earned this money: it belongs to you. Take it and make whatever use you like of your money.' Instead, I told them: '£8 is soon spent, and it will not do you much good if you send it down your throats in the form of bottles of whiskey, bags of sweets, and fat geese for Christmas. On the other hand, if you leave this money with me, I shall use it to provide for you everything which makes life pleasant . . . Besides, I am disposed to allow profit sharing in no other than that form.'[6]

The arrogance of William Lever's double bluff approach to money did not extend to his children, who presumably had greater maturity and good sense than soap workers. His son William, sent to Eton so that he might acquire the education that would allow him to escape the taint of his father's grocer's upbringing, was provided with a bank account and an annual allowance, not to mention a Panhard car with a specially requested number ten sprocket. Nor did that arrogance extend only to the pressing needs of life on earth. The LeverPearson Effect produces an obsession with immortality, an almost insatiable desire to guarantee the permanence of your dynastic power by building it into the fabric of the spiritual domain as well. Stained glass windows or monuments mark every spot deemed by William Lever to have witnessed important steps on his passage through earthly life. Perhaps the most celebrated site now is that of St George's Congregational Church in Thornton Hough, close to the Leverhulme family seat of Thornton Manor near Port Sunlight.

The style of St George's is classic Norman, the stained glass modelled closely on continental examples and executed only after considerable study of early Norman churches around Europe. And, not to be dominated by any spiritual presence, William Lever first ordered that the foundations of the new church be dropped five feet below the level of the upper road. The west window was to become the framework for a stained glass window in memory of Lady Lever. At every turn it is a Lever church, down to the organ case carved from oak taken from the house in Bolton in which Mrs Lever was born. Attending a service there produces the eerie impression that it was built not to the glory of God but to a soap maker and his wife. If the rest of William Lever's life is any guide, the impression is not accidental. The building of St George's was the next best thing to creating for himself the feudal right of running a parish and placing a vicar in his living.

On the whole, biographers of William Lever have been kind. They have concentrated on the benevolent despotism that he brought to the industrial life of Lancashire and Cheshire. They have stressed the part he played in the founding of an immense commercial enterprise that gave Britain a worldwide foothold in consumer goods. They tend, nevertheless, to overlook the negative effect of his patronising and overbearing style, a manner that stifled independent thought or a desire for change. They omit the megalomanic tendencies that drove the man to gigantic projects designed more for his own gratification than to create a new generation of industry in Britain that would establish a base for an economy to compete with the rest of the world in the future, when everyone else had mastered the art of making soap.

In this sense he was not even a man of his time. Instead, he was a product of Britain's feudal subconscious, anxious only to re-create the social system of the Norman era, albeit with a touch of modern concern for simple welfare. His fixation with Napoleon – an entire room at the Lady Lever Art Gallery is given over to idols and memorabilia exalting the Emperor – suggests a mind that pursued empire for itself, and spent millions on building the townships for the workers to guarantee a captive citizenry. A page in the *Port Sunlight Magazine* in 1967, dwelling on the strange atmosphere that permeates the Lever-built community overlooking the soap complex on the banks of the Mersey, unconsciously defines the medieval style of William Lever's philosophy: 'as if you'd strayed

into private property, a trespassing into another age where everything is intensely ordered and correct'.

Thus, the LeverPearson Effect took hold of the twentieth century. The first generation of industry was overtaken by the curse of
Buddenbrook. The wealth that came to the captains of Britain's first
industrial revolution turned them into generals, whose only desire
was to transform their industrial army into loyal conscripts. In
future years that loyal army would content itself with the lifestyle of
Prutopia – of living in the past while serving the daily needs of their
high technology employers. Forty years after the death of William
Lever a casual reading of the winter 1967 issue of the *Port Sunlight
Magazine* would yield a passage that fits exactly into the Prutopian
mould, where a loyal workforce finds escape from its high technology serfdom in the pursuit of crafts and the restoration of steam
engines:

> *Tickets to the Past*
> Long before summer holiday advertisements began to appear in
> mid-December, Brian Bushell, of Port Sunlight's Data Proces-
> sing Unit, has made up his mind where he will spend *his* vacation.
> He will travel to Towyn-on-Sea, Merionethshire, where he can
> forget the marvels of electronic computers and recapture some-
> thing of the magnificence of the age of steam.

The observation is not a random point of no practical relevance.
The managers of industry act through example. In Britain the social
pattern pushes those managers to escape the dirty surroundings of
the factory in favour of rural peace. At its extreme it pushes the
leaders of industry to seek for themselves a ticket to the past
through patronage and the creation of an aristocratic lifestyle. The
energy that created an industrial structure is dissipated in frock-
coats, country houses and royal audiences. It encourages and perpetuates an unmodern set of values. Translated into hard, practical
fact it means that industry, in Britain, is inevitably a matter of
sudden and short-lived achievement which is then overtaken by the
pursuit of personal grandeur. The vital issues of technological
change, production engineering and design are abandoned. In the
end the accumulated neglect of industry turns into inexorable
decline.

One recent biographer, W. P. Jolly, does capture something of

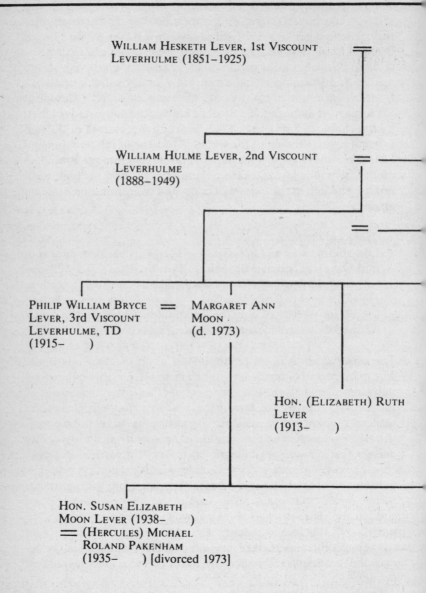

WILLIAM HESKETH LEVER, 1st VISCOUNT
LEVERHULME (1851–1925)

WILLIAM HULME LEVER, 2nd VISCOUNT
LEVERHULME
(1888–1949)

PHILIP WILLIAM BRYCE   ═   MARGARET ANN
LEVER, 3rd VISCOUNT   MOON
LEVERHULME, TD   (d. 1973)
(1915–   )

HON. (ELIZABETH) RUTH
LEVER
(1913–   )

HON. SUSAN ELIZABETH
MOON LEVER (1938–   )
═ (HERCULES) MICHAEL
ROLAND PAKENHAM
(1935–   ) [divorced 1973]

ELIZABETH ELLEN HULME
(d. 1913)

⊢ (1) MARION BEATRICE SMITH
        [divorced 1936]

⊢ (2) WINIFRED AGNES (FREDA) MORRIS, *née* LLOYD
        (d. 1966)

HON. ROSEMARY GERTRUDE ALEXANDRA
LEVER
(1919–   )
= WILLIAM ERSKINE STOBART
↓ WHETHERLY

HON. VICTORIA MARION
ANN LEVER
(1945–   )
= (1) (JOHN) RICHARD WALTER
        REGINALD CAREW POLE
        (son of SIR JOHN GAWEN CAREW
        POLE, 12th BT, DSO, TD)
        (1938–   ) [divorced 1974]
= (2) ROBERT GORDON LENNOX
↓ APSION

HON. (MARGARET) JANE
LEVER (1947–   )
= ALGERNON EUSTACE
  HUGH HEBER-PERCY
↓ (1944–   )

the flavour of the Leverhulme dynasty and its view of industry and, in doing so, he pinpoints the elusive quality of the LeverPearson Effect. It is, in simple terms, a peculiarly British failing that offers *social* rewards for *economic* achievement, and by doing this it destroys the will to continue along the path of further economic achievement. If the death of British industry can be explained by any social mechanism, then the perennial hankering for escape from industry into the pastoral peace of aristocratic gentility, so typical of the successful British entrepreneur, must come top of the list. In his book on the first Lord Leverhulme, W. P. Jolly finishes with a precise summary of the mainsprings of William Lever's outlook:

> For the King, or Gladstone, or Lloyd George, he was quite prepared to sit up and beg, round up sheep, or dig a few truffles. For labour, for his workpeople, he had a conscientious regard, attending to their education and welfare as one of them might have devoted himself to the training of a promising and well-loved whippet. His paramount regard was for himself and for the extensions of himself in his family, the small group of friends of his childhood and the firm of Lever Brothers.[7]

Significantly, the Leverhulme title disappears with the third viscount, who has produced no male heir.

But what of the Pearson family? Have not they avoided the curse of Buddenbrook, and instead brought to British industry further generations of enthusiasm for the manufacturing ethic? A close examination of the Pearson dynasty, now graced by the aristocratic title of Cowdray, will reveal the same tendencies as those that afflicted William Lever, and the same longer-term consequence of an abandonment of the worldly art of making things in favour of a lordly lifestyle surrounded by horses and royalty. The Pearson family of the 1980s is escaping from traditional industry into the safety of the landfax economy about as fast as its financial advisers can advise it. In three generations the Cowdray empire has moved away completely from the concrete and clay that made it rich. The fourth-generation heir prefers the comforts of his luxury yacht to the rigours of the daily grind of industry.

The rise of Pearson began within a year of the turn in fortune of William Lever. In 1884 Weetman Pearson moved to London from his Yorkshire home to begin bidding for major building contracts. Over the next few decades he was to reap the immense rewards that came from the business opportunities of Britain's Victorian might. A prosperous provincial construction firm was turned into the most powerful building company in the world. Weetman Pearson trod the same path of overseas expansion as William Lever; while Lever sought out and captured the supplies of palm oil and other raw materials needed for soap-making, Pearson built ports and other distribution facilities to ease the flow of commodities from distant territories to the factories in Britain. The Pearson company constructed harbours in Vera Cruz and Valparaiso, docks in Para, a dam on the Nile, railways in China and Spain; the list stretches around the world.

In Mexico, Weetman Pearson discovered his own Eldorado to match the soap gold mine that gave to William Lever untold wealth. Through his friendship with the Mexican President Porfirio Díaz, Pearson had his pick of plum contracts for massive construction projects. He bought up thousands of acres of Mexican land in the hope that they would yield oil. And they did. It is said that Weetman Pearson took more money out of Mexico than any man since Cortez. He was a cowboy in the world of business. He formed the Mexican Eagle Oil Company and sold it to Royal Dutch Shell in 1919, not too long before the revolutionary government nationalised the oil industry. Even in Britain a mixture of cowboy bravado and low cunning made money. According to legend, on the day he was awarded a lucrative contract for work on Dover Harbour, he sped to Dover before the award was made public to buy surrounding land before the prices soared.

This rapidly growing wealth pushed Weetman Pearson inexorably into the Buddenbrook groove. He became a Member of Parliament but saw the office as little more than a natural reward for his business success. He was dubbed 'the Member for Mexico' because he spent so much time there in the pursuit of profits and so little on the benches of the House of Commons. He never spoke in the House and rarely, if ever, listened to speeches made by other Members. To Pearson the life of politics seemed an empty exercise, suitable merely as a badge of prestige that reflected his business glory. His only contact with practical British politics came through his wife, who is remembered for the fashionable Liberal Party salon she ran in London.

Inevitably, Weetman Pearson climbed the aristocratic tree in parallel with William Lever. Pearson was made a baronet in 1894, a baron in 1910 and a viscount in 1917. He had come a long way from his humble roots; his grandfather had been a day labourer in the Yorkshire building trade. And he saw the objective of his climb as the creation of a feudal kingdom. In 1908 he bought Cowdray Park in Sussex; it was to give the Pearson family its aristocratic title. 'A princely estate' was how the first Lord Cowdray described his newly acquired domain of some 17,000 acres. That family was to grow and prosper through a relentless pursuit of assets, a pursuit that eventually took the dynasty away from industry into the land and data-based services of the landfax system.

When Weetman Pearson died in 1927 he left a vast conglomerate with interests in manufacturing, mining and banking. But already the high point of that Pearson dynamism had passed. The construction business had been closed by then. The second Lord Cowdray preferred life in the country to the world of business. The Pearson enterprise was run by Clive Pearson, the second son. And from there the company management was to fragment through the branches of the Pearson dynasty: a company run by blood relatives but not by the heir. Instead, the Cowdray business became a dynastic affair. Today it is run by a vast interlocking network of senior executives, many connected to the family through birth or marriage. The Cowdray family trust owns more than 6 million shares in the parent company of S. Pearson and Son, and effective leadership of the key components has passed to the aristocratic offspring of this three-generation noble line. A perusal of the complex structure of the Pearson group will identify a series of names interlinked through the pages of Burke's *Peerage*. Lord Gibson, Churchill, Lord Poole, Viscount Blakenham, the Duke of Atholl, Baron Cranworth, the Earl of Bradford and a long succession of ancient English and Scottish titles all adorn the Pearson letter-heads or the pages of ancestry into which Pearson heirs have married.

But the aristocratic character of the Pearson management is only one small part of the saga. In itself it is little more than a minor comment on the self-evident enthusiasm of the Cowdray family for the pursuit of noble credentials. More important is the drift of the Pearson company away from its industrial and constructing foundations, towards the non-industrial activities of the landfax economy.

The evolution of S. Pearson and Son since the 1960s shows a consistent concern with land, banking and information; the claims of large-scale manufacturing of the kind that produces 'democratic wealth' have, it seems, been of no interest to the Pearson board of directors. And the shift of concentration in recent years towards acquiring assets overseas rather than in the domestic economy suggests a company that sees Britain's profit-earning days as quite clearly numbered.

The Pearson record on acquisition offers a picture of conquest on the grand scale. The most recent edition of *Who Owns Whom* sets out a staggering list of some 375 company names owned by the parent S. Pearson and Son which cover a broad range of money-making activities. The Monocle Investment Trust, Insitu Double Glazing, Leach Plant Hire, Silicon (Organic) Developments, Rabbit Promotions are but a random sample. A closer examination adds shade to this otherwise dazzling view: more than half of them are dormant companies apparently bought by Pearson only to be allowed to fade away.

The true picture of S. Pearson and Son, 1980s model, is of a company abandoning mass production industry in favour of high-profit financial services, land, craft activities and amusement parks – a first class landfax conglomerate. The financial and banking activities of S. Pearson and Son, principally through the work of offshoot bank Lazards, are now among the most significant in the City of London. More than £1,000 million in landfax funds, much of it from pension funds, is handled by the bank. And Lazards itself now boasts assets of more than £600 million.

There is, too, a considerable investment in the information component of landfax enterprise, chiefly through a Pearson-owned newspaper chain of comprehensive power. An enormous fraternity of provincial newspapers carries the word to daily and weekly readers in such communities as Milton Keynes, Southend, Hillingdon, Darlington, Oxford and Hull. In all, the Pearson family control 11 evening papers, one morning paper, 56 weeklies and 18 controlled circulation publications. Around 6 million readers a week leaf through the pages of the Cowdray information network. It is especially significant that the vital heart of the landfax economy, the City of London, is all but monopolised by Pearson publications. The *Financial Times*, *The Economist*, the *Banker*, the *Investors Chronicle*, *Money Management*, *World Business Weekly*

Figure 13:2
THE PEARSON DYNASTY

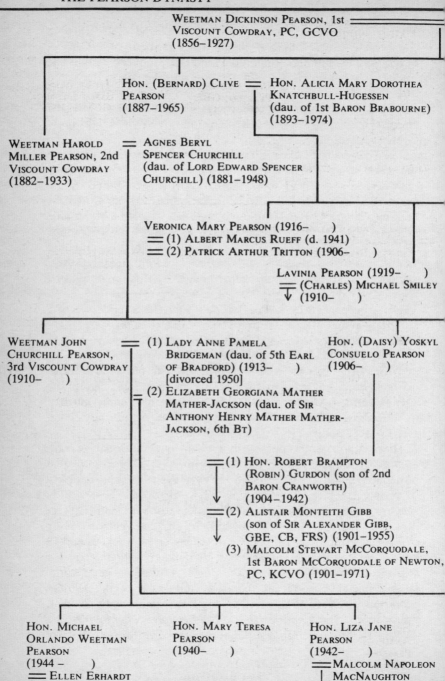

WEETMAN DICKINSON PEARSON, 1st
VISCOUNT COWDRAY, PC, GCVO
(1856–1927)

HON. (BERNARD) CLIVE ══ HON. ALICIA MARY DOROTHEA
PEARSON   KNATCHBULL-HUGESSEN
(1887–1965)   (dau. of 1st BARON BRABOURNE)
                         (1893–1974)

WEETMAN HAROLD ══ AGNES BERYL
MILLER PEARSON, 2nd   SPENCER CHURCHILL
VISCOUNT COWDRAY   (dau. of LORD EDWARD SPENCER
(1882–1933)   CHURCHILL) (1881–1948)

VERONICA MARY PEARSON (1916–   )
══ (1) ALBERT MARCUS RUEFF (d. 1941)
══ (2) PATRICK ARTHUR TRITTON (1906–   )

LAVINIA PEARSON (1919–   )
══ (CHARLES) MICHAEL SMILEY
   (1910–   )

WEETMAN JOHN ══ (1) LADY ANNE PAMELA   HON. (DAISY) YOSKYL
CHURCHILL PEARSON,   BRIDGEMAN (dau. of 5th EARL   CONSUELO PEARSON
3rd VISCOUNT COWDRAY   OF BRADFORD) (1913–   )   (1906–   )
(1910–   )   [divorced 1950]
              ══ (2) ELIZABETH GEORGIANA MATHER
                 MATHER-JACKSON (dau. of SIR
                 ANTHONY HENRY MATHER MATHER-
                 JACKSON, 6th BT)

              ══ (1) HON. ROBERT BRAMPTON
                 (ROBIN) GURDON (son of 2nd
                 BARON CRANWORTH)
                 (1904–1942)
              ══ (2) ALISTAIR MONTEITH GIBB
                 (son of SIR ALEXANDER GIBB,
                 GBE, CB, FRS) (1901–1955)
                 (3) MALCOLM STEWART McCORQUODALE,
                 1st BARON McCORQUODALE OF NEWTON,
                 PC, KCVO (1901–1971)

HON. MICHAEL   HON. MARY TERESA   HON. LIZA JANE
ORLANDO WEETMAN   PEARSON   PEARSON
PEARSON   (1940–   )   (1942–   )
(1944–   )   ══ MALCOLM NAPOLEON
══ ELLEN ERHARDT   MacNAUGHTON
                                             (–   )

══ Annie Cass (dau. of Sir John Cass, of Bradford)
    GBE   (d. 1932)

Hon. Gertrude Mary ══ Thomas Denman,
    Pearson, GBE   3rd Baron Denman,
    (1884–1954)   PC, GCMG, KCVO
                        ↓ (1874–1954)

Hon. Francis Geoffrey ══ Ethel
Pearson   Elizabeth
(1891–1914)   Lewis

Elisabeth Dione Pearson (1920–   )   Joan Cinnetta Pearson
══ (Richard) Patrick Tallentyre   (1912–   )
    Gibson, Baron Gibson (Life Peer)   ══ (William) Anthony
↓   (1916–   )   ↓   Acton (1904–   )

Hon. (Beryl) Nancy   Hon. Brenda Ruby
Pearson   Pearson
(1908–   )   (1912–   )
══ John Hugh Hare,   ══ (1) Paul Willert (son of
    1st Viscount Blakenham,   Sir Arthur Willert, KBE)
↓   PC, OBE (1911–   )   ↓   (1909–   ) [divorced 1948]
                                   ══ (2) Hugh Carter
    Hon. Angela Pearson   ↓
    (1910 (twin)–   )   Hon. (Helena) Daphne
    ══ (1) George Anthony Murray, OBE   Pearson
        (son of Sir George Evelyn Pemberton   (1918–   )
        Murray, KCB) (1907–1945)   ══ John Lakin, TD
    ══ (2) Robert Mordan Thorne Campbell Preston,   ↓ (1910–   )
    ↓   OBE, MC, TD (1909–   )

Hon. Charles   Hon. Lucy   Hon. Rosanna
Anthony   Pearson   Pearson
Pearson   (1954–   )   (1959–   )
(1956–   )   ══ Luis Hector Juan
                           Sosa Basualdo
                        ↓   [divorced 1978]

and a number of other key financial journals and newsletters have fallen under the Pearson spell. And with the coming of high-technology fax the Pearson group has moved into electronically transmitted information; through FINTEL, a million facts a day will be available on TV screens everywhere at the blink of an electronic eye – provided your purse will stand the cost of joining the elite club of TV data-bases.

The hunger for land is also very much a part of the Pearson strategy. Apart from the thousands of acres held personally by the Cowdray family – the Sussex estate near Midhurst is a mere bagatelle compared to Lord Cowdray's 60,000 acres at Dunecht in Scotland – there is a considerable stake in Millrayne Holdings, a company managing, in Pearson's words, 'a large and soundly financial portfolio of properties'. There are, in addition, the 1,700 acres of land near Grays in Essex, known as the West Thurrock Estate. This is used in part to house industrial units; but the Pearson board seems reluctant to take the plunge to the point of actually building and managing plant for the production of real things on the estate. The Pearson policy is to let the land to others so that they can take the risks of manufacturing. More than a hundred acres of the land are leased out for rubbish tips. And indeed, true to the landfax ideal of preferring farms to factories, more acres at West Thurrock are leased for agriculture than for industry.

The other half of the S. Pearson land hunger takes them to oil, the very same commodity that financed the first steps of the Cowdray dynasty three generations ago. Oil is, after all, an asset of the land, not of industry. It lies beneath it rather than on its surface, but it is in every sense a non-industrial resource that is exploited by those with rights over land or sea. Its myriad uses include industrial ones, but the pursuit of the black gold beneath the ground stems from the same landfax instincts that push funds into farmland and urban dwellings. The Midhurst Corporation, named after Lord Cowdray's country seat in Sussex, is geared almost entirely to the discovery and exploitation of oil. Through a shareholding in Ashland Oil, for example, the Pearson family have a stake in a company with total sales of more than £2,000 million a year.

But the most significant trend in the Pearson strategy is the mounting tendency to move assets out of Britain altogether. The work of Lazards favours foreign economies to a considerable extent. Indeed, the Pearson board point to their involvement in

overseas ventures as a facet of their corporate strength. To quote
from a recent company publication: 'a considerable proportion of
the funds managed is invested in foreign markets.' The same publication gives further details of the special experience of Lazards
bankers in the use of overseas tax havens and in the management of
offshore funds. A key component in this machine for funnelling
money abroad is a subsidiary bank in Jersey which specialises in
offshore activities.

Above all, the entire financial structure of the Pearson company
increasingly reflects a strategy of expanding abroad in preference to
investing in Britain. In particular, there has been a massive concentration of company growth in America. In 1969, for instance, the
turnover of Pearson activities in America represented only 0·1 per
cent of overall corporate activities. Ten years later, by the end of the
1970s, this level had grown to 16 per cent.[8] Nearly one-fifth of total
net assets were now to be found on the other side of the Atlantic
from the corporate headquarters on Millbank in London.

The major vehicle for this escape to America is the Midhurst
Corporation. The strategy is best described in the words of
company chairman Lord Gibson, who is linked to the Cowdray
name through his marriage to a cousin of the third viscount. In April
1980 he looked forward to the new decade with a message which
seemed to sum up so much of the mood of the City fraternity as it
surveyed Britain's sombre prospects: 'I give pride of place to
Midhurst, where we have a long-term programme of redeploying a
significant proportion of our substantial United States assets into
direct investments carrying control.'[9] A major investment of
Midhurst in the United States is in land; it has a large stake in the
Blackwell Land Company, which owns and operates 22,000 acres in
the San Joaquin Valley in California. In keeping with the Pearson
attraction to land plus information, the growth plan for Midhurst
is being accompanied by a programme to spread Cowdray information sheets all over Florida. In the midsummer of 1980 Pearson
Longman announced the purchase of the Manatee Group, a US
company specialising in shopping guides and advertising literature.

The future for Pearson interests in Britain therefore seems no
more optimistic than for the economy as a whole. The manufacturing sector of S. Pearson and Son – now concentrating more and
more on craft activities – has stagnated as a contributor to the
company balance sheet. In 1975 the ceramics, glass and engineering

division represented 52 per cent of total turnover and just 34 per cent of profits. Five years later this share had slipped to 49 per cent and 28 per cent respectively. The areas of growth were those most favoured by the rules of landfax economics: the information division of Pearson Longman and the Midhurst Corporation were the focal points of new profits, which rose threefold over the five-year period. If the shape of the Pearson corporate structure changes in parallel with the de-industrialising tendency of the British economy as a whole, this already discernible trend will lead eventually to a corporate mix of true landfax proportions, with manufacturing activities fading away.

Symbolically, a buoyant sector in Pearson's British empire is its amusements division, which includes such popular leisure centres as Madame Tussaud's waxworks museum, the London Planetarium, Chessington Zoo, Wookey Hole in Somerset – which is used to house relics from Britain's Roman and Celtic past – and Warwick Castle. It seems appropriate that the castle is one of Britain's best reminders of the Norman conquest, built by Henry de Newburgh, a close ally of William the Conqueror. William Lever, that conqueror of the industrial revolution, would have approved of this acquisition by the heirs of his doppelgänger, Cowdray. He would have approved, too, of the Cowdray preoccupation with stained glass windows. As with Lever, the rise of the Pearson family is framed for posterity in the leaded glass of dozens of ornate monumental windows throughout Britain, from Worth Abbey in Sussex to the unlikely surroundings of Leeds Polytechnic, close to the simple origins of the Pearson name. There, an entire circular, windowless room is given over to a carefully arranged group of Pearson stained glass relics. It has the eerie atmosphere of a tabernacle, built for a man obsessed with the pursuit of immortality, who could not, it seems, come to terms with not being God.

The sting in the tail of the LeverPearson Effect is hidden among the Cowdray amusement parks that now form an increasingly important part of Pearson's British interests. As industry falters, and the Doulton division of glass, engineering and ceramics falls behind its counterparts in the Pearson portfolio, the zoos and wonderlands take over as the profit-earners. While the Pearson financial strategists move steadily into banking, offshore activities and overseas purchases, the long-suffering manufacturing sector suffers on. The moral seems unavoidable: while Pearson's bread is made increasingly overseas, poor Britons are left with the circuses.

The LeverPearson Effect is not, by itself, an exhaustive explanation of Britain's industrial demise. It is but one facet of a social failing that conspires to demote the claims of industry within the broader framework of allotting resources. It has helped to create an economic class structure in which industry is seen as second best beside the attractions of land and finance. The City of London is a vast temple that calls to prayer each day the best and the brightest, more especially the best as denoted by birth. And the call of the aristocratic, feudal dream has played its part in sapping the energies of those who built British industry, turning them in the direction of a life of music, far distant from the pressing needs of twentieth-century Britain. Now, high technology is magnifying the impact of the LeverPearson Effect, accentuating the hold over information of the huge conglomerates and the tight-knit financial networks. Only they can spare the profits to buy into the information revolution, and by doing so build up the protective system that will keep them safe through the new dark ages. Thus do the new aristocrats make their alliance with the old.

14

Black Knight rules OK

For several decades after the Second World War it was possible to say that Britain's old class divisions were breaking down. The lubricating effects of modest prosperity had begun to blur the edges of complex sub-divisions based on birth, accent and, above all, work. The old social adage 'What you are is what you do' was being overcome by an expanding economy. The rise of the meritocracy put brains and creative impulse along with the old standards as the measuring sticks of status. Princesses married photographers; pop groups visited the Palace. The ambitions of Joe Lambton in *Room at the Top* became socially respectable. But this upstart culture didn't last for long. As the economy gathered momentum on its downward slide, the people already at the top took to the backwoods, where status doesn't grow on trees. As the money runs out the old class principles will once again become the only ones that count.

There are, in fact, two class systems at work in Britain. The one can trace its ancestry back to the Conquest, with its emphasis on landed power. The other is more subtle: it can best be described as the division between Church and Chapel. Both are dominating influences on the way Britain is organised. And now that the writing is on the castle walls both are taking command once again.

By its nature, class is an elusive topic. It eludes the mathematician with her elegant formulae. It provokes incredulous rejection when discussed by social scientists. This elusive quality nevertheless is the reason for the continuing hold of class over Britain's lifestyle. During the two hundred years of British industrial history the effects of class thinking were overshadowed by the immensity of change brought by factory production. Now that industry is disappearing and the economy is reordering itself around simpler principles, class is once again becoming a powerful factor.

All the evidence now points towards a return to a class-based lifestyle. The most comprehensive studies, those conducted by John Goldthorpe and his colleagues at Nuffield College, Oxford, have amassed considerable statistical support for the argument that Britain's experiment in classless society has failed. Surveying the record of British social history in the wake of the post-Second World War reforms, their conclusion is blunt and depressing:

> Such reforms had the explicit aim of reducing class influences on processes of 'social selection', and thus of creating greater openness in our sense; that is, greater equality of chances of access, among individuals of all class origins, to positions differently located within the social division of labour. However, what our findings . . . must suggest is that these reforms have in fact failed to achieve their objectives . . . the general underlying processes of intergenerational class mobility have apparently been little altered, and indeed have, if anything, tended in certain respects to generate still greater inequalities in class chances.[1]

Again, the technical language obscures a comparatively simple point. Despite the reforming efforts of post-war politicians and despite the egalitarian pressures of economic growth, the resilience of Britain's class system won the day. More specifically, people beginning their working lives in manual tasks have seen their opportunities for class 'improvement' actually deteriorate. Over the full span of their working careers, the chances of people of working class origins being found in service class rather than working class positions have worsened. In John Goldthorpe's words: 'The results of our enquiry lead clearly to the conclusion that . . . no significant reduction in class inequalities has in fact been achieved . . . the only trends that may arguably be discerned are indeed ones that would point to a widening of differences in class chances.'

The reasons for the failure of Britain's post-war experiment are varied and complex. The strategy adopted by several governments, of attempting to achieve reform through changing the law, clearly misjudged the resistance of the long-established class structure in the face of any challenge. But whatever the explanations, the experiment failed; the reasons are of little interest to those left imprisoned by the limiting barriers erected in any society domina- ted by class. The 'room at the top' that should have been created by the expansion of the British economy just never materialised. Put another way, the national cake that lay at the centre of the double bluff system did not grow larger; there was thus no chance of bigger slices for all. Instead, those that already had, kept. And they began to see the value of privilege and rank in keeping hold of what they had salvaged.

Thus, the pre-industrial lifestyle of Britain reasserts itself. The collapsing economy seems guaranteed to make the revived class structure of Britain 1986 one defined, as in the past, by growing inequalities of wealth and income. Already, a vast zone of poverty spreads upwards from the ranks of the low paid, unemployed and retired. The one section of the working class – in the sense of those who survive by earning wages and salaries – that has been pro- tected so far is the aptly termed 'service class'; the description has its roots in the Latin *servus*, the same origin as the 'serf' of feudal times. Even this group's prospects are clouded by the technological challenge of the electronic cottage; and the image of a service class in a cottage industry setting needs no elaboration to convey its medieval flavour.

It is only one small leap of imaginative liberty to a social system in which all the pomp and ritual of castle politics is resurrected. After all, the paraphernalia of chivalry is still bright and in good repair, polished regularly over the years by cohorts who must have known that, one day in the future, their princes would come again. Turn to any page of Burke's *Peerage* or Debrett's *Correct Form*: the jargon of feudalism is splendidly preserved. Much of it is in constant daily use; for instance, in the introduction, by Sir Iain Moncreiffe of that Ilk, to *Correct Form*:

> We have only two hereditary knights, the Knight of Kerry who is the Green Knight, and the Knight of Glin who is the Black Knight; for the White Knight has gone a-missing these many years. It may therefore seem rather unnecessary to need to know the correct way of addressing them. However, I was asked this very question by the barman of one of my clubs which one of the two hereditary knights had just joined. The correct answer, which is given in this book, is just 'knight'. So, if staying at Glin Castle, you will know to say 'Goodnight, Knight'.

That introduction was published on the eve of 1980, as Britain prepared for the new decade. There follow more than 400 pages of closely reasoned detail on the correct mode of address for every high social butterfly, from a divorced Scottish peeress to the 'widow of one who would have succeeded to a Peerage had he survived', to 'Marchionesses of the United Kingdom and Ireland since the Union'. A Table of Precedence in England and Wales, listing the pecking order of notables at formally correct gatherings, stretches over more than seven pages, excluding the pages covering Precedence in Scotland, which has been given its own, devolved, brand of official snobbery.

The pillars of Britain's social structure are being rebuilt on feudal lines. New centres of power emerged with the rise of industry after 1750: the business class of the factory regions, the trade unions. But the death of industry will take away their power base. The business class will be forced to function on the margins of the landfax economy: the growth of speculative businesses in land and finance from the mid-1960s was the first sign of this changed entrepreneurial climate. Even the pioneering spirits who are chasing success in oil exploration and production – Algy Cluff of Cluff Oil is a notable 1980s example – are merely carrying the hunger for land one stage further by seeking wealth in offshore land and the mineral riches that lie beneath the sea. The civil servants will adapt, as they always have, to the changing status quo. Their motto will remain what it has been since the power of esoteric knowledge was first recognised: 'No to change of the wrong kind.' At heart they will stay loyal servants to the people who own Britain.

The trade unions, having grown enormous on the back of industry, face a major challenge that will almost certainly destroy the power they have amassed since 1870. They will be savaged by the rapid increase in unemployment over the 1980s. Up to 5 million of their 12 million members could be out of work by the end of the decade, weighing heavy on the union funds that have been accumulated to support them. But more important, the changing shape of the economy will progressively erode the power base of organised numbers that has been the unions' chief political weapon in the twentieth century.

The impact of the video-electronic revolution will break up the huge factory constituencies that have given the trade unions their mass strength. The world of white collar work is being transformed by high technology into small units of employment, without the hordes of clerical workers filling acres of desk space. The electronic cottage is taking over, along with the small technology-based firms and craft enterprises. Where work still exists in the Britain of the future it will be in fragmented units, where political organisation and wide-scale strikes are difficult to achieve. In the land of Prutopia small will be beautiful for the employers, freed by technology from the need to negotiate with large-scale unions. And the energies of rebellious workers will be absorbed in the baking of bread and the restoration of steam trains.

Oligarchy is not by definition a calamity. A governing body can be modern, efficient and fair and, therefore, a force for good. But Britain's class structure is held together by a thread of myth and magic that puts ritual before practical value and status before any ideal of social progress. The result is a country where sentiment rules and where two different realities exist side by side. On the one hand there is Britain as it appears to outsiders: a country in which the evidence of economic and social crisis is now overwhelming; on the other there is the dream world created by Britons for themselves.

In this respect Britain is no different from many primitive cultures. In her book *Patterns of Culture*,[2] Ruth Benedict has described the potlatch system common in Pacific communities and amongst certain North American tribes. There the status seekers indulged in a maniacal kind of conspicuous consumption and conspicuous waste through feasts and giveaways. The underlying cause was a 'drive for prestige'. It has its counterparts in the British pattern of social rewards, which operates through honours and patronage and through the unspoken codes of class distinction. It drives an industrialist such as William Lever to seek escape from the soap vats that made him rich into the plush comfort and prestige of the House of Lords. Through building museums, amassing several fortunes in art treasures, designing villages for his workforce and buying entire island communities he thunders down the road to potlatch megalomania, and eventually to the prestige and recognition that Britain's tribal lifestyle readily offers him. Meanwhile, back at the soap factory . . .

Pacific cultures have also developed a series of bizarre 'cargo cults' since the Second World War that bear a striking resemblance to a modern British phenomenon. During the wartime years British

and American troops arrived by air in primitive South Sea communities to prepare for the invasion of Japan. The huge aircraft and
ships and manufactured wealth they brought with them were seen
by the islanders as nothing less than miracles. The visitors were seen
as children of the gods. And 'cargo' became the prize of salvation
offered to converts to this new religion. In the Britain of the 1980s
the blessing of offshore oil is seen by a desperate country as a vital
instrument of economic salvation. Stripped of its veneer of sophisticated statistical jargon, however, Britain's oil wealth is little more
than a North Sea cargo cult. And, as with its South Sea counterparts, it will guarantee nothing by way of salvation. Indeed, an
appraisal published in the *Financial Times* set out the probable *cost*
to British industry of the supposed gift from the sea. The net effect
of North Sea oil is a cut in the output of Britain's manufacturing
industry of 9 per cent. Not surprisingly, the effect on the landfax
economy, where land, services and information are the vital factors,
is a noticeable growth. The *Financial Times*, it is worth noting, is
owned by the leading aristocrat of the landfax system, Lord
Cowdray. The article carried the headline 'De-industrialisation is
good for the U.K.'[3]

Unfortunately, the resurrection of class as the dominant force in
Britain's economy has immediate practical effects, too. The drift
back to pre-industrial ideas of rank means that the pivotal positions
in the main economic institutions are captured by people who
favour the constipated rule of family and social pull. The directors
of the Prudential Assurance Corporation, for example, are obliged
to act on behalf of the millions who have saved in order to make the
Prudential Assurance Corporation grow rich. At the last count the
Prudential board included four peers and an assortment of figures
chosen from the City establishment, collectively paid more than
£220,000 a year. They run a financial institution of massive power,
with invested funds worth more than £7,000 million. In keeping
with the landfax system, more than £2,000 million has been invested
in land and property, including nearly 100,000 acres of agricultural
land. The remaining funds are invested in stock market paper and
government securities. According to recent company pronounce-
ments, the management of these considerable landholdings is to be
steadily transferred to men from the Pru.

The same drift has already overtaken the central pillars of the
government. The Civil Service is still dominated by entrants from

public schools and from Oxford and Cambridge Universities, and will be until well into the twenty-first century. In the mid-1970s, of external candidates who passed the Final Selection Board en route to becoming future Permanent Secretaries, more than half came from public schools, almost two-thirds came from Oxbridge and most were graduates in arts subjects, with little expertise in the technological challenges of the next thirty years. These are the people who will be in charge of the key Whitehall departments in A.D. 2010.

In politics, too, the drift back to class-ridden government is quite marked (see Tables 14:1, 14:2 and 14:3). A modern Labour Cabinet is less 'working class' in composition than it would have been thirty years ago. Both major parties are being taken over once again by the products of the public schools. The hope of creating a classless political system, enshrined in the reforms of the 1940s, is becoming a hollow memory. All this, of course, would be unimportant if a surge of economic democracy had swept away the power or significance of class background. A 'middle class' Labour Cabinet, for instance, would make some sense if the 'working class' that had founded the Labour movement had withered away in a climate of general prosperity. But this has not happened. The social value of a public school background would become worthless in a country where popular education were successfully installed. But again, the economic pressures push the other way. The collapse of Britain's Welfare State since 1975, presided over by both political parties, has made private education the one sure guarantee of future survival for the children of an anxious population. It was, perhaps, fitting that just four days before the *Financial Times* was proclaiming the joys of de-industrialisation, the *Sunday Times* published figures that showed that local authorities were spending more on public school fees than on buying books for local secondary schools. The local authorities covered in the survey, more than thirty in all, were a mixture of Labour- and Conservative-led councils. The drift to the new feudalism is an all-party affair.

But of more practical impact still is the pervasive effect of status ranking in the everyday world of industry, commerce and the professions. There always has been a discernible pattern of class preferences when it comes to taking a job in Britain. 'You are what your work is' has long been the unwritten code that has maintained Britain's social divisions. The 'tradesman's entrance' to the homes

THE BACKGROUND OF LABOUR POLITICS

Table 14:1

Social and educational background of Labour MPs

| | % of total: Main occupation | | | % of total: Education | | |
	Profes-sional	Business	'Worker'	Private	Univer-sity	Oxbridge
1918–35	33	5	39	18	31	12
1945	35	8	28	19	34	15
1955	37	7	25	24	38	16
1964	41	10	18	23	44	18
1974 (Oct)	51	10	12	16	56	21

Table 14:2

Social and educational background of Labour Cabinets

	Aristoc-racy	Middle class	Working class	Public school All	Eton	University All	Oxbridge
1924	3	5	11	8	–	6	6
1945	—	8	12	5	2	10	5
1964	1	14	8	8	1	13	11
1974	1	16	4	7	–	16	11
1976	1	13	7	7	–	15	10

THE BACKGROUND OF CONSERVATIVE POLITICS

Table 14:3

Social and educational background of Conservative Cabinets

	Aristoc-racy	Middle class	Working class	Public school	Eton	Oxbridge
1922	8	8	–	14	8	13
1935	9	11	2	14	9	10
1955	5	13	–	18	10	14
1963	5	19	–	21	11	17
1970	4	14	–	15	4	15
1979	3	18	–	19	6	16

Source for Tables 14:1, 14:2 and 14:3: Ivor Crewe, Department of Government, University of Essex

of polite society speaks paragraphs for the paranoia displayed by the better placed about being contaminated by contact with those who fetch and carry for a living. Even such areas as industrial management or the specialised professions have been overtaken by considerations of status, and here the damaging consequences have a direct effect upon economic activity.

To begin with, the role of 'manager' has always been regarded as that of a feudal steward. As the English reformer Robert Owen put it in 1811: 'My intention was not to be a mere manager.' To witness the British manager of today, on a visit to some foreign capital, humbly confessing to the job of industrial manager − when the local culture invariably ranks such a man high up the scale of social significance − is to see the damning effects of a social rule book that has split the entire world of economics into Dirty and Clean. The Dirty Hands Disease is an accurate term for the socially rooted rejection of work in industry by entire classes of the British population. As the Australian-born businessman and inventor Alistair Mant has observed, the British obsession with Dirty and Clean cleaves right through the world of work.[4]

Part of this obsession is expressed through code-words or a simple choice of vocabulary. Nowhere in continental Europe, for example, does one find the British division of science into 'pure' and 'applied'. In Britain the arts are definitely OK; the recruitment system of the senior Civil Service is geared to the superiority of the 'arts' mind over the mind skilled in practical engineering or of scientific bent. And 'pure' science is *fairly* OK. But *'applied'* science is definitely rather too low down the league table of social point-scoring. Put at its most basic, 'applied' science is too near the unseemly world of manufacturing to be recommended socially. The distinction spreads right through the hierarchy of Britain's sensibilities. Clean is OK; it is the City, the better professions (though they all have their own in-built aristocracies), the effortless generalist with his public school and Oxbridge education. It is hardly surprising that a society that has encouraged its citizens to seek social status above everything else should place the Clean above the Dirty, and spend all its energy striving to become as pure as the soap that put Lord Leverhulme where he is today.

As with Britain's ornate class structure, where Black Knight still rules OK, the status system in the world of work produces its share of absurdities. Research by Liam Hudson, for instance, has uncovered some startling observations about the social origins of doctors and the parts of the body on which they later specialise. He found there was a statistically valid correlation between social background and U and non-U specialisms.[5] Doctors who had been educated at public schools tended to specialise in work on the head as opposed to bodily areas below the waist. They preferred the exterior surface of the body to the innards, the living body as opposed to the dead body, even the male body as opposed to the female. The moral seems clear: the distinction is deeper than mere professional status. It is a matter of subconscious calculations of cleanliness or dirtiness. All doctors belong to the clean side of working Britain, certainly in comparison to work in industry. But because of the absurd mechanics of a finely-tuned system of social ranking, British medicine (in common with most other professions) has developed an Orwellian rule book of its own. All doctors are clean, but some doctors are cleaner than others.

The most costly result of the application of British Binary Thought, as Mant observes, is that it polarises the workplace. It is usual for British commentators to speak of 'both sides of industry' when discussing management and workers, as if managers do not work and workers are not part of the operational framework of the company that employs them. In a very telling though quite accidental allusion to the world of Lord Leverhulme, Mant summed up the British ethic in a single sentence: 'While applied science has to mean machines, grime, oily rags, soot, effluent, etc, "pure" is the word most preferred by the soap manufacturers, almost as though soap were not the end product of a manufacturing process.' The force of this was brought home to me on a visit to a pottery in Stoke, where I was taken round the workshops by a man in a white coat. 'What branch of pottery are you in?' I inquired. 'I'm not,' came back the reply, 'I'm a manager.' The pottery, part of the Royal Doulton group, was a small outpost of Lord Cowdray's business empire. I wondered if the good Lord and the pottery manager would feel themselves to be kindred spirits on the U side of British life.

But the rule of Binary Thought spreads wider than the British workplace. It permeates every layer of every slice of British life (see Table 14:4). There is the class structure so beloved of Sir Ian Moncreiffe of that Ilk ('a quaint name we have used since the Middle Ages because it gives other people such fun'); there is the coded

BRITISH BINARY THOUGHT

Table 14:4

Class and the British workplace

Clean U	Dirty Non-U
Effortless	Hard working
Pure science	Applied science
The professions	Industry
Gentlemen	Hard men
Brains	Hands
Generalist	Specialist
Management (just)	Workers
Eye specialist	Gynaecologist
South	North
Landfax	Manufacture
Wealth/fees	Income/wages
Dress for work	Undress for work

Derived from Alistair Mant, *The Rise and Fall of the British Manager*, Macmillan, 1977

world of Dirty and Clean. Through them both, like a great religious divide, runs a tribal confrontation that touches politics, money, work, school and play. It can best be defined as Church and Chapel (see Table 14:5). And in the Britain of Prutopia it seems clear that Church will hold all the trump cards, as it did when the first Domesday Book was written nine centuries ago.

The English Church, of course, has always had a stake in the pre-industrial order. For hundreds of years the tithe on farm produce was the lifeblood tax that supported the priesthood and maintained the fabric of the local parish buildings. It is understandable that the coming of industry was seen as a diabolical threat to the wealth and privileges of the traditional Church hierarchy. The vast factories became the dark Satanic mills that figure so centrally in the hymn 'Jerusalem'. The fire and smoke of the great iron furnaces and ovens of the eighteenth- and nineteenth-century industrial towns were regarded as evidence of a Faustian pact with the Devil that posed a direct challenge to the rural strongholds of old Church England. In this fear the Church found an ally in the landed aristocracy, who saw the town only as the means by which their landed wealth could be turned into money. The City of London became a

BRITISH BINARY THOUGHT

Table 14:5

Church and Chapel

Church	Chapel
Monarchy	Parliament
King	Country
South	North
Landfax	Industry
Professions	Jobs
Esoteric knowledge	Exoteric knowledge
Oxbridge	Redbrick
Plutocratic	Meritocratic
Charles II	Cromwell
County	Town
Status quo	Dissent
The past	The future
Cricket	Football
Monetarism	Equality
Troops in Ireland	Troops out
Nuclear war	Staying alive
EEC	Siege economy
Civil Service power	Trade union power
Oil	Coal
Winning	Following

vast laundering mechanism that relied on the gentlemanly reputa-
tions of the country squirearchy to spin fortunes out of nowhere.
The town nevertheless remained a place to be treated with suspicion; like the factories that had given it life, the town founded on
industry has always been seen as a potential enemy, ready to steal
away the lifestyle of the rural elites at the first opportunity.

Thus, the Church has remained the protective cocoon within
which pre-industrial Britain has stayed strong and safe, waiting for
the day when the upstart culture of factories and trade unions,
building societies and equal pay, women's rights and popular education would all run out of steam. The Chapel, with its provincial,
unadorned façade, stands for the enemy. And within these two
brick-built temples the two sides of Britain's social framework
congregate. They listen to different sermons and have visions of
Britain's future which are diametrically opposed. The people in the
Church look forward to Prutopia, where the landfax aristocrats will

rule. Those in the Chapel are still waiting for Cromwell's unfinished revolution to be completed, and some semblance of modernity to be grafted on to Britain's feudal ways. Church has a stake in economic sloth; Chapel needs industrial success to pay for the changes it has prayed for over the years. Church believes in the power of esoteric knowledge. It will make certain it captures control of the computer nerve centres of the economy. Chapel believes in the freedom of all information on the premise that the truth shall set you free.

In the long run the battle between Church and Chapel will decide Britain's social future. All the odds are stacked in favour of Church. It controls the sinews of status quo Britain: Oxbridge, the Civil Service, the Conservative Party, the landfax system. Organised through a system of elites, it is far better equipped to act quickly and effectively when the day of judgment comes. And if the battle runs to a close finish, Church has Black Knight on its side – and quite a few other soldiers, too.

It was Church that welcomed William the Conqueror. And did very nicely out of it. Now that the shape of Britain's social system is going through another revolutionary transition, Church will see its chance.

KEEPING DOWN
THE PEASANTS

15

CS isn't just a gas; it stands for Civil Service

It was no coincidence that Britain's Civil Service was born in the Valley of the Shadow of Death. Seven months after the disastrous Charge of the Light Brigade in the Crimea in October 1854, the Palmerston government answered the growing clamour for reform by creating the Civil Service Commission. It was a tactical victory for Palmerston, a strategic defeat for Britain. In the century that followed, this new Civil Service created for itself a power base at the very heart of the economic and political structure. An elite was born; nobody noticed as it slowly took command of the controlling levers of everyday life. And nobody realised that, by its very make-up and attitudes, it was taking control not in the interests of change but in support of the same ethos of pre-industrial amateurism that had driven the light cavalry to their doom in Russia.

Britain in the 1980s is governed in the same way that it is educated, informed, defended and organised for economic purposes. It is governed by a tight-knit mafia whose principal quality is its devotion to the static present rather than to issues of the future, to traditional ideas rather than new, to the last war rather than to averting the raging battle that will surely come when the awful dimensions of Britain's Prutopian fate begin to dawn on the populace. To repeat the final paragraph of a comprehensive and critical examination of Britain's Civil Service, published in the first year of the new decade:

> Whitehall's mandarins have helped inflict, and now defend, this malaise and call it good government. To challenge the character and operation of the Civil Service is to assault the very citadel of

Britain's closed corporate state. Possibly the biggest question facing the British political system in the 1980s is whether it has the will and the ammunition to mount that assault.[1]

Perhaps the second biggest question is whether the assault will be more than a replay of the charge of 1854, an empty gesture against the wrong guns at the right time.

The assault will almost certainly be defeated, for a very simple reason. Britain's Civil Service elite is purely a manifestation of a set of attitudes and social principles which pervades every crevice of the pillars of British society. To attempt to reform the outlook and practices of those 'Whitehall mandarins' is to call into doubt the entire panoply of elite-producing machinery, from public school to Oxbridge to polite social pressure. And that is little less than to call for social revolution. The optimist will say the attempt is essential; the pessimist will point to the elegance of the self-reinforcing network of loyalties, prizes and inbred attitudes that gives those pillars their rock-hard mortar.

The size of Britain's government machine provides it with a ready-made first line of defence. The growth of welfare politics after 1945 brought millions of people into public sector employment. More than 4,500,000 men and women work as public servants, paid from taxpayers' contributions. More still are employed as administrators in the nationalised industries. This weight of numbers produces a great, inert outer wall of humanity behind which the Whitehall elite shelters for protection against critical attack.

The central government Civil Service has a strength of nearly three-quarters of a million, a figure against which the pin-pricks of public spending cuts have made only slight progress. But the figures are deceptive. Of this enormous contingent only 4,000 are actual 'policymakers', the London-based Principals and above. It is here, in this relatively tiny group, that the power of government is vested. It is here, therefore, that the great dragon Attitude can wreak such havoc if let loose unchecked. Or, as in the case of The Four Thousand, checked to the point of awe-inspiring uniformity.

The philosophy of Britain's modern Civil Service can best be gauged from the comment of *The Times* when Sir Ian Bancroft was appointed Head of the Home Civil Service in 1977: 'Sir Ian's profession is vital to the country's fortunes. It is a sheet anchor of the constitution and a great bulwark against change of the worst kind.'[2]

The key issue, therefore, is the one that leaps out from the cautious syntax of the second sentence: how is 'change' categorised? The answer lies behind the steep, forbidding walls of the Civil Service citadel. And it is a familiar one.

Lord Balogh, a former adviser to Prime Minister Harold Wilson in Downing Street, put his finger on it in 1959:

> The image of a smoothly and efficiently working parliamentary democracy is one of the most extravagant of all British myths. Its rise has to a large extent been due to the vanity of the politicians and the genius at public relations of the heads of our bureaucracy . . . Effective power without responsibility, the complete freedom from all criticism, and last but not least, the attainment of higher salaries than their ministerial chiefs – such are the rich rewards of their skilful efforts.[3]

Balogh went on to attack the method of Civil Service recruitment which, he said, favoured 'the smooth, extrovert conformist with good connexions and no knowledge of modern problems'. The attack was driven home five years later, in a Fabian tract called *The Administrators*: Britain, it said, was governed by a closed monastic order, isolated from industry, local government and the pressing social problems of daily life. Nothing had changed, it seemed, from the medieval days of mass illiteracy, when clerics used their learning to take control over the running of the earthly, as well as the heavenly, estate. Even in the 1980s, the clerics still rule.

As with Britain's other elite fraternities, that of the modern Civil Service is filtered through carefully constructed stages of education and breeding. The selection process that replenishes the upper echelons of the Service favours white against black, amateur against technician, public school against state school, Oxbridge against redbrick. The objective is the perpetuation of a governing habit that is biased in favour of stability within the kingdom, a best-of-all-possible-worlds in which the doubting of administrative decisions taken in Whitehall is seen as akin to treason. Certainly, the model of the ideal recruit seems designed to foster a general euphoria in the status quo, preferably *in statu quo ante*; and certainly the governing elite which supervises that recruitment makes sure that the model is kept brightly polished.

The point is made quite unconsciously by one Oxbridge careers adviser, in replying to a question concerning work in a Whitehall department:

> One of the attractions is not the work as such but the fact that people are conscious that they want stimulating colleagues; it's the environment rather than the job. The Civil Service is one of the few employers who look kindly on post-graduate students in medieval history.[4]

Indeed, the entire balance of the recruitment procedure for senior civil servants is tilted in favour of those post-graduate historians with their taste for the feudal past. The Civil Service Selection Board, known to close observers of Whitehall folklore as Cizbee, is not so much concerned with the objectives of a candidate as with his origins. It seems less interested in where you wish to go in your career than where you have been. And at the back of the collective mind of Cizbee there pulses an overriding question: are these candidates before us PLU – People Like Us?

The Selection Board scrutineers reject this accusation; the tests they supervise and interpret are not, they say, designed to recruit in the image of the existing mandarinate. As far as plain statistics can prove anything, however, these remonstrances are a transparent sham. Despite the efforts of the Fulton Committee, which reported in 1968 with the central conclusion that the so-called cult of the generalist 'is obsolete at all levels and in all parts of the Service', and despite the persistent criticism of recruitment procedures by committee after committee in Parliament, entry into the citadel is still most readily achieved through the code-words of nineteenth-century gentlemanly life; the arts training received by Oxbridge undergraduates is still the most favoured passport.

Between 1948 and the beginning of the 1970s, when the minor reforms resulting from Fulton altered the structure of the class divisions within the Civil Service, recruitment to the Administrative Class was dominated by graduates of Oxbridge (see Table 15:1). If anything, the dominance grew stronger over those years. Since then, although the rules of entry and promotion have been tinkered with, little has altered in the corridors of Oxbridge power. Ten years after Fulton, in 1978, the qualifying test pass rate for Oxbridge candidates was still twice that of candidates from other universities; that from private schools was 50 per cent better than from maintained schools. Above all, the pre-industrial flavour of the intake shone through: less than a third of the degrees taken by the successful candidates were in the practical world of science and technology.

But this qualifying test is only one stage in the scaling of the citadel walls. After successfully passing through the first filter, the candidate goes before the Cizbee judges – the Civil Service Selection Board. In that 1978 intake, the selection stage showed the same in-built bias in favour of Oxbridge and public school education, despite the neutralising effect of the first stage of qualifying tests. Thus, a disproportionate number of 'privileged' candidates ('privileged' by their access to the best teaching and the most status-orientated pieces of paper) won through on the second round. Again the technical specialisation of the candidate seemed of little importance, arts graduates performing just as well as their science-trained rivals. The result is summed up in the comments of a constitutional expert, Lord Crowther-Hunt, who served as constitutional adviser to the Prime Minister in the 1970s, as well as on the Royal Commission on the Constitution and on the earlier Fulton Committee itself: 'The Cizbee system appears not to mind what you have studied, but it does favour a privileged background.'[5]

The effects of such a selection system on the practical art of government are shattering and probably account, more than any other single factor, for Britain's economic crisis. One celebrated story, rarely repeated outside the closed world of Whitehall, tells of a senior civil servant in charge of motorway policy. When asked by a

OXBRIDGE RULES IN A.D. 2000

Table 15:1

Recruits to Administrative Class since 1944 Education Act[6]

	1948–50 method		1951–55 method		1956–60 method		1961–65 method		1966–70 method
	1	2	1	2	1	2	1	2	both
% with fathers in routine manual or non-manual work	51	44	48	21	43	14	25	18	25
% at state school	43	22	39	21	47	26	25	29	38
% at Oxbridge	65	74	75	89	77	93	81	80	62

Source: Ivor Crewe, Department of Government, University of Essex

member of an inquiry team whether he had studied road construction techniques in North America and elsewhere as a means of improving the expertise of his own department, he replied that he saw no point in such an exercise since the Civil Service wanted generalists who could be moved easily from post to post, from education to pensions to fisheries. A specialism, therefore, would be regarded as an unwanted drag on that career-ladder mobility. The episode is one small part of an overall vendetta against technical specialisation in Whitehall. In this particular case it goes far in explaining why Britain now faces a ten-year period of motorway decay, vast expense in repairs and a disastrous decade of traffic delays on the main arteries of road transport.

There can be no prospect of changing the operational characteristics of Britain's government machine, and of opening up avenues for new policy for the economy, until the outlook of the Civil Service is shifted in the direction of twenty-first-century needs. A change of attitude does not appear likely. The Fulton Committee was a frontal assault on that 'citadel of Britain's closed corporate state'; it was expertly smothered by the mandarins, with a little assistance from high-placed friends. The Central Policy Review Staff, installed in the Cabinet office in the early 1970s as a buffer around the Prime Minister to protect him against the unfettered influence of the career Civil Service, has been slowly steamrollered into irrelevance. Much the same fate had befallen the old Department of Economic Affairs, set up in 1964 by a zealous Wilson administration to protect Labour's economic programme from the weight of Treasury inertia. By the time Edward Heath became Prime Minister in 1970 the DEA had gone. And the so-called 'chocolate soldiers' – advisers brought in from the outside world and financed by grants from the Rowntree confectionery company – were neutralised by the Civil Service self-preservation machine.

Even if this Whitehall machine is overturned and selection procedures are reformed in favour of broad-based recruitment and highly specialised personnel able to confront the challenges of a high-technology age, the damage has already been inflicted. The shape of Whitehall things to come has already been determined by the Civil Service career structure, for that carefully chosen intake of the 1970s will provide the heads of government departments for the year 2010. By then their grasp of medieval history could serve them well in the governance of the new feudal Britain.

For the moment, the only direct challenge to the high-minded moralising of top civil servants like Sir Ian Bancroft comes from Ministers themselves. In this respect it seems fitting that British television ushered in the 1980s with a series that poked sophisticated fun at the efforts of a new Minister to overcome the serried ranks of prejudice offered by his senior departmental advisers. It is not surprising that *Yes Minister* proved popular; so many in Britain secretly prefer the rule of mandarins to that of the elected. But it is not just the Confucian minds of people like Sir Ian that guarantee success in the Whitehall battle against *The Times*'s 'change of the worst kind'. Sheer weight of numbers plays its part. In 1900 there were roughly 50,000 civil servants in Britain, serving (if that is the correct term) about 60 Ministers. This means a ratio of civil servants to Minister of a little over 800 to 1. In 1980 the Civil Service establishment stood at some 700,000 with just over 100 Ministers. The ratio had risen to 7,000 to 1, a trend that speaks paragraphs about the impossibility of politicians getting on top of the massive edifice that drafts policy and supervises its implementation.

Backwards to the guns

A Civil Service created in the aftermath of monumental disaster on the battlefield can be expected to have a special contribution to make in military policy. With the mandarins busily fending off change and the generals equally busily planning for the last war, the chances of backward progress are high. Much of Britain's defence sector has long suffered from over-bureaucratisation and endless back-stabbing between the armed services in the pursuit of favoured treatment by politicians in the defence budgets. With the annual level of spending on defence now running at above £8,000 million, such official warfare is likely to have enormous, and expensive, consequences.

The most significant area of turmoil is in procurement, involving the building of weaponry, the purchasing of supplies and the funding of new designs for equipment. This sector involves considerable expenditure; in the Estimates for 1980–1, for example, £4,300 million was set aside for purchases of equipment and some £1,200 million for miscellaneous stores and services. Yet a brief examination of the Whitehall approach to procurement will yield a depressing picture of administrative mayhem and ambition-tainted bowler-hatted imperialism. The light and shade in that picture are graphically reproduced in a recent report of the House of Commons Expenditure Committee, published after taking extensive evidence of the bureaucratic wonders of the Ministry of Defence:

> The examples quoted suggest that decision-making at the highest level in the Ministry may have been influenced more by the fear of making mistakes than by the possible rewards of taking risks. While the Ministry may thus have avoided more serious errors, the policy has resulted in prolongation of the lives of projects which eventually were cancelled and in damaging delays to projects which might have been pressed ahead with earlier. The effects have also included disillusionment and damage to morale in industry and impairment of military preparedness.[7]

No better illustration of this failure can be found than the strange story of HMS *Invincible*. The Royal Navy, of course, has shrunk in parallel with Britain's political and economic demise. At the outbreak of war in 1939 Britain boasted the largest navy in the world: some 300 ships and 161,000 men. By 1980 the strength of British naval personnel stood at 71,000; the complement of major surface combat vessels stood at 72. This contraction was offset, in some measure, by the decision to base the small deterrent force in the submarine fleet, but the scale of reduction in naval strength had a massive effect on morale. The most humiliating blow to naval prestige was the loss of the great aircraft carriers. At one point there were seven of the 50,000-ton monsters capable of carrying four squadrons of fighters, and they were the very touchstones of British naval pride. In the Defence White Paper of February 1966 – as if in celebration of the ninth centenary of the Battle of Hastings – the government announced that the aircraft carriers were to be scrapped.

There then began a bitter struggle in Whitehall, a struggle that could be traced back to a decision at the start of the Second World War that Britain's navy would be given long-term replacements for its main capital ships. The decision to scrap the carriers was regarded by senior officers and their allies in the ministries as a betrayal of this promise. And they were ready to use all the weapons of bureaucratic guile, political string-pulling and moral blackmail to achieve victory – no matter what the cost to the taxpayer or even to the strategic efficacy of the navy itself. As the then Prime Minister, Harold Wilson, recorded:

> There was a tremendous battle within the Defence Department, involving Service ministers as well as Chiefs of Staff, on the carrier controversy. The final advice was to phase the carriers out. There was a sharp revolt from the Navy and, in the event, the First Sea Lord, Sir David Luce, resigned with quiet dignity. The Minister of Defence for the Navy, Christopher Mayhew, resigned as well.[8]

No new orders were to be placed for carriers. As the existing ones became obsolete, they were to be taken out of commission. By 1978, the last of the seven, *Ark Royal*, was on her way out of the navy. It seemed like a victory for those who had argued for a reduction in our forces.

But for the navy, no battle is ever over until the last shot has been fired. By 1980 a new aircraft carrier, *Invincible*, was coming *into* service, to be followed by two more – the *Illustrious* and a new *Ark Royal*. They are 'disguised' aircraft carriers, technically called 'through-deck cruisers', but classified in *Jane's Fighting Ships* as 'light aircraft carriers'. The *Invincible* carries a total of eighteen aircraft – ten Sea King helicopters and eight Sea Harrier jump jets. By 1979, even the navy was forced to admit that she was something more than a mere cruiser. 'An aircraft carrier, perhaps,' was the description of the Flag Officer Naval Air Command, Vice-Admiral Sir Desmond Cassidi (quoted in the *Guardian*, 28 March 1978).

The story of how the navy – in complete contravention of the wishes of the 1964 government – managed to get its new generation of aircraft carriers after all, is a classic example of the power of the bureaucracy; having dug its heels in on the issue, it proved more than a match for the strength of four successive Defence Secretaries. It also provides a salutary demonstration of spiralling costs, wrong-headed strategic thinking, and a blinkered resistance to uncomfortably original thought.

In sounding the death knell of the aircraft carriers, the 1966 Defence White Paper laid out the strategy that in future air support for naval operations was to be provided from shore bases. *Invincible* thus began life as a through-deck cruiser carrying helicopters. Its job, the primary job of the Royal Navy this century, was to protect convoys. Only by securing the vital convoy routes across the Atlantic can Britain hope to survive in a conventional war; around this premise our whole naval strategy is supposedly built. Convoy protection requires a special sort of ship – fast, cheap and manoeuvrable. Unfortunately, such ships are not the stuff of which naval traditions and impressive naval reviews are made. It is also true that the building plans for such small ships are far more likely to be cut back than those of larger ships in which a big capital investment has already been made. Thus, as the navy's planners settled down to design the *Invincible* and the new cruiser class, there were already strong institutional reasons for making the ship as large and powerful as possible.

The 1964 plans for *Invincible* were for a ship of some 10,000 tons, to be built at a cost of £60 million. By the time the various departments of the navy had added their recommendations, the size of the ship had almost doubled. The ship that was finally laid down at the Vickers yards in 1973 included successive modifications which ensured that, when she was fully loaded, the *Invincible* would have a displacement of 19,500 tons.

By 1979 when she was launched, *Invincible*'s costs had soared to £250 million. By the time the ship went into full commission in late 1980, her total cost was around £400 million – an increase of 650 per cent in sixteen years. (Such hyper-inflation is not uncommon within the Ministry of Defence: the Sting Ray, Britain's new light-weight torpedo, was estimated in 1969 to cost £82 million; by 1977 the project, still uncompleted, had so far cost £700 million.)

The *Invincible* is completely unsuited to Britain's modern strategic needs. It will not protect convoys; in fact it represents so large a capital investment that at least five other frigates will have to be assigned to protect it – at a cost, according to NATO sources, of £500 million. Thus the *Invincible*, with a total crew of around 1,000 and a highly expensive communications system, becomes the 'command and control' centre of a task force – implying an aggressive stance quite out of keeping with the current underlying strategy of the navy which is defensive, and certainly quite different from the role envisaged for it a decade earlier.

The chief difference between the plans for the *Invincible* of 1964 and the ship which exists today is in its planes, the eight Sea Harrier jump jets which at one time threatened the whole through-deck cruiser project.

The navy managed to convince the Ministry of Defence that it needed the new class of ship, with its multitudinous technical sophistications, only after the aircraft carriers had been abandoned. The development of the Harrier, the world's first V/STOL (Vertical/ Short Take-Off and Landing) aircraft, was a grave embarrassment. Here was a plane that clearly could have applications to the needs of the navy – but because of the labyrinthine politics of the Ministry of Defence it had to be ignored. For the navy to have admitted, at a crucial stage in the development of the through-deck cruiser, that they might now need some form of aircraft carrier, would have brought down upon them the wrath of the air force, and might have threatened the whole *Invincible* project. They pointed out that the vertical take-off involved a massive fuel payload, reducing the Harrier's fire-power.

It was into this delicate situation that Lieutenant-Commander Doug Taylor wandered, in 1970, with an original and revolutionary idea: using a 'ski jump' ramp, the Harrier could take off from the deck of a ship in almost storm force conditions, with a dramatic improvement in performance. A take-off along a 500-ft runway enabled the plane to lift only 8,000 lb. of fuel and weapons, whereas a 250-ft runway and a ski-jump enabled it to take off with over 10,000 lb. The ski-jump would cost £250,000. A similar improvement using engine power would have cost £35 million.

Taylor's bright idea brought him a reprimand from the Director of Naval Air Warfare for putting the *Invincible* in jeopardy. He was forbidden to mention the subject in public. In 1974 Taylor went back to the ministry again with more detailed plans. Once again he met with a hostile response.

It was to be six years before Taylor's proposal was accepted. Only after the *Invincible* and the *Illustrious* had been laid down and the navy had been granted the right to purchase Sea Harriers was Taylor's idea considered politically possible.

Over the course of sixteen years the 10,000-ton through-deck cruiser became a 20,000-ton 'command centre for maritime forces' and now, finally, 'an aircraft carrier, perhaps'. In the intervening period, the Icelandic Cod War showed just how overly sophisticated the British navy had become. Its sophistication left it unable to face the real tasks; the highly technical frigates sent out to protect fishing trawlers in the early 1970s could not compete with the more manoeuvrable Icelandic gun-boats.

In full battle readiness, with SAM and twin Sea Dart missiles, with a speed of 28 knots and a range of 5,000 miles, the *Invincible* is one of the most impressive ships of any of the world's navies. There is no doubt that it is a powerful status symbol. It is unfortunately also true that it is quite irrelevant to Britain's needs. Meanwhile, a vast army of men from the ministry can claim victory. And the proud tradition of planning for the last war has been upheld with valour.

16
Preparing for the feudal peace

A society shows its true colours by the way it prepares for war. To echo the words of Franklin D. Roosevelt in 1940: 'The core of our defense is the faith we have in the institutions we defend.' As much was true in England's feudal years seven or eight centuries ago, when the knight on horseback fought for the feudal values that gave him his rank and power. Now, technology has given the man on horseback massive destructive capability, the power to annihilate entire cities. The aftermath of nuclear war will be a society in which industry has all but gone and local communities will be thrown back on the limited resources of feudal times, chiefly the produce of the land. Nuclear war in Britain would, in effect, be a sudden, concentrated version of the slow death that is steadily overtaking Britain's industrial sector. In the plans for nuclear survival drawn up by the Whitehall mandarins you will find all the elements needed to defend the fabric of Britain's status quo from the rebellion and conflict that the slow death of industry through peaceful decline will increasingly generate. Nuclear war, or industrial collapse through neglect – the result is the same for the economic and social structure. And for Britain, planning for nuclear war is no different from planning for the social confrontations that will scar the feudal peace of Prutopia.

During the preparation of this book the author took part in an exercise mounted by the Emergency Planning Service of Humberside County Council (see Document 2 of the appendix). The exercise was based on the assumption that Britain had been the victim of a massive nuclear attack and that powers of government had thereby fallen to the local controllers designated by the Home Office to wield ultimate power in the post-nuclear period. The exercise confirmed what seems apparent from a superficial reading of Britain's official war planning: that the elimination of industry will re-create the economic structure of the medieval era, and that the natural bias of our administrators – and through them of the controllers who will govern Britain in the vital days after nuclear attack – is towards the model of feudal society as the basis of post-war politics.

It is already acknowledged by specialists in civil defence that the economic sector best geared to survival in Britain is the agricultural sector, and that those people best protected against nuclear bombardment are prosperous landowners living in large, thick-walled country houses built over their customary cellars. It is also certain that the vital commodity after a nuclear war would be food. Put more simply, the nuclear destruction of industry would have the effect of returning power to the landed gentry who have been so busily entrenching themselves in the countryside during the past two decades of British industrial demise. The other vital factor in a post-nuclear Britain would be information. The computer networks of the government would be the backbone of the post-war capacity to govern: they would provide all the details of pre-war life from criminal records to income tax arrears. Access to data-banks of big commercial companies would be essential for any attempt to re-create a primitive economy. The telephone network, much of it strategically protected through a carefully designed long-term programme of double-routing and hardened tunnels, would become the lifeline of the government machine.[1] In short, nuclear attack would push Britain prematurely into its landfax future, where land and information become the twin pillars of power.

But what of the peasants in this post-nuclear feudality? It is here, clearly, that the point of tension would arise, for a vast mass of disillusioned, bereaved and terrified people would pose a revolutionary threat of unparalleled proportions. And it is here that the most significant – and chilling – observation is to be made about the nature of Britain's official plans for nuclear war. The underlying philosophy of Home Office policy is that the primary objective must be to preserve Britain's governing elite, so that the transition to feudal peace should not be interrupted by an unnecessary debate amongst the populace about who should rule what is left of the country. Reading between the lines of the Home Office circulars, the glossy pamphlets on survival and the prognoses of the planners at regional level who are already well trained in the staging of mock nuclear holocaust, the message seems a clear one: when the sirens sound the peasants can go to hell. And many millions of them most certainly would; Britain's grossly inadequate civil defence would see to that.

Planning the elitist war

Technology has given the military the power to wreak massive, accurate destruction. A 5-megaton weapon-burst on a typical indus-trial city would destroy the whole of the central area and kill almost the entire population within a circle six miles across. Even beyond this central area the damage and death rate would be catastrophic. The side-effects of radiation would spread across hundreds of square miles, depending on wind movement and other climatic factors. People living in cheaply-built highrise flats would have no protection. Such a level of weapon power is contained in warheads carried by US Titan II missiles and by Soviet weapons such as the SS-17, SS-18 and the older SS-9. All these weapons have ranges sufficient to reach British targets. And both the United States and the Soviet Union have several other weapons systems that can deliver comparable destructive power through multiple-warhead rockets or by the grouping of target zones.

It is by no means certain that the third world war will be fought by nuclear weapons; all the arguments militate against a strategic exchange that turns victory into an unstable and unrewarding emptiness. But the likelihood or otherwise of strategic suicide is of secondary concern. For political and psychological reasons the Whitehall planners have adopted the maxim of Professor Harold Urey, the discoverer of Deuterium: 'The next war will be fought with atom bombs and the one after that with spears.' Whatever the longer-term motives, those planners have chosen to encourage the popular belief that a nuclear war will be so destructive that any attempt to survive it will be doomed from the start. If one is not killed by the initial blast, one will die a lingering death from radi-ation sickness – and if, by some freak chance, one should survive *that*, the world that is left will not be worth living for. As General Sir John Hackett – who turned his expertise into the best-seller *The Third World War*[2] – recently described it:

After a nuclear war the whole of Europe would become a vast, uninhabitable desert. No industrial society, nothing that we would recognise as government would survive. There would be a state of total anarchy, with all those who remained alive prey to bands of savage marauders, with disease rampant and violent death commonplace. In an all-out nuclear war, to use the word 'survival' is idiotic.

'Most houses offer reasonable protection against radioactive fallout from nuclear explosions. Protection can be substantially improved by a series of quite simple do-it-yourself measures.'

William Whitelaw, Home Secretary, 12 February 1980

'There is no defence against a ballistic missile and it is a waste of time to erect one.'

Lord Carver, former Chief of Defence Staff, 6 March 1980

'The five risks can be reduced by white-washing a coat of light-coloured emulsion paint on windows (even though these will soon be shattered by the blast).'

Civil Aid pamphlet

'For the entire building, without including the mutual shielding of the adjacent building, the Reduction Factor is calculated from the previously computed Protection Factor,

$$Rf = \frac{1}{Pf} = \frac{1}{17} = 0.0588$$

Home Office instructions for Protection Factor Estimator

'They make a desert, and call it peace.'

Tacitus, *Agricola*

Publicly at least the government appeared to support this view. In 1968, Home Secretary James Callaghan announced the disbanding of the civil defence corps. Since then, government advice for the public in the event of nuclear war has been simply to stay at home and keep indoors, a policy the British public has accepted with customary fatalism.

In fact, however, opinion has recently been swinging round to the view that nuclear war – appalling in its consequences though it would be – need not be the 'final catastrophe' of traditional repute. Many civil defence planners believe that, given adequate precautions, around 70 per cent of the population could survive an all-out nuclear war. The other side of the coin is that 30 per cent would die: a horrendous figure, but by no means Armageddon. Recent tests by the Boeing Corporation in America have established that even sophisticated machine tools can survive close proximity to a nuclear blast, provided they are carefully lagged and buried, and agricultural experts have shown that crops retain less radiation than previously thought.

In the view of Peter Laurie, author of *Beneath the City Streets*, the destructive power of the hydrogen bomb has been deliberately oversold by the military, along with the view that it will be used against civilian as distinct from strategic targets. Laurie argues that 'each side's possession of nuclear weapons is an invaluable bogy in the woodshed for the other', to frighten populations into granting the military the billions they need to counter the potential enemy:

> It is as if the nuclear governments were in tacit agreement to overawe each other's people . . . Instead of war being a relatively remote business involving professionals, it is now aimed at *us* – the taxpayers. It is a device which enables a government to hold its *own* citizens hostage in peacetime, to involve their hopes and fears more directly in the arms business than any modern government has managed before.

Providing shelters for the civilian population is not part of the defence establishment's plan (in Britain, anyway, civil defence comes under the control of the Home Office). It is because of this that Britain arrived in the 1980s with a commitment to spend at least £5 billion developing the Trident missile, and a mere £26 million on the whole of its civil defence (see Table 16:1). Given that nuclear war may be survivable, the people of the United Kingdom are now dangerously and needlessly exposed. We no longer have a large-scale evacuation policy. Our civil defence equipment is gathering dust in warehouses, and while Switzerland and Sweden have comprehensive shelter policies, we have none (see Table 16:2).

DEFENDING THE FEW

Table 16:1

Priorities in UK defence spending*

UK defence budget: £8,240 million
UK home defence budget: £26 million
UK home defence spending as % of total defence budget: 0·003%

UK home defence budget by category	£
Home Office and UKWMO	4·7 million
Wartime regional government	2·4 million
Local/central planning and training	3·0 million
Emergency oil and ports	9·7 million
Stockpiled food and equipment	6·0 million
Total	25·8 million
Provision for Humberside in local category:	£40,000

*The above figures reflect the position as it was in July 1980. Since then the British government has announced certain increases in the budget for home defence. The increases do nothing to change the vastly disproportionate levels of expenditure on 'active' and home defence. The new home defence budget provisions of some £45 million by 1983 should be seen against the fact that by that year the main defence budget will have risen by another £500 million.

Table 16:2

Nuclear shelter places in selected European countries

West Germany	2 million
Sweden	7 million
Norway	1·7 million
Denmark	2·6 million
Soviet Union	175 million
Switzerland	5·4 million
Britain	nil

That is to say, there are none for civilians. For the government, however, the situation is very different. The extent of government planning for *its own* survival after nuclear war suggests that it, at any rate, believes protection is possible, and has invested heavily to ensure it.

The scale of official preparation for war was first revealed publicly in 1963 when eight members of the Committee of 100, calling themselves 'Spies for Peace', broke into an underground bunker near Reading. What they discovered was what the Home Office planners called 'RSG6' at Warren Row: the Regional Seat of Government from which the area would be ruled by one Cabinet Minister and 400 civil servants in the event of a national catastrophe. Gradually, over the years since then, it has been possible to piece together the network of highly secret underground bunkers which stretches over the whole of the United Kingdom. They are evidence that, while up on the surface people were being told that civil defence was useless and too expensive, beneath ground the government was spending large sums on its own life insurance.

In the event of a full-scale nuclear strike, central government will be dispensed with altogether. As the Home Office Circular No. ES 7/1973 to local authorities put it:

> In any future war involving the widespread use of nuclear weapons, it would be impossible to rely on exercise of powers of government from the capital. The basis of the wartime machinery of internal government is therefore the decentralisation and concentration of all functions within 10 home defence regions . . . Wartime regional government would be headed by Commissioners having full authority to govern internally; an authority derived from emergency powers approved by Parliament in the latter stages of a deteriorating situation before an attack.

Each of the ten regions would be ruled from a secret underground location. Government would be in the hands of one man – the Commissioner, the only elected official underground. He would be a Cabinet Minister, supported by a top team of Whitehall civil servants of the rank of Permanent Secretary and below; he would enjoy sweeping powers. With him in the Regional Seat of Government would be police and military commanders.

The second tier of government is at sub-regional level. There are seventeen sub-regions in England and Wales, three in Scotland and one in Northern Ireland. Here, as in the case of the RSGs, the concern would not be primarily with helping the wounded above ground: the job of the Sub Regional Headquarters, according to the Home Office (ES 7/1973), would be 'the conservation of resources, both manpower and materials, for longer-term survival – rather than immediate short-term aid to the hardest hit areas. Sub Regional Commissioners would be concerned with the administration of justice, with the maintenance by the police of law and order and with the general behaviour and morale of the survivors.' Such relief effort as could be mounted would come at local authority level. Here, the man in charge would be known as 'the Controller' – the area's peacetime Chief Executive, a non-elected official who would nevertheless, like his superiors in the RSGs and the SRHQs, have power of life and death. As Humberside's Chief Executive, an accountant by trade, coolly remarked in a *Panorama* programme: 'If people were looting, it would be within my competence to instruct that they be executed.'

Figure 16:1

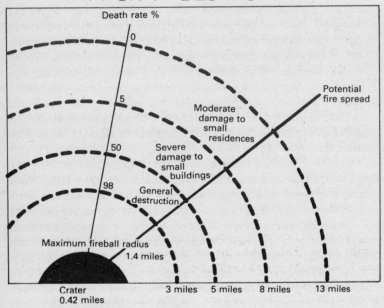

A CITY DESTROYED

The whereabouts of RSGs and SRHQs are a strict secret. However, on 21 March 1980, in the magazine *Time Out*, several locations were disclosed. Working on the evidence of documents salvaged from a derelict government bunker, the magazine revealed, for example, that an innocent-looking bungalow on a wooded hillside at Kelvdon Hatch near Brentwood was actually the entrance to SRHQ 51 – an underground bunker with office space and accommodation for over 200, which would be responsible for ruling the whole of Greater London. SRHQ 42, from which Bedfordshire, Essex and Hertfordshire would be ruled, is hidden beneath Sovereign House in Hertford, the local DHSS office. The headquarters of Surrey Constabulary conceals SRHQ 61 which would administer Kent, Surrey and Sussex. RAF Alconbury would be RSG 4, in overall charge of the whole of eastern England.

This complex network of underground government installations, with room for around 10,000 politicians, civil servants, members of the security forces and advisers, linked by telephone and teleprinter, with their own radio studios (maintained by the BBC), stands in sharp contrast to the protection offered to those on the surface.

For the mass of the British people, civil defence boils down to a thirty page leaflet, *Protect and Survive*,[3] priced 50p and available from H.M. Stationery Office. It lays down, in very basic language, aided by simple diagrams, the sort of primitive precautions the individual can take against nuclear war. The main advice is to stay put:

> Your own local authority will best be able to help you in war. If you move away – unless you have a place of your own to go to or intend to live with relatives – the authority in your new area will not help you with accommodation or food or other essentials. If you leave, your local authority may need to take your empty house for others to use.
>
> So stay at home.

A population that is static is much easier to control than one that is on the move. Threats like the one above, and the solemn warning at the front of the booklet, that because of 'radioactive dust falling where the wind blows it . . . No part of the United Kingdom can be considered safer than another,' are useful methods of coercion. Another method could be ration cards valid only in the area in which they are given out. (Home Office Circular No. E/1/1974 reveals that plans for rationing are already prepared.) *Protect and Survive* instructs each family to lay in a stock of food sufficient to last fourteen days.

For actual protection against the blast and against the effects of radiation, the booklet advises the building of a makeshift shelter within your own home. A cellar or basement, or failing that a hall or passage on the ground floor, should be chosen as a fall-out room. Boxes of earth, sand, books and furniture are then used to surround the room. Within it, an inner refuge is then constructed, preferably by propping two doors against a wall and covering them with sacks of earth. In this tiny, enclosed space, a family will have to eat, sleep and perform all their bodily functions for at least forty-eight hours – possibly even a fortnight. For those unfortunate enough to live in any but the bottom five storeys of a block of flats, or who live in a bungalow or caravan, *Protect and Survive* can only lamely advise 'alternative shelter accommodation', with neighbours, relatives or friends: 'arrange to shelter with someone close by you'.

'Tax exile Michael Pearson, son and heir of the immensely wealthy Lord Cowdray, has amazed the natives of the Balearic island of Ibiza by building a fall-out shelter in his new £250,000 house.
    'Pearson, 36 two days ago, now plans to spend six months of the year in Monte Carlo and the rest of the year in Ibiza.'

Daily Mail, 19 June 1980

In confronting the greatest horror facing civilisation – the threat of nuclear war – *Protect and Survive* offers the language and intelligence of the nursery. Many experts in the civil defence field regard it as worse than useless; one refers to it as 'Neglect and Die'. Only occasionally does the optimistic prose allow a glimpse of what life after a nuclear war might actually be like:

If a death occurs while you are confined to the fall-out room place the body in another room and cover it as securely as possible. Attach an identification. You should receive radio instructions on what to do next. If no instructions have been given within five days, you should temporarily bury the body as soon as it is safe to go out, and mark the spot.

(A further impression of 'life' after nuclear attack is set out in Document 3 of the appendix.)
    The Home Office plans to distribute a copy of *Protect and Survive*

to every home during the run-up period to war, assuming such a useful three-week phase presents itself in an age when intercontinental ballistic missiles can be primed within hours. It is to be issued in conjunction with a series of twenty short television films which are held, ready for use, by the BBC and the IBA. Of all the Home Office circulars on preparation for war it is ES 2/1975, entitled 'Information Services in War', which gives the most revealing insight into current official planning:

> Normal peace-time television and sound broadcasting would continue until the Government decided to introduce the special wartime broadcasting service (WTBS) . . . At the time specified, all television services and local radio stations would close down, and sound broadcasting would be restricted to a single programme, consisting primarily of news, official announcements and advice on the measures that should be taken to increase the prospects of survival, although there would be, for morale purposes, an entertainment element.

For most people, the loss of a free and independent broadcasting service at a time of nuclear war would be the least of their worries. The important question, however, is for how long *before* an attack would the government be in control of the media? 'To facilitate the work of planning', the Home Office divides the 'pre-attack period' into three phases. The passage is worth quoting at length as it shows official thinking on how we will be 'eased' into war-readiness:

a. Low-level crisis
During this period, which might last for several weeks or even months, very little material would be released to the public. The general aim would be to allay public concern and to prevent, so far as possible, any disruption of the normal life of the country. Government broadcasts might give the first indication of the possibility that war might not be averted, but the emphasis would be on assurances that everything possible was being done to prevent war and on references to the effectiveness of the nuclear deterrent.

b. Preparatory period
It is envisaged that, in a deteriorating international situation, there would be a period of some 3–4 weeks during which the

Figure 16:2

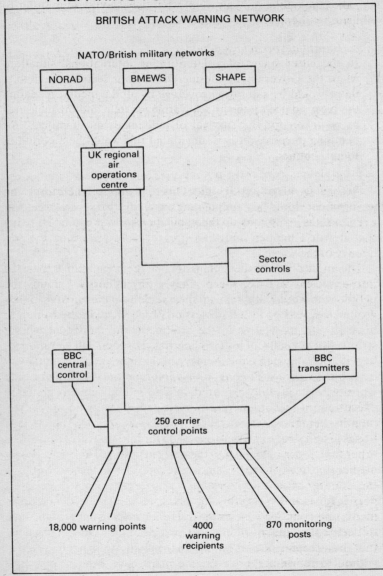

PREPARING FOR WAR WITH THE BBC

BRITISH ATTACK WARNING NETWORK

NATO/British military networks

NORAD   BMEWS   SHAPE

UK regional air operations centre

Sector controls

BBC central control

BBC transmitters

250 carrier control points

18,000 warning points   4000 warning recipients   870 monitoring posts

necessary steps would be taken to place the country on a war footing. During this period, the Government's efforts to avoid war would continue unabated, but all the media would be used to make the public fully aware of what they should do in order to increase their prospects of survival.

c. Immediate pre-attack period

In the latter stages of a deteriorating international situation, when the Government considered that war seemed inevitable, there would be saturation coverage by all the media, repeating the basic advice on the attack warning system and the measures to be taken for the survival of individuals and families. For planning purposes, it is assumed that this would be a period of some 72 hours.

According to official Home Office planning, therefore, the government would be manipulating the media 'for several weeks or even months', softening up the population for war by first stressing that it won't happen and then progressively increasing the frequency of the warnings.

The implications of these plans are that the population is to be led into a nuclear war like sheep. Only a tiny minority – mainly the people who would later take up their stations in the bunkers underground – would be in full possession of the facts. In the run-up to nuclear war, as well as in the aftermath, the individual will be stripped of virtually all his civil liberties. His food will be rationed, he will probably be unable to leave his local area, his property will be subject to requisitioning; all his information about the outside world will be carefully censored, and he will be liable to summary execution on the orders of a non-elected official who only a few months before was a so-called 'public servant'. As far as it is possible to judge, there is no provision for the survival of politicians other than those belonging to the party in power. There is certainly no mention of any form of democratic control over the authorities in the country after the attack, in a situation which will certainly persist for months, possibly for years. As the Home Office documents point out, it will be at 'the discretion of Parliament at the time to decide the content of emergency legislation'. One would hope that the sweeping powers implicit in the plans would not be voted in without a murmur. However, the plans have been in existence since, at the very least, the mid-1960s. Neither of the two parties which have been in power since then has seen fit to alter them. If we should ever actually find ourselves on the brink of nuclear war, it may well be too late.

Britain's defence planning gives us some useful insights into modern military thinking. It is clear that both before and after an attack, the population will only be fed those items of information useful to the government – items that sustain morale and keep the population malleable. For the ten Commissioners and seventeen Sub Regional Commissioners, the restoration and maintenance of law and order would be the first priority: 'The aims of Home Defence are defined as those defensive measures necessary in the United Kingdom: a) To secure the United Kingdom against any internal threat . . . ' (Home Office Circular E 3/1973). The bunkers are built to be bomb-proof – but also to be concrete bastions of government order, difficult to locate or enter.

'YOUR struggle will bring US Victory' ran a propaganda poster in 1939. The slogan, with its implications of Us and Them, was deeply resented by the population, and later abandoned. All wars have been controlled and directed by a minority while the majority have carried out their instructions and borne the brunt of the consequences. In conventional wars, this has often been glossed over. During the Second World War, for example, some form of democratic control continued to be exercised. Parliament remained in session throughout – indeed it even managed to force an unpopular war leader, Chamberlain, out of office. By-elections were held, and anti-government candidates returned. But in nuclear war, there will be no such opportunity. Both the planning and the waging of a nuclear war are the prerogative of a few. As Bertrand Russell described the situation in the 1950s:

> Whether the populations of the world are to live or die rests with the decisions of Krushchev, Mao Tse-tung and Mr John Foster Dulles, not with ordinary mortals like ourselves. If they say 'Die', we shall die. If they say 'Live', we shall live.[4]

The names may have changed, but the situation remains the same, and Britain's civil defence reflects this. In a nuclear war there is no need for a large conscript army. The weapons of the third world war can only be operated by small groups of highly trained professionals: the nature of the weapons, their effects, the language used to describe them, the grandiose and complex strategic theories which govern their use – all these are alien to the mass of the population. All that remains for us to do is to take cover in makeshift shelters and listen to the radio for instructions.

In the third world war, control resides in those who understand and have possession of the technology of the various weapon systems, just as in the economy of the 1980s knowledge and control of the micro-processor revolution is the prerogative of the elite. The parallels between the two are striking. In both the modern economy and the modern war, large numbers of the population are not only superfluous – they actually threaten the well-being of the elite. The threat to the masters of the new micro-industrial revolution is posed by the millions whose skills are no longer required – thwarted, cut off from decision-making, relying on hand-outs from their rulers. The threat to the Commissioners and Controllers in the event of nuclear war comes from a similar source: the secrecy and fortification of their underground citadels, the extensive plans for armed protection of food and medical convoys, and the frequent references to the danger of 'subversives' make it all too clear that the perceived threat after a nuclear war is not the attacker, but the ignorant, frightened and possibly violent civil population.

One of the great perils for democracy lies in the correlation between the aims and structures of these two elites. They are not in conflict, they are complementary, and one could conceivably aid the other.

For example, the way that wars and the great fluctuations in the world's economy run in tandem has been frequently noted. In this century, both world wars were preceded by a slump, and followed by an economic boom. As our modern economy has moved into crisis, so the threat of war has, in the words of Jimmy Carter, come closer than at any time since 1945. Might the economic conditions generated by the micro-revolution trigger a war? Would a war in fact *solve* many unpleasant side-effects of the micro-chip society? A drastic cure, but not a fatal one. Factories are moving out of the towns and into the less strategically vulnerable countryside. It is in the decaying cities they leave behind (14 million people live in Britain's five biggest conurbations) that the highest casualty rates would be suffered in a nuclear war. Dispensing with a third of the population – provided industry was protected – might one day be seen as the 'purge' our society will have to endure in order to survive.

There is only one historical precedent for such a dramatic drop in population. The Black Death, the great plague which swept across the face of Europe in the mid-fourteenth century, carried off between 30 and 50 per cent of the population. What the historian G. M. Trevelyan describes as 'the reduction of the English subjects of Edward III in sixteen months, from perhaps four million to perhaps two and a half million souls' shattered an economic system which had been in place for centuries. Serfs and villeins struck for more money; many fled. 'The world', writes Trevelyan, in his *Shortened History of England*, 'seemed coming to an end.' In fact the catastrophe contained the seeds of a new beginning for Britain's economy:

> Part of their difficulties the landlords solved well and wisely, by substituting sheep pasture for tillage. It was not for more than a century later, when the population had nearly filled up the gaps left by the Black Death, that there was any need for the landlords to evict ploughmen in order to make room for the shepherd. In 1350 death had evicted the ploughman, and 'the deserted village' was ready to hand . . . The export of raw wool to the Flanders looms, and the concurrent growth of cloth manufacture in England . . . made demand for all the wool that English flocks could supply. In this way a national policy and distant markets were beginning to disturb and improve the parochial economy of the old manor, and to offer alternative occupations for the emancipated or runaway villein.[5]

This new economic order was the result of a wholly unexpected natural calamity. Today in Britain, we have laid contingency plans for our modern Black Death. Our baronial castles are the underground fortresses that house RSGs and SRHQs. The historians of future centuries may look back and see more clearly than we can the effects of the linking of our political, military and industrial elites.

What one can deduce today is that civil defence, once an activity designed to *protect* the population, has become increasingly concerned with *controlling* it. Provision for war has supplied a handy excuse for the existence of an alternative 'underground government'. By 1972, the government had broadened significantly its definition of the role of 'Home Defence':

> It is considered that there is much common ground between war planning and the preparations required for and the organisation appropriate to a major peacetime emergency . . . Accordingly there are many advantages in creating a closer relationship than hitherto in local planning for the different emergencies of peace and war.[6]

In December 1973, at the height of the miners' strike, the Heath Government put the RSGs and SRHQs on standby, following the disturbance at the Saltley Coke Depot. It was the first tacit admission that our planners had something other in mind with these underground fortresses than the speedy recovery of the country from nuclear attack. Any future government now has an almost invulnerable underground redoubt to which it can retreat. In war and in peace, our rulers have carefully planned their protection, both from the H-bomb and from the subversive.

During the 1960s there was a general feeling that nuclear war would be a great big, democratic bang that would wipe out everything alive. 'When the air becomes uranious/We will all go simultaneous/We will all fry together when we fry,' sang Tom Lehrer.

In the 1980s we will not all go 'simultaneous', neither will we all 'fry'. A carefully chosen few won't even get their fingers burnt. And if the BBC doesn't tell anybody, the secret will never leak out that everything went according to plan.

17

Here is the news?

Britain began the 1980s with a highly appropriate choice as the new chairman of the BBC. George Howard, who was elevated to the chairmanship after nearly nine years as a BBC governor, is the perfect encapsulation of the values and social mores of Britain's landfax elite. Descended from a line of eighteenth-century Whigs, Mr Howard has lived long in the true landfax style. His 130-room house, Castle Howard in Yorkshire, was for years the home of the earls of Carlisle. The 10,000 acres of farmland that surround it, much of it let to tenant farmers, puts him firmly into the mould of the pre-industrial aristocracy. Nor will it be long before his reign at Television Centre matures into a real-life lordly title. As a former chairman of the Country Landowners Association he has the reputation of a stalwart defender of the rights of the landed wealthy. Now, with Britain's most powerful disseminator of information at his finger-tips, George Howard has completed his journey through the corridors of landfax power, and has arrived at the innermost sanctum.

Mr Howard's appointment seemed the product of a carefully balanced appraisal of Britain's approaching crisis, in which the loyalty of the BBC to the status quo would be the essential guarantee against popular dissent. He had been for twenty years a friend of the Home Secretary, William Whitelaw, with whom he would henceforth have closest political contact. His schooldays with Lord Carrington, his time at Oxford with Edward Heath, put him in the inner circle of Conservative thinking. His view of the role of the chairman can be summed up in the remarks he made to the press after his appointment was announced: 'It is our function, if a programme is made and put out that it later appears ought not to have been put out, to take extremely stern measures.'

Chairman Howard brought a stamp of feudal sensibility to the output of BBC news and current affairs programmes. The *Sunday Times*, a newspaper openly opposed to Britain's subtly effective methods of official censorship, caught the significance of his appointment. Ran the headline to their story covering his promotion: 'George Howard: Yes, I'll defend the BBC's castle'. But the case of George Howard is only one small example of the erosion of independence in the conduits of news and information that is overtaking Britain's mass media.

There is, in any event, a permanent danger that purveyors of information on a large scale will cut the corners of truth in the interests of commercial or political survival. As Walter Lippmann put it: 'When distant and unfamiliar and complex things are communicated to great masses of people, the truth suffers a considerable and often radical distortion. The complex is made over into the simple, the hypothetical into the dogmatic and the relative into an absolute.' The only way to guard against this distortion is to ensure that information is widely and freely distributed, within basic controls on moral and personal vilification. Put another way, a free press is best found in large numbers rather than in few, in unfettered distribution rather than restricted, in open presentation of salient facts rather than circumscribed. If Britain is ever given a proper, written constitution, or a modernised Bill of Rights, such a freedom would figure as a dominant and guiding principle; perhaps that is the very reason why these charters have not emerged. Since the birth of welfare politics on a mass scale, with the passing of the Education Act in 1944, there have been three Royal Commissions on the press. The latest, in 1977, committed the same error as its predecessors, in omitting any real scrutiny of the access to distribution in the publishing industry. In France, commercial wholesalers have been required by law to take any periodical, whatever its politics or circulation level. In Britain the rationale of commercial expediency merges with political or other tactics to create a selective distribution network in which publications that fail to join in the game of polite politics and social comment are sent to the publishing equivalent of Siberia.

This selective distribution system, organised through the explicit operation of a blacklist, has ensured that magazines such as *Camerawork*, *Private Eye*, *Gay News*, *Undercurrents* and the

Leveller – all of them legitimate publications representing widespread sectional interests – have undergone persistent ostracism at the hands of major national distributors. These same distributors nevertheless seem happy to give permanent shelf space to soft pornography, children's comics (often politically mischievous) and tabloid newspapers of dubious objectivity and with a taste for sensationalism.

The net result is a distribution system that buttresses the power of a small, established group of publishers. In magazine publishing, for instance, some twelve publishing firms enjoy a combined market share of 70 per cent. They are owned in large part by companies equally well established in newspaper production, companies owned by leading landfax aristocrats such as Lord Cowdray – who counts amongst his flock a vast network of provincial papers, the key financial publications of the City, as well as shares in such groups as Haymarket Publications.[1]

It is not surprising, given the attraction of such aristocrats to the pastures of information distribution, that they have made considerable efforts to break into commercial television. Applicants for the 1980 round of TV franchise awards included Cowdray himself, Lord Matthews's Trafalgar House, a family group funded by the estate of Lord Beaverbrook, Lord Nathan, Lord Weidenfeld and a string of merchant banks and pension funds with blue-chip boards of directors. Their interest in the small screen is nothing new but the incentives are higher, now that high technology has transformed the ordinary domestic TV set, almost overnight, into a conduit for information on a potentially limitless scale. Much of British television has long been run by companies with peers of the realm hovering in the background: D. C. Thomson, Associated Newspapers and Lord Grade's Associated Communications Corporation are typical examples.

Thus, both press and broadcasting seem set on the road to domination by a noble fraternity, a trend enhanced by the tendency of the patronage lists of the Prime Minister of the day to dispense titles to favoured servants in the world of information. But it is the BBC, with its massive and traditional hold over radio and television, that sits at the crossroads of mass communication and information. And it is to the BBC that the government looks for support in the constant effort to inform the British public with the aim of maintaining the status quo.

Every night in Britain millions of people sit down in front of their TV screens to watch the major news bulletins. In the space of less than fifty years, broadcasting has usurped the leadership in opinion-forming once enjoyed by the printed word. By the early 1980s, with some 20 million licence-holders having access to TV and radio, broadcasts of news items had become the unchallengeable source of popular information about the way the world is working. To judge from a poll conducted recently,[2] the intimacy of the small screen, coupled with a carefully designed gravity in the mode of presentation, has succeeded in convincing people that broadcast news is the best. In answer to the question, 'Which of the five media do you consider "always trustworthy", or "trustworthy most of the time"', the results were quite strikingly in favour of television and radio:

BBC TV	86 per cent
ITN	78 per cent
BBC Radio	74 per cent
Own newspaper	40 per cent
Newspapers in general	30 per cent

It is hardly surprising that BBC output in particular, and broadcasting companies in general, are subject to self-imposed controls over programme content. And it is no surprise that such controls are seen by many as a primary instrument of stability at times of social stress. As much was realised by the creator of BBC standards, Lord Reith. To borrow his own words: 'If there had been broadcasting at the time of the French Revolution, there might have been no French Revolution.' Put more crudely, broadcasting is the principal means by which otherwise unruly peasants can be 'informed' into a condition of all-believing complacency about their political and social prospects. The mass audience attracted by television and radio is thus safely entertained, all thoughts of the Bastille pushed into oblivion by soap opera and the autocued bulletins delivered by perfectly formed newscasterettes. The size of the audience is matched only by the self-satisfaction of the broadcasters. Thus the 1978 *IBA Guide* proclaimed:

. . . a short television news item, well written and presented, balanced, well-illustrated, expertly putting its finger on the significant points, is probably the most valuable and graphic way of imparting information . . . News coverage on Independent Television has raised the threshold, albeit gradually, of public sophistication in understanding many of the complex economic, industrial and political problems facing the world.

And writing in the recent special anniversary issue of the *Stage*, the editor of BBC Television News, Alan Protheroe, declared: 'It is only by being scarifyingly honest with ourselves that we can ensure television news programmes remain the most consistently success-ful output in the history of British television.' In addition to the self-congratulation, Mr Protheroe used his article – on twenty-five years of television news coverage – to take a swipe at his critics.

The 1980s will, again, bring its crop of 'sociological investiga-tions' into the way television does its job.

I shall remember the past years, and the 70s in particular, for the plethora of idiocies perpetrated in the name of the pseudo-science of sociology, for Masterships and Doctorates gained for the scribblings of 'social scientists' who apparently neither understood nor wished to understand what television news is trying to do.

They will, again, come knocking at the door, eager, bright-eyed, totally biased, not-understanding, wet-behind-the-ears young men and women speaking a language only they can under-stand . . .

There will be those 'professors' (all of them self-described 'experts' in communication) who will, in that incestuous and self perpetuating pseudo-academic circus that passes for a science, coin new phrases to supersede 'gatekeepers' and the like.

'Colonel' Alan Protheroe, as he is known to his colleagues, received the MBE in 1980 – for his services to the Territorial Army. (He was one of a number of senior BBC TV News staff who had connections with the military. Defence Correspondent Christopher Wain is a former major; Managing Editor Tony Crabb was an officer in Military Intelligence.) His attitude is typical of that of many broadcasting professionals towards the people who have made it *their* business to study the media's methods. At the end of *More Bad News*, the second onslaught from the Glasgow Media Group against what they see as the 'one-sided' nature of television, there is quoted a revealing exchange from a recent top-level BBC meeting:

> DG (Director General) said there would be no sense in attacking *Bad News* in detail . . . he thought however that the ideology of sociologists was a subject which would repay a little study and hoped that it would be possible for a programme like *Analysis* to tackle it . . . Desmond Wilcox felt it would be dangerous to launch a widespread attack on the discipline of sociology, which included some perfectly responsible practitioners. It should attack, where necessary, particular arguments and . . . the standpoint from which they were presented. Michael Bunce repeated his view that the BBC should attack spurious communicators and academics . . . DG agreed that the BBC should examine the aims and politics of sociology.

The self-evident hatred for 'sociologists' shown by the BBC Director-General was, perhaps, understandable. Sir Ian Trethowan, who was granted a knighthood by Margaret Thatcher, is regarded by a great many current affairs journalists who worked with him over the years as a man of limited academic horizons. He has, it is said, a deep distrust for anyone prone to displays of cleverness. His efforts to cajole editors into employing presenters untainted by the contagious curiosity about Britain's institutions that so blackened the records of the 'sociologists' are now a part of internal BBC legend. It so happens that *Analysis*, the current affairs radio programme recommended by Sir Ian to put the record straight, was presented by Mary Goldring, a journalist with views very close to those of Sir Ian himself. Miss Goldring was for some time a senior writer with the flagship weekly of Lord Cowdray's publishing empire, *The Economist*.

The point is not that *Analysis* would not have produced an objective programme on the issue of 'sociology', merely that it is odd for a BBC Director-General to have a ranking of programmes in his mind at all, with each one given a rating for its political demeanour. There are, after all, dozens of programmes in the current affairs broadcasting schedules that could have tackled the subject with equal, if not greater, skill. But then, perhaps Sir Ian had taken to heart the ironic observation of the American writer James Reston, when commenting on his own government's discomfort at the robust actions of the US press: 'If it's far away it's news, but if it's close at home it's sociology.'[3] And having recalled those words, perhaps Sir Ian deemed it wiser to have his 'sociology' concocted by friends. However, not even the best of friends could prove the existence of, as Sir Ian put it, an 'ideology of sociologists'. As professional people they happen to thrive on the diversity of their opinions, not on the joys of conspiracy.

The Glasgow Media Group has not found the answers that will make Britain's news coverage more informative and bias-free. But through its several publications it has elicited defensive reactions, of the kind seen above, that prove its point many times over. The proof was ever-present in the room when those senior BBC men revealed their attitudes to social questioning. As the Glasgow Media Group has remarked: 'That a basis for a sociological critique of broadcast news might exist at no time seems to have entered the apparently fevered discussions of the Editor of News and Current Affairs' fortnightly meetings in the BBC.'

Both the BBC and the IBA stoutly defend themselves against charges of bias. The 1977 *BBC Handbook* pointed out that, 'The Licence requires the BBC to refrain from "editorialising"; that is, to refrain from expressing a point of view of its own on any matter of public controversy or public policy. Careful safeguards have been erected within the BBC to prevent breaches of this rule.' And according to the IBA, 'There is an immense unspoken tradition at ITN – almost an obsession – with balance.'

'Balance' is generally held to be a refusal to favour one particular point of view or another: Right or Left, industry and management, each has its allotted time. During an election campaign, for example, the various lengths of time given to commentators of all parties are carefully logged to avoid giving one side more exposure than another. But the *BBC Handbook* does, in its own words, add 'one footnote': ' . . . impartiality does not imply an Olympian neutrality or detachment from those basic moral and constitutional beliefs on which the nation's life is founded.'

The point was perhaps most starkly made by Lord Reith, at the time of the General Strike in 1926. He vigorously opposed the view held by the many Cabinet 'hawks', among them Winston Churchill, that the BBC should come under the direct control of the government. 'I told him,' wrote Reith in his diary on 9 May 1926, 'that if we put out nothing but Government propaganda we should not be doing half the good that we were.' In other words, the BBC was more use to the government if it sustained the illusion of inde- pendence. The point was reinforced two days later, when the Cabinet agreed that the BBC should remain unrestricted, and Reith wrote: 'The Cabinet decision is really a negative one. They want to be able to say that they did not commandeer us, but they know that they can trust us not to be really impartial.'

It is the contention of the 'wet-behind-the-ears young men and women' of Mr Protheroe's description that this lack of true im- partiality is still the case today. The problem for social scientists has been to prove it. It is all very well, for example, for Anthony Smith, a 'television professional' himself, to say that, 'News tends to lay out the orders of "priorities" among the issues which confront society; it creates some of the doubts and fosters the certainties of that society, placing them all in a context of its own.'[4] But such gener- alities carry little weight among sceptics. The Annan Committee reported that this outlook 'naturally raised resentment, not to say bewilderment, among the journalists in broadcasting with whom we discussed [it].' They quoted the Editor of ITN who remarked that news 'was dictated primarily by events that had happened that day'.

To tackle this argument, the Glasgow Media Group undertook to monitor all news bulletins on television in the first four months of 1975. At that time, the major political issue in Britain was the fight against inflation, with Chancellor Denis Healey claiming that rises in wages could no longer match rises in prices, and that living standards had to fall. During that time the group was able to analyse the 'buried conventions and beliefs' which produced slanted cover- age of the issues (see Table 17:1). The central 'consensus' belief, that inflation was being caused by excessive wage settlements, was continually rammed home in supposedly 'impartial' coverage, such as the BBC's Budget preview on 19 March 1975 (BBC–1, 9 p.m.), which 'conveyed uncritically Mr Healey's call for a "tough budget"':

If we don't tighten our belts the implication is that foreign creditors from whom we borrow will insist that we do before they lend us any more. Without more moderate wage deals and better productivity on the shop floor Mr Healey says our prices will soon be rising twice as fast as our competitors'. So his message called for belt-tightening and the party meeting rejected a call for an opposite give-away budget.

As the research team comments: 'Not only was the alternative view not explained; but the whole tradition of Keynesian economics was dismissed in a single phrase ("an opposite give-away budget")'. Throughout the period that the Glasgow group was monitoring the news, control of wages was overwhelmingly presented as the sole means of bringing down inflation. In their eagerness to put this view across, the media repeatedly distorted the facts. Thus ITV's *News at Ten* (24 April 1975) reported that the Price Commission 'firmly blamed wage-cost increases' for increasing prices. In fact, as the researchers point out, 'The contribution to price increases that was directly attributable to increased labour costs *was in fact calculated by the Price Commission as only 20 per cent of the total.*'[5] Other factors, notably the rise in oil prices, were completely ignored. Over the four months that the study was in operation, the twenty million or more viewers of television news each night were given a one-sided view of the economic crisis. Television news, in the view of the Glasgow group, distorts because it relies upon an essentially partial view of the world – the part of the world that puts up 'spokesmen' and employs people to handle public relations. The prejudices of the establishment and of the journalists who write about it buttress one another. As Tom Burns has described it:[6]

The television news journalists slipped easily into a set of 'attitudes and expectations, truisms and commonplaces' current not among their audience (of whom they knew no more than did anyone else in Britain) but among colleagues in the BBC, in ITN and in the newspaper world. By the mid-seventies, that is, television news had indeed become a mirror, at least mentally, but a mirror reflecting not society at large, but the *Weltanschauung* – the vision of society – held by television journalists.

The findings of the *Bad News* team support the influential arguments of John Birt and Peter Jay – that television news contains an inherent 'bias against understanding'. The boiling down of complex issues, the bewildering succession of stories, the natural tendency of news bulletins to home in on the dramatic and the visual – all these factors militate against any real grasp of what is happening. No main bulletin in Britain lasts longer than half an hour, a time span that allows only a superficial treatment of the issues. This sketchiness lends itself ideally to the consensus view. It ensures that there are certain fixed reference points (for instance, that wage costs are the overwhelming reason for inflation) which may be treated as read, speeding up presentation of news and allowing the impression, at least, that all important viewpoints have been covered.

POLICIES OR 'SOLUTIONS' TO ECONOMIC CRISIS IDENTIFIED ON TV NEWS

Table 17:1

Proposed solution	Number of references
Wage restraint/lower wages	287 (+ 17 negative)
Defence of living standards	79 (+ 15 negative)
Expansion of the public sector, need for a government investment programme, proposals to reverse decline in industrial investment	47 (+ 50 negative)
Cuts in govt expenditure	21 (+ 1 negative)
Better communications in industry	14 (+ 6 negative)
More progressive taxation ('Cuts at top', 'Tax the rich' etc)	12 (+ 4 negative)
Abolition of price control	11 (+ 6 negative)
Increased profits for industry	10
Statutory wage control	8 (+ 20 negative)
Increased investment in private industry (including govt aid)	9
Import controls	7
Reduction of 'complex' VAT rates	6
A ban on the export of capital	2
Lower interest rates	1

It is a way of looking at current events which consolidates the belief that modern society is made up of a set of more or less fixed power blocs. If news journalists wish to get a view on, say, industry or the economy they turn to senior industrialists, politicians or favoured union leaders. When the shopfloor is shown at all, it is generally represented by a figure ranting on the back of a lorry at a mass meeting, or by *vox pops* of workers outside factory gates. TV journalists go to the top for opinions, wrote Dick Francis, the BBC's Director of News and Current Affairs, because these 'are the people whose decisions largely determine the way things will be run in our democracy'. This constant seeking-out of a 'charmed circle' who appear regularly on television must inevitably foster an illusion of consensus which either excludes people with a different set of views or, when they do appear, ensures that they come over as weirdly out of tune with the 'real' TV world:

> The mass media cannot assure complete conservative attunement – nothing can. But they can and do contribute to the fostering of a climate of conformity – not by the total suppression of dissent, but by the presentation of news which falls outside the consensus as curious heresies, or even more effectively, by treating them as irrelevant eccentricities which serious people may dismiss as of no consequence.[7]

Groups which are viewed as being beyond the pale seldom, or never, make it on to television at all. The BBC's coverage of Northern Ireland is a good illustration of the straitjacket in which broadcasters work. Night after night, news bulletins have carried pictures of burnt-out shops or wrecked cars. Yet when the BBC *Panorama* programme attempted to make a documentary film about the *perpetrators* of terrorism – the IRA – the project had to be abandoned. The IRA had set up a roadblock in the Northern Ireland village of Carrickmore and invited the BBC crew to meet them there. Not knowing what to expect, the team from *Panorama* went – and filmed the incident. The uproar which ensued, with the Prime Minister denouncing the BBC on the floor of the House of Commons, was a sledgehammer reaction which killed the project stone dead. All film – which included interviews with senior IRA leaders, who describe secret meetings with William Whitelaw, Ulster Secretary in the Heath administration – has been locked away. The Director-General of the BBC privately assured Mr Whitelaw – Home Secretary and the Minister responsible for broadcasting – that the programme will never be transmitted. The reaction illustrates the way in which a consensus view, which the media themselves have helped to foster, can rebound upon the broadcaster. Television has cut away the ground from under its own feet when it comes to Ireland, and created a dangerous precedent in bowing to Government pressure and accepting that some issues are just too hot to handle. It is significant, moreover, that the BBC gave in on a matter that did not even exist; after all, the *Panorama* 'programme' at the centre of the storm had not even been made. It remained only a glint of courage in the eye of a single editor. And even that proved too close for official comfort.

'Disasterville' is the description used by senior BBC management of the Carrickmore affair and the attendant publicity. Since the incident, every news and current affairs editor has been issued with the 'Red File', a developing set of BBC guidelines on filming in sensitive areas. (Document 4 of the appendix describes these guidelines.) The reason for the fear within the BBC – and the IBA – about, for example, talking to terrorists, is not that the *public* necessarily object (BBC audience research found that four-fifths of viewers approved of the decision to show an interview with the Irish National Liberation Army on the *Tonight* programme), it is the fact that such things are deeply unpopular with the government.

Unhappily for the BBC, the increasing control the government seems to wish to have over the media comes at a time when they are facing their worst-ever financial crisis. 'The way things are going,' the Controller of BBC–2, Brian Wenham, was quoted as saying, 'the BBC might well finish the 1980s with one TV channel instead of two.' Part of the reason for the panic in the BBC over Carrickmore was that the storm broke on the day the Cabinet met to decide the size of the Corporation's licence fee increase.

The increase awarded raised the cost of the colour licence from £25 to £34 and brought the BBC over £1 billion for the period 1980–2. Even so, it left a shortfall of £130 million from what the BBC had asked for (a licence fee of £41). In 1980, the Corporation was forced to shed 1,500 jobs. The licence fee system – theoretically not a government handout – has helped bring the BBC much more firmly within the control of the government. The system was originally designed to keep the BBC free of interference, but as inflation has accelerated, so the broadcasters have had to go back to the government more and more often. For thirty-two years, between 1922 and 1954, the BBC licence fee was raised only once – from 10 shillings to £1. From 1954 onwards the story has changed. Since 1965 the BBC has asked for an increase in the fee *eight times*.

Regular pilgrimages from Broadcasting House to the Home Office in Queen Anne's Gate have taken their toll of the BBC's independence. The questioning, liberal days of Sir Hugh Greene's tenure as Director-General have given way to introspection, and a fear of appearing too far out of step with the government. The road has been a long one, the loss of freedoms gradual, but nevertheless the route is clearly marked:

July 1967. 'I have done something the BBC won't like,' announces Harold Wilson at a cocktail party. 'What this naughtiness was the Prime Minister at this point kept *in petto*,' writes Stuart Hood, a former BBC TV Controller, 'but as the evening wore on, the need to communicate his prank became too strong for him . . . he revealed that he had appointed Lord Hill to be Chairman of the BBC.' By moving over the retiring head of ITV to take charge of the BBC, Wilson both gave the Corporation a public snub and brought its liberal Director-General to book. As Richard Crossman describes it: 'Charlie Hill has very much run the ITV to suit the convenience of the politicians and in particular he has made sure that their treatment of news and current affairs does not offend the establishment, including the leaders of the two big parties. He has carefully avoided all the irritating things the BBC do . . . So Harold has coolly switched Hill to the BBC to discipline it and bring it to book and, above all, to deal with Hugh Greene. And in Charlie's place he is going to pop an absolutely safe politician – Herbert Bowden. A bureaucrat, an establishment man if ever there was one, who has always done what Harold required.'

April 1969. Sir Hugh Greene is forced to leave as Director-General. The change delights Mrs Whitehouse. His broadcasting obituary is written in the *Financial Times* by T. C. Worsley: Greene 'carried the BBC struggling and kicking out of its auntie image into something more relevant to the decade. Instead of reflecting the respectable, old-fashioned, middle-class values of the past that were over and done with, the BBC began to mirror at least equally the aspirations and attitudes of the newly enfranchised young who had come up via the grammar schools and the red-brick universities . . . Sir Hugh gave them their chance.'

October 1971. Following the *Yesterday's Men* controversy, the BBC Programmes Complaints Commission is set up. The Commissioners are Sir Edmund Compton, Sir Henry Fisher and Baroness Serota, their brief is to investigate 'complaints from people or organisations who believe themselves to have been treated unjustly or unfairly'. Described by Greene as 'the deplorable surrender by the present Board of Governors of responsibility and authority.'

November 1979. Mrs Thatcher denounces the BBC in the House of Commons following news of filming in Carrickmore. 'This is not the first time we have had occasion to raise similar matters with the BBC. The Home Secretary and I think it is time the BBC put its own house in order.' The editor of *Panorama* is sacked, only to be reinstated after the threat of a walk-out by television journalists. The police raid the *Panorama* offices and take away film of the Carrickmore incident – the first time a search warrant has ever been used to seize film belonging to a television company. This incident, together with that of the *Tonight* interview with the killers of Airey Neave, was referred to the Attorney General for decision on whether or not to prosecute under the Prevention of Terrorism Act. A new set of 'guidelines' on filming in Northern Ireland is introduced.

Over the past few years, the IBA too has come under heavy government pressure. In June 1978, a report by the Thames TV programme *This Week* on police brutality in Northern Ireland was cancelled on the day it was due to be transmitted. 'The ban was an act of political censorship, pure and simple,' commented Peter Taylor, the reporter who made the film. 'The Independent Broadcasting Authority is one of the biggest menaces to free communication now at work in this country,' claimed an editorial in the *Sunday Times* (11 June 1978). 'This is only the latest in a long line of cases in which the IBA has shown itself to be on the side not of freedom but on that of the State, authority and censorship.'

Thus, television, the sharp end of the Fourth Estate, moved into the 1980s with its journalists feeling themselves under siege. The distance that should exist between the state machine and those who comment on it is being eroded by the month. The BBC, that trusted friend in news coverage for 86 per cent of men and women in the street, slides ever closer to the bosom of Westminster. Abroad, the Corporation is seen as an extension of the British government. Soviet newspapers carry stories of the use of BBC overseas transmissions to communicate coded messages to intelligence agents in the field. They point to the integration of BBC networks into the NATO nuclear warning system as evidence of the politico-military connections of the Corporation and its commitment to a fixed view of east–west relations. Much the same is said of several Fleet Street newspapers, not least because of their long associations with various sections of the intelligence services.

In Britain such accusations are greeted with undisguised mirth. Perhaps the outcome of the 'Steel Papers' case will mark the beginning of a change of mind. In late July 1980 the House of Lords ruled that Granada TV must release the names of those who had supplied the producers of *World in Action* with six cardboard boxes filled with documents relating to the management of the British Steel Corporation by Sir Charles Villiers and his colleagues; at the time of the House of Lords' decision BSC was losing taxpayers money at the rate of £500 million a year. The decision was roundly condemned by even the most cautious amongst the British press. The editorial column of *The Times* captured the growing sense of outrage at this legal endorsement of Britain's siege mentality: 'The decision of the House of Lords in the Granada Television case is restrictive, reactionary and clearly against the public interest.'[8] But the editor of The Thunderer had missed the point; the right to define the public interest has now, in the new feudal Britain, become the monopoly of a tiny band. Perhaps it is the same band that played so well on board the *Titanic* as the great ship sank inelegantly beneath the waves. Certainly, Lord Cowdray had no illusions; the editorial pages of his own *Financial Times* carried not a word about the case. The editorial column was used instead to defend the right of 'families to send, by dint of their private wealth, children to schools which are not open to each and any of the country's children'.[9] The news coverage by the paper of the House of Lords decision reflected the same critical rejection of the right of freedom of information on such a vital public issue. The story repeated the strictures of Lord Denning, who had sat in judgment on the case in the Court of Appeal two months before and who had attacked Granada TV as 'disgraceful'.

If Britain's purveyors of news can count few sociologists within their ranks, their grasp of history is more tenuous still. A glance at the records will remind them that the Fourth Estate of the press grew up to impress honesty upon the Third, the Third being the French bourgeoisie in the years of ferment before the Revolution. As Britain confronts the 1980s the leaders of its press community have already begun to pack their survival kits; many of them have even reserved their places in the bunker.

Perhaps they know a secret.

18

Shhhhhh . . . you know who

Anxious governments can be forgiven for spying on their enemies; survival is the ultimate goal in politics. And there is much respectable precedent in Britain's history for arming the state machine with larger-than-life ears. The Tudor monarchs spent much time and wealth on the perfection of their secret services, as did the Stuarts after them. In both cases the heavy rhythm of history won in the end; even big ears cannot guarantee perpetual rule. But science has come increasingly to the aid of rulers under threat. The rise of terrorism on an international scale, of subversion as a respectable military weapon – recognised by such classical strategists as von Clausewitz, it is a common tool used by all modern governments – and the scope of sensitive technical information jealously guarded by the average defence ministry, have all helped to create a state of paranoia, and a paranoia of the state. Nowhere is that condition more acute than in Britain, where the mounting crisis of confidence has turned surveillance, wire-tapping and computerised curiosity into a major growth industry.

The British ethos of self-congratulation about a national prowess in secrecy and cloak-and-dagger expertise, exemplified in the adventures of 007, has its roots in the considerable achievements of intelligence services in two world wars. Even in peace it has reflected concern about foreign enemies seen by the majority of Britons as unwelcome visitors. But times have changed; Britain has become an introvert country, looking frantically for enemies within. And the weapons of secret protection, so expertly created by Britons over the years, are now turned inwards. Big Ears has moved in next door.

As the 1970s have given way to the 1980s, the methods used by the state to protect itself have been increasingly in evidence. For many, Britain today is a place where civil liberties are under serious attack. With the Official Secrets trial[1] has come the revelation that the jury system – traditionally one of the proudest examples of British liberty – has been tampered with by the 'vetting' of potential jurors. The Prevention of Terrorism Act – introduced at a time of national emergency, but still in force – removes many civil liberties, and is brandished over the heads of a number of television journalists. Government phone tapping is on the increase. The Special Patrol Group has become active on British streets, and has been implicated in the violent death of a demonstrator. And in May 1980, television viewers were treated to The Storming of the Iranian Embassy – an hour-long, live-as-it-happens, full-colour drama, in which for the first time the power of the Special Air Service was unleashed in central London. With their array of sophisticated listening devices, stun grenades, plastic explosives and the like, precisely and ruthlessly applied, the SAS in the summer of 1980 seemed to exemplify the interlinking of government control, state security and high technology.

The 1970s saw the introduction of computers into everyday police operations: data banks of information on millions of people, criminal or not, are now at the finger-tips of any policeman with a two-way radio link. At the same time, phone taps have been used on a much more extensive scale than before, and technology is about to be introduced that will render them virtually untraceable. Typically, Parliament – which has never debated police computers, nor legalised phone tapping – appears to be completely powerless to prevent the increasing encroachment of technology into civil liberties. Even that most innocuous document, the driving licence, has been turned into a rudimentary identity card, with the date of birth of the holder encoded upon it, and the threat that the Driver Number code might one day be used to carry more information, scrambled into seemingly random numbers intelligible only to civil servants or the police.

Most drivers can now be quickly checked out anyway, by reference to the Police National Computer at Hendon. In 1979 it held 30·2 million records. Among them were over 23 million entries on vehicle owners: their names and addresses, their car's year, make, model, colour and type, and the date that the owner acquired it.

Other information which the computer now makes instantly available includes 4 million criminal names and 2·5 million fingerprints. It will also, according to the Home Office, ' . . . include details of persons wanted or suspected of offences, vulnerable persons reported as missing, persons found, and other categories of people such as deserters, escapees, or people we need to locate for many reasons.'[2] By 1979, there were 100,000 people included in this category.

Every day during 1979 the computer handled 160,000 requests for information – almost 60 million inquiries per year. The sort of information that the computer makes available is a matter of controversy. A Home Office watchdog, the Data Protection Committee, created to look into the subject warned that:

> the linking of factual personal information about an identifiable individual with speculative data about criminal activity could pose a grave threat to the individual's interests . . . [This] should only be done . . . in special circumstances . . . with caution and subject to the most stringent safeguards.[3]

In fact, the computer carries a wide range of information which can, according to the Home Office, be linked 'when a police officer has judged it relevant'. A case in January 1977, for example, proved that the computer was carrying details of one vehicle owner's membership of the Anti-Blood Sports League. If such seemingly harmless information is included, what else might be? In trying to judge this, the Data Protection Committee reported: 'In relation to the Metropolitan Police, we do not have enough evidence to give a firm assurance . . . that the public need [not] be unduly alarmed by the use of computers for police purposes.'

Fears about what might be contained in files to which the individual has no access are paralleled by increasing concern about just what the police now perceive their role to be:

> I think that from a police point of view that my task in the future, in the ten to fifteen years from now, the period during which I shall continue to serve, that basic crime as such – theft, burglary, even violent crime – will not be the predominant police feature. What will be the matter of greatest concern to me will be the covert and ultimately overt attempts to overthrow democracy, to

subvert the authority of the state, and, in fact, to involve themselves in acts of sedition designed to destroy our parliamentary
system and the democratic government in this country.

The words of James Anderton, Chief Constable of Greater
Manchester (quoted here from the BBC programme *Question
Time*), give an indication of how the police today see themselves.
They consider their role to be far less neutral and far more actively
political than has traditionally been the case. Sir Robert Mark, for
example, Metropolitan Police Commissioner between 1972 and
1977, has attacked the 'Socialist philosophy' which has reduced 'the
standards of the wealthy, the skilled and the deserving to the lowest
common denominator'. He has referred to Churchill's description
of Hitler as 'this Nazi guttersnipe' as a term which 'warmed our
hearts in 1940': 'Poor Neville Chamberlain's references to Herr
Hitler and Signor Mussolini caused as much dismay then as the
Shadow Employment Minister's respectful touching of his forelock
to the trade unions on television causes now.'[4]
  Thus James Prior (the then Shadow Employment Secretary)
becomes Chamberlain, his 'softly softly' approach to trade unions a
policy of appeasement, and the trade unions – by extension – are
Nazis. Sir Robert's views, appropriately aired in the journal
Security Gazette in 1979, are disturbing because they suggest the
type and number of people the police feel they must now regard as
potential 'subversives' – of the millions of trade unionists, there are
presumably thousands whose political aims would bring them under
suspicion. The danger today is that modern surveillance techniques
allow the police to keep tabs on huge numbers of people. When the
Police National Computer had to be closed down between 29 and 31
July 1978, according to the review of police methods in *Policing the
Police*,[5] Scotland Yard's Peter Nievens wrote to Fleet Street's
editors asking them not to report the incident: 'There is a slight risk
that some subversive elements or criminals might attempt to take
advantage of the reduction of this facility should this become publicly known.' Who, it would be comforting to know, do the police
regard as 'subversive elements'? And how might they be expected
to profit from the two-day absence of the computer?
  In an increasingly sophisticated electronic age, the Police
National Computer – soon to be joined by other computers
attached to individual regions – represents only one method of

surveillance. Over the past two decades, the police, along with the intelligence services, have made increasing use of new bugging techniques. Telephone tapping in the 1970s was much more wide-spread than in the 1960s (see Figure 18:1). By 1979, the number of taps authorised by the Home Secretary was 411 – more than three times the figure for 1958. In addition there were 52 warrants issued to allow the interception of mail. There were a further 56 telephone taps authorised in Scotland in 1979, compared with just *three* in 1967 (see Figure 18:2). According to the White Paper, *The Interception of Communications in Great Britain* (1980), 'without interception the police view is that their effectiveness in tackling organised crime, particularly in London, would be substantially diminished.' The White Paper revealed that phone tapping had helped catch the Great Train Robbers; that 62 per cent of the heroin and 56 per cent of the cocaine seized by the Customs and Excise in 1978 was brought in as a result of phone tapping; and that 'over the years a number of serious terrorist attacks and threats to national security would not have been countered had it not been for the interception' (although 'for obvious reasons of security' the White Paper declined to go into specific examples).[6] The circumstances in which interception might be authorised were left vague. For the police, it would have to involve a 'serious crime' (defined as 'an offence for which a man with no previous record could reasonably be expected to be sentenced to three years' imprisonment') *or* 'an offence of lesser gravity in which either a large number of people are involved or there is good reason to apprehend the use of violence'. This second definition would appear considerably to negate the civil liberties safeguards inherent in the first. It is not difficult to conceive of the kind of demonstrations, for example, that the police might argue *could* involve a number of arrests or *could* lead to violence. Here there seem to be no rules to prevent, for instance, the phone tapping of organisers of pickets or of large public protests. In much the same way, the Security Service can obtain a tap if they can convince the Home Secretary that it involves 'a major subversive, terrorist or espionage activity that is likely to injure the national interest'. One man's 'subversive' could be another man's trade union leader.

According to the revelations in the *New Statesman* (1 February 1980), the main centre for phone tapping in Britain is at 93 Ebury Bridge Road in London's Victoria, where there is a capacity to tap 1,000 lines simultaneously. Although on the face of it that figure

Figure 18:1

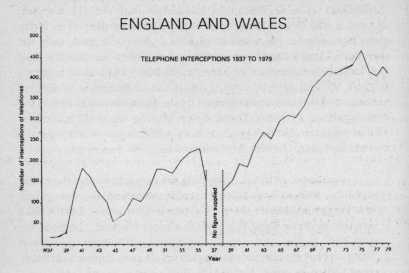

ENGLAND AND WALES

TELEPHONE INTERCEPTIONS 1937 TO 1979

Figure 18:2

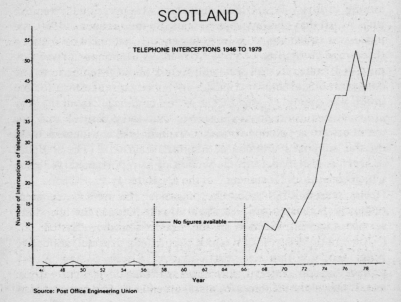

SCOTLAND

TELEPHONE INTERCEPTIONS 1946 TO 1979

Source: Post Office Engineering Union

would seem to be vastly in excess of the number of taps actually authorised, it is important to remember that the 411 warrants quoted in the White Paper may be only half the story. The figure does not indicate the number of actual phones tapped, only the number of times the Home Secretary has signed warrants; it does not include the monitoring activities of MI6 (keepers of Britain's biggest 'official secrets', overseers of the interception of foreign signals, and the service authorised by the Prime Minister to bug the conversations of the Patriotic Front during the 1979 Lancaster House talks on Zimbabwe); nor does it reveal just how long a tap can remain in operation. According to the *New Statesman*:

> . . . a national network of tapping connections covers the entire country, with 12 lines at least usually connected to every 'group' exchange in major cities. To prevent ordinary Post Office engineers recognising this system and its purpose, the lines are included in the Defence Communications Network, which is installed for military communications. It runs through ordinary Post Office facilities, but details of its operations are secret.

The paper also reported hostility to the work of phone tappers among ordinary Post Office engineers, who occasionally remove bugs which they spot attached to lines. By the summer of 1980, the union was sufficiently concerned to put out a statement calling for a three-man committee of Privy Councillors to monitor phone tapping in Britain. 'It's all very well to talk about listening in to the conversations of known criminals by police,' a spokesman for the union was quoted as saying, 'but we are concerned about the grey areas of unauthorised tapping. We want to be assured that our members are not going to be asked to undertake any illegal activity on the supposed grounds of national security.'[7] (The POEU's concern is also evident in the section of its report on surveillance which constitutes Document 5 of the appendix.)

The reason for the union's concern at this time is the great technical expansion which is about to take place in the telephone service – the introduction of the sinister-sounding 'System X'. ('You can do things with it which people only dreamed about five years ago.') Within ten years, all over Britain System X will replace the conventional mechanical switching devices currently in use. It will be the ideal tool for mass surveillance. Every aspect of its operation is miniaturised into small electronic devices, so that to bug it would involve no tell-tale signs, simply the provision of a couple of new programmes in the computers which control it. As part of its normal function, System X will automatically generate records of who calls whom and for how long.

The introduction of computer technology into the operations of police and security services is fast outstripping Parliament's ability to keep pace. There have been no debates on the implications of such developments as the new police data banks, and MPs are rarely given satisfactory answers to Parliamentary Questions. In October 1972, for example, Les Huckfield tabled thirty-seven detailed questions on the Police National Computer – and was rewarded with a brief, two-paragraph reply.

As the new technology increasingly lends itself to the maintenance of the state's security, so the obsession with secrecy – for so long the hallmark of British democracy – continues to grow.

Why is it that Britain today is, by general consent, one of the most secretive societies in the West?

The desire of Whitehall to assert its power at home appears to have grown as Britain's opportunity to assert its power abroad has declined. Paradoxically, while we now have fewer truly important secrets, our concern about secrecy has never been higher. It is tempting to see the Official Secrets Act as a sort of virility symbol for our senior civil servants: brought up to rule an empire, they find their power severely curtailed. But secrecy carries with it an illusion of real power – *they* know something *we* don't. Such trappings are useful. The civil servants can preserve their image as inscrutable possessors of knowledge, keepers of secrets too great to be entrusted to ordinary taxpayers. At the same time, the sweeping powers of the Secrets Act allow them to cover up mistakes; as the Labour MP Michael Meacher put it 'Official secrecy has more to do with protecting the government from embarrassment than with the nation's security.'

The Official Secrets Act (1911) passed through all its stages in the House of Commons in just twenty-four hours: it was never properly discussed, despite the enormous powers it introduced. The Act made it an offence for any government employee to pass on any information he gained in the course of his work. Anyone coming into the possession of such information is also guilty. In short, everything the government does but doesn't choose to tell us about is secret. This ludicrous legislation remains on the statute-book today, having successfully survived the recommendation of the Franks Committee that it be abolished, the Labour Party's 1974 Manifesto commitment to repeal it, and a couple of Private Members' Bills which aimed to replace it.

Unlike other countries, Britain has no Freedom of Information Act. It is impossible for the public to discover even the most innocuous details of what the government is up to. It is, for example, impossible to get government reports and statistics on car safety tests; on the safety of food additives; on the incidence of food-poisoning on liners; on the cause of gas leaks and explosions; on the risks of fluoride poisoning; and on incompetence or fraud at MOT testing stations. The absurdity of the situation is pointed up still further when information relevant in this country is officially secret, but freely available in the United States. A recent *Panorama* programme, for example, revealed that the Triumph TR7 – a British car – was unsafe, and had a tendency to catch fire. Between 1971 and 1977 there were 13,125 replacements for faulty wiring; acting on this information, 25 American TR7 owners filed law suits of a million dollars each against the manufacturer, British Leyland. In Britain, the information which formed the basis for the *American* complaints is secret. The programme, entitled 'Listen, Do You Want to Know a Secret', was scheduled to be repeated in the summer of 1979. After pressure from BL, the repeat showing was cancelled. The men at the top in the BBC decided that the British public did not, after all, want to know this particular secret. How many others are they being denied?

19

Good night, Knight

Britain, as much as any other country, is entitled to have its secrets, if only to give to its bureaucrats a sense of power and pride. But one secret will prove difficult to protect for long – the devastating extent of Britain's economic and social disintegration is fast becoming apparent. Some in Britain will welcome the collapse and disappearance of industry; for them it has always been identified with the vulgar pursuit of material comfort. In the decade of the 1970s their view was put in a series of essays and reports that cast scorn on that pursuit: the reports of the Club of Rome, the studies of the *Ecologist*, books such as E. F. Schumacher's *Small is Beautiful*.[1]

Some, too, have long yearned for a return to the morality and social texture of pre-industrial times. The following observations by the Cambridge historian Peter Laslett in his book *The World We Have Lost* suggest a deep nostalgia for the simple social structures and the predictable lifestyle exemplified in the household of an English baker in the years before the noise and turmoil that came with large-scale industry:

> We may feel that in a whole society organised like this, in spite of all the subordination, the exploitation and the obliteration of those who were young, or feminine, or in service, everyone belonged in a group, a family group. Everyone had his circle of affection: every relationship could be seen as a love relationship. Not so with us. Who could love the name of a limited company or of a government department as an apprentice could love his superbly satisfactory father-figure master, even if he were a bully and a beater, a usurer and a hypocrite?[2]

The yearning for a feudal age, with its orderly tyranny, clearly has its attractions for the besieged psyche of the average individual of the industrial era, beset by the pressures of factory noise and faceless technologies. The psychologist Dr Erich Fromm, in *The Fear of Freedom*,[3] suggests that the twentieth-century phenomena of German and Italian Fascism were the result of a mass desire to escape from modern industrial life back into the predictable, though unfree, world of feudal despotism.

But then, the professors will always have their explanations; the romantics will always have their nostalgic dream. After all, on a sunny summer day what can be a richer experience than to bask in the silence of the open fields? Alas, the age of choice has gone. The coming of industry changed the chemistry of everyday life. And having been changed, it can only be restored to its pre-industrial flavour at immense social and political cost.

No society in the western world has yet attempted to rediscover 'the world we have lost'. Put to the popular vote, none would choose to. But because of the inexorable process of industrial degeneration, urged on by the feudal spirit which underpins so much of life in twentieth-century Britain, millions of people have already embarked on that journey. By the year 2010, who will care what they found when they reached their journey's end?

Until 2066, when an invading army arrives, full of hope for the land it is about to conquer. By then, true to its Prutopian vocation, the country the invaders see before them will spend much time in the baking of bread. There could well be many 'superbly satisfactory father-figure masters', languidly enjoying the benefits of their new feudal power. And scrawled on a nearby castle wall, the graffito of a world that was lost some time around 1986: 'Why didn't anybody tell us?'

APPENDIX

APPENDIX

Document 1

The Protopian Manuscripts

Document 1 presents an idealised version of life in the post-industrial phase. In this sense this book is a critique, not an endorsement, of the Protopian scheme. Protopia is a society where high technology is used for the benefit of the many; Prutopia is a society where it is owned and used for the benefit of the few.

The *Protopian Manuscripts* set out a conceptual model for a self-supporting community of the future, developed by Andrew Page for the Dartington Hall Trust; the scheme has been given concrete form in a 1:250 scale model designed in collaboration with Tetra Design London. The project was a prizewinner in the lay category in a competition related to community life in the year 2000, held in collaboration with the British Town and Country Planning Association in June 1980.

The *Manuscripts* describe a number of key characteristics of life at the beginning of the twenty-first century, when the economic environment has concentrated on self-sufficiency on the land coupled with high-technology, knowledge-based activities and pre-industrial crafts. Some major elements of life in Protopia are:

1 A community size of around 2000.
2 A social and physical environment where all the necessities are close at hand: home, work, school, recreation, shops, community government, caring schemes.
3 A high degree of self-sufficiency through full use of the land, local energy supplies, local crafts and markets.
4 The appropriate use, within a single communal lifestyle, of

high and low technology: high technology in information, low technology in the production of food, clothes, utensils and many household goods.

Here is an extract from the *Protopian Manuscripts:*

The synthesis of the two revolutions – the high-tech– low-tech composite

A vital consideration underlying my attempts to integrate ideas, values, and technological objectives for a sustainable future is the awareness of the need for a synthesis of the two revolutions worldwide: the one – the ecological movement, enthusiasm for alternative technology, E. F. Schumacher's principles of 'small is beautiful' and the 'economics of permanence', a life of more direct participation in primary production and assumption of responsibility for local community services; the other – the micro-electronics revolution, heralding an age of automated production and of one-world communications and universal access to information.

Although the way forward promises to be rough, a possible pattern may be discerned in which (due to the increasing costs of energy, the desirability to reduce transport, the high risks of capital intensive industry and, of greatest importance, the urgency for authentic employment) automated production would appear to be self-limiting to such products as electrical installations, information and communications systems, tools, and other products not amenable to crafts production methods.

On the other hand, there is the growing interest in, and signs of economic viability of, crafts occupations and small industries. There is every reason to encourage the situation in which products such as clothing, household furnishings (pottery, tableware generally, furniture, etc.), detail work in shelter construction, and production of small runs of industrial products would come within the province of employment intensive, crafts process, local production methods.

Together with planning for increased participation of many people in local food production and processing, allowance has been made in the Self-supporting Community model for a large number of small workshops interspersed among dwellings within the community. Workshops for low-tech, artisan production; but also to accommodate high-tech cottage industries for small-scale manufacturing and/or assembling of specialised electronics components. Thus:

10 One or more purpose-built structures for high-tech automated production with special design features for access (perhaps, as mentioned earlier, underground passageways to the village Trans-

port Depot); then several workshop areas for high-tech cottage industries; and many small crafts workshops with combined retailing and nearby dwelling space.

By means of such a High-tech–Low-tech Composite, the objective is to secure economic solvency as well as full employment in meaningful occupations. It is projected that, within this conceptual framework, a community could achieve a salutary balance in provision of its own primary needs with some degree of product and service specialities to assure generation of surplus revenues by trade outside.

As regards economic organisation, three sectors are envisaged within the conceptual synthesis: *individual enterprise* – personal and family businesses and crafts workshops; *co-operative enterprises* (occurring upon 'hiring' other persons on a full-time basis and/or as a means for purchase of capital equipment appropriate for shared usage, e.g. pottery kiln); and *community enterprises* (i.e. the maintenance of public services and amenities).

The social value at issue is that mentioned earlier of one person : many jobs (with the intangible benefit of mutual appreciation for all that it takes to sustain one's community).

A schematic pattern of employment could be of each person working for, say, 10 per cent of the time in a high-tech occupation, then 60 per cent in a low-tech, primary production, craft, and 30 per cent in varying occupations within the community enterprise sector.

The operatives of such a system could be a labour-credit arrangement in association with various job-sharing formulae. Children and old people could be included in the local employment scheme. Leisure would largely consist of alternation of productive occupations.

In order to assure equitable participation in maintaining community facilities, a village levy could be set, not unlike present income tax and local authority rates. However, in distinction to tax and rates, one would have the option to work off the amount of the levy in one or more community enterprises, and the system could be financially arranged to encourage working off rather than paying off the amount.

The co-ordination of such a multiple and diversified occupations programme could be facilitated by electronics technology. Therefore:

11   Village Cottage Office – a central community building housing a wide range of electronics technology for use in the co-ordination of occupations (for needs and skills matching) – in this function, then, the Cottage Office would serve as back-up to the café (the *primary* communications centre).

  The electronics technology would also be of use to individual, co-op, and community enterprises for handling accounts, tax details, stock control, supplies ordering, outside marketing, etc.

  Routine aspects in education could also be facilitated by computer and video software. Additional hardware and software at the Cottage Office could be telex, telephone answering service, Xerox machine, citizen band radio, video tape deck and library, and adapted programmes of Teletext and Viewdata; in general, an expanded range of facilities similar to those offered at a university Resources Centre.

One person : many jobs

Further towards the re-integration of community life is the principle of one person : many jobs – one predominant job (held for an average of, say, twenty hours per week), job sharing, many part-time responsibilities including especially the maintenance of community facilities – another reason for high density nucleated planning: the close proximity of homes, workplaces, and public facilities to overcome the disincentive of distance as a reason for non-participation in community life.

Land for the people

An essential principle for re-integration of living is allowance for the re-establishment of relationship between people and the land. More people on the land, more land under cultivation; organic, low energy input, mixed crop agriculture; increased cultivation of perennial crops; private horticultural conservatories, gardens, and allotments, co-operative undertakings for grains and livestock; a shift from farming the land to gardening, tending the land – as a way of life and not simply as a source of profits.

8   Conservatories as nurseries or kitchen gardens attached to each dwelling. Allocation of an allotment with each dwelling. Communal greenhouses and co-operative smallholdings.

In a community for 2,000, the relatively small size and high density, nucleated planning allows for sufficient proximity to allotments and smallholdings encircling the village within the green belt. However, in regard to existing communities of populations greater than c. 2,000, allowance should be made for allotments closer to dwellings – this policy is urged in distinction to present policies of infilling new housing within communites.

9   Local food processing workshops in conjunction with local food production and retailing, e.g. flour mill, bakery, cheesemaking, brewery, bottling of jams and preserves – all perhaps organised as a local food co-op which would also trade village surplus for foods not grown locally and buy in bulk from outside. As in the case of food production, participation in food processing on a part-time basis should be available to as many residents as possible.

Local production by the people, from local resources, for the local market

Seasonally, then, through built environment planning and revived arrangements regarding work and school, the opportunity is provided for the lifestyle such that, at spring sowing and harvest time, the entire population can be involved in the life-cycle of the land.

Document 2

Humberside plans for war

In July 1980 an emergency planning exercise was carried out at the Humberside County Wartime Control at Wawne near Hull. A full dress rehearsal for official life 30 days after a nuclear attack was based on planning assumptions outlined in this scenario, which is an abridged version of the document prepared by staff of the Humberside Emergency Planning Service.

Dateline: 30 days after nuclear attack

In keeping with the tradition of earlier European wars, hostilities did not commence until after the harvest had been gathered.

The strike against the United Kingdom consisted of about 180 nuclear warheaded missiles being delivered onto centres of population, industry and communications in the space of three hours. The obvious intention of the attack was to paralyse the country in order that it could no longer influence the course of events militarily, politically or economically.

In addition, the electro-magnetic pulse from a high powered nuclear burst in the troposphere over Northern Europe had the effect of rendering unusable all radio communications facilities which had not been previously protected and burning out the majority of surviving electrical transformer and distribution equipment.

The nuclear strike, when it arrived, affected Humberside in the following degree:

A 2-megaton groundburst weapon detonated over the civic centre of Hull leaving a crater half a mile across and forty yards deep. Simultaneously a half-megaton airburst at Immingham Dock breached the banks of the Humber to a distance of a quarter of a mile inland. In addition to the

physical damage, a massive tidal wave swept along the estuary, tearing at
the foundations of the Humber Bridge and causing the already weakened
structure to collapse. All shipping, moored or otherwise, was inundated as
far as the Trent Falls. The Saltend petro-chemical complex dissolved in a
flash of light which was lost in the silver brilliance of the enormous heat
flash which enveloped Hull.

Scunthorpe also disappeared, in a mushroom pillar of dust and debris
under the impact of a 1-megaton groundburst, and the ancient walled city
of York ended its two thousand year history in a split second, despatched
by a 1-megaton groundburst. The electro-magnetic pulse, generated by
the high airburst weapon, could not be seen but its effects were immediately felt by the breakdown of all but the most effectively protected
communications equipment and the failure of the electricity generating
system.

The resultant clouds of radio-active fallout were carried by the wind to
the North-East causing high levels of radiation on the coastal strip of the
county.

At a point in time ten days after the air attack warning sounded in the
United Kingdom, heralding the approach of the first nuclear missile, the
Controllers at the Humberside County and North Wolds District Wartime
Headquarters were in a position to assess the situation in their respective
fields of responsibility. Each faced a bleak prospect. Massive destruction
had been caused in large centres of population in or near to their areas with
an appalling death roll, but in the surrounding countryside, casualties had
been surprisingly light.

Apart from a few 'hot spots', the effects of radioactive fallout had
decayed to an acceptable level, and thanks to timely warnings issued by
the Warning and Monitoring Organisation and the good sense of many of
the population in constructing and stocking fallout shelters on their own
initiative, a high proportion of the population in these areas had survived
and were now able to move about freely. The destruction or disablement
of those facilities to which civilised man has become accustomed, electricity, fuel, transport and the availability of food and water, and the
traumatic shock of the holocaust on the morale of the population were by
now exacting their toll.

In the following twenty days, the Controllers and their staffs had
struggled to cope with the most urgent survival problems, those of the
rescue of trapped persons, the provision of food, water and shelter for
survivors, the obtaining and distribution of fuel, the prevention of disease,
the care of the sick, the restoration of utilities and the maintenance of law
and order. Thirty days after the attack, the Controllers took stock of the
situation. It was indeed a bleak prospect. The chill winds of autumn were
now blowing and soon winter would arrive – a winter to be faced with
inadequate shelter, food or fuel by a population shocked, bewildered and,
in many cases, suffering from sickness and disease.

EFFECTS OF BRIEF EXPOSURE OF WHOLE BODY TO IONISING RADIATION

Table D2:1

Dose (rad)*	Effects	Probable mortality rate	Notes**
0–50	No characteristic symptoms. An individual may experience mild symptoms, such as nausea and loss of appetite.	Zero	–
50–200	Some nausea and vomiting within 24 hours. (<50% of those exposed)	< 5% (after 60 or more days)	All those in this band capable of performing tasks.
200–450	Nausea and vomiting soon after exposure and illness for a few days (>50% of those exposed). Subsequent latent period of 1–3 weeks, followed by further illness.	< 50% (within 30–60 days)	Most of those in this band would need some medical care.
450–600	Nausea and vomiting very soon after exposure in majority of cases. Subsequent latent period of 1–2 weeks followed by further illness.	> 50% (after about 30 days)	More serious degree of illness described for previous dose band. Intensive medical care needed to survive.
Over 600	Early onset of vomiting which, without medication, may last for several days or until death. Possible latent period of no more than 2 days before serious illness.	90–100% (within 2 weeks or less)	Accelerated version of illness described for previous dose band.

NOTES

1 Dose is expressed as rads in surface body tissue. This is roughly equivalent to exposure as registered on an instrument in roentgens.
2 The Operational Equivalent Dose (OED) can be regarded as equivalent in effect to a brief exposure dose of the same numerical value, the OED being defined as the maximum value of (accumulated dose – 150 – 10t) where t is the number of days elapsing after the initial exposure to radiation.

   *1 rad = 10 mGy
  **For those exposed to the higher doses in each of the above dose bands the early effects of exposure will be more serious and the chance of survival relatively poorer.

General notes

In the preparatory period and following the conventional attacks, many of the population of urban areas, not only from Hull but from the Leeds and Bradford areas, self-evacuated to the coastal strip of Humberside, flooding into caravan sites, holiday camps and inland villages where they became an embarrassment to the Local Authority in the early stages and a source of the highest level of radiation casualties post-attack due to the lack of protection in the lightly-built structures they were occupying.

A Community Advisory network was set up before hostilities and as a result all villages and many parts of small towns have their own voluntary organisation, although most are working in isolation. This at least includes members of the community responsible for emergency feeding, first aid and emergency sanitation.

At County and District Controls, sufficient staff took post in the preparatory stage to enable operations to continue during the period of fallout and more staff reported for duty when they were clear of the danger from radiation (in the period D+5 to D+15) with the result that all Controls are adequately staffed and have moved in many cases from protected accommodation to normal offices as the fallout danger passed.

Food

Stocks accumulated by householders have been exhausted during the period in which they were in shelter. Food held in shops and small warehouses has been distributed (officially or unofficially) and some feeding centres are operating. No Government emergency food stocks are available or anticipated. Warehouse stocks of unprocessed food are largely intact as are many farm stocks. A 'Black Market' shows signs of emerging. Priorities include the setting up of a food collection and distribution chain to husband existing stocks in a situation where transport is in short supply and power unavailable. The County has 'lived on its fat' up to this point but must make plans to survive the coming winter.

Industry

Power-based industrial production has ceased. Commerce is virtually at a standstill, no imports are being received or can be expected. A massive reinstatement of the vital industries is a priority which must be dealt with from this stage.

Information services

Some personnel with hand-operated printing equipment and small stocks of supplies are available. An embryo information service has been started but this needs to be rapidly reinforced so as to maintain public morale.

Communications

Surviving external communications have already been set out. In the absence of mains electric power and the extreme fuel shortage for the use of standby generators, it is important that only essential lines of communication are used. The telephone system has been patched to give minimum cover but priorities include the extension of this so that effective control and co-ordination may be achieved in the recovery stage.

Document 3

The effect of nuclear war on a small community

A scenario presented by Julian Allason to a seminar at the Home Defence College, Easingwold, in September 1979.

In Manton, for that is the name of our village, not a great deal of attention was paid to the build-up of Soviet armour around Erfurt and Magdeburg. The only event which seemed out of place was the arrival of large numbers of holiday-makers, relations and friends; more than was usual for the time of year. Certainly, no one thought of them as refugees.

Historians will argue about exactly how much warning was given. Certainly the County Emergency Planning Officers were notified a week before the attack.

The international situation continued its decline. The Government remained reluctant to order any overt action which might heighten international tension.

On D-4 the order to print 'Protect and Survive' was finally given. There was still to be no reference to the campaign in the Press. The television advertisements were not to appear, in the event.

In Cabinet the rapid increase in unofficial stoppages in certain key industries was noted. Docks, printing and railways were particularly badly hit. There had been a number of mysterious interruptions of communications. Sabotage was suspected and three GPO engineers were being questioned. The union was demanding their immediate release.

On D-3 the Emergency Planning Department telephoned their volunteers. Their instructions were to consult privately with the community leaders, and to ensure that the UKWMO carrier warning point was continually manned, and to note in general terms the resources situation in the village.

On D-2, the Chairman of the parish council, a retired military man, called his meeting to order. Only 8 people were present. They were, if you like, the natural leaders of the community.

The situation was critical, he explained. Due to the delicate state of negotiations, no official war warning had been issued by the Government, although it could now be expected at any time. The telephone preference scheme would shortly be implemented.

At his invitation, the Community Advisor made his report. The Management Committee received it in silence.

Copies of 'Protect and Survive' were unfortunately not available, due to industrial problems in the printing industry, a shortage of paper and the deplorable state of the posts. Nor had they yet appeared in advertisement form in the newspapers, due to strikes.

However, he, the Community Advisor, had had roneoed off 1,000 broadsheets of instructions to householders. These could be distributed from door to door.

A brief summary of the local water sources, livestock situation and availability of fuel was given. The stock of both village shops had been seriously depleted by a sudden surge of buying during the previous 48 hours. The position was the same with petrol. There was plenty of grain in store, however.

The Committee then considered a list of key personnel, prepared by the Community Advisor. No doctors lived in the village, but there were two former nurses and a research physicist who commuted.

After some disagreement, a retired serviceman was nominated to organise a peace-keeping force. For the time being its role would be restricted to distributing the broadsheets and advising on protective measures.

The Committee adjourned.

The following day at a hastily called public meeting in the village hall, the Chairman of the parish council introduced the Community Advisor. His speech was short and many questions followed.

In the other three neighbouring villages, no such preparations were in hand. These villages received no advice.

At approximately 5 a.m. the following morning, Soviet tanks rolled across the German border. An hour later, two high altitude electromagnetic pulse detonations terminated the BBC's pretaped attack warning. Throughout Europe radio and telephone communications went dead. Only the steady rise and fall of sirens was to be heard.

At 7.30 the police arrived to arrest a retired teacher active in fringe politics.

Throughout the village, the scene was one of frantic digging. Plastic rubbish sacks full of earth were piled up in front of windows and doors, and inner refuges constructed.

The majority waited fearfully indoors, ears attuned to silent radios or straining for the sound of sirens.

A skeleton staff of GPO engineers, the few who had reported for duty, struggled to restore the carrier warning system, its switch gear having been damaged at several points by EMP.

Due to the prevailing wind, not everyone at Manton heard the hand-operated sirens. But news travels fast in a small community and by 9 p.m. the following day, when the war went nuclear, almost everyone was in cellars or hastily constructed inner refuges.

The three-man crew of the Royal Observer Corps bunker, just to the south of the village, rated the groundburst up to 5 megatons. A pretty large bomb by any standards, but given the relative inaccuracy of Soviet targeting, probably the minimum needed to destroy the strategic stockpile hidden in the rock caverns 20 miles away.

For fifteen seconds there was the most brilliant and searing light, causing spontaneous fires to break out several miles from ground zero. It would be many years before the radiation at the centre decayed enough to allow anyone to approach the crater.

Slowly and majestically the familiar mushroom cloud grew. Three-quarters of a minute later the blast wave struck the village, like an invisible tidal wave.

At that distance the damage was principally to roofs and windows. A number of villagers were severely injured by flying glass and a caravan was demolished. Surprisingly the church spire, for years the subject of a repair fund that never quite matched inflation, survived intact.

A number of gipsies, who had ignored the warnings, suffered mild skin burns and eye damage.

There was one heart attack.

Forewarned, the villagers knew that they had a few precious minutes before the fallout descended.

Frantically they moved to cover the previously filled baths. As advised in the broadsheet, water and oil supplies were shut off. Broken windows were hastily blocked.

All of this was in contrast to the scenes of confusion which reigned in the other three villages. Without benefit of proper advice, their casualties were already substantial.

Three bangs echoed across the valley separating the villages, heralding the descent of the deadly and invisible dust.

Silence enveloped the village as families crammed themselves into cellars, barricaded themselves under the stairs or in the hastily constructed inner refuges.

Only the older houses, with their 13½-inch brick walls, really gave sufficient protection. The bungalows, their large picture windows blown out, afforded their inhabitants even less than the officially calculated protection factor of 25.

Of those who suffered the threshold dose of 150 roentgens, almost all had sought shelter in houses of modern construction.

Ignorance contributed to a number of tragic misunderstandings about release periods and the need to cover food. Inadequate hygiene precipitated stomach upsets which were mistaken for radiation sickness and vice versa. This bred a panic which drove some out into the street in search of help. At this stage there were also rumours of biological attack.

The radios remained silent during the first twenty-four hours. And then a weak broadcast was received from the Sub-Regional Control. The message was 'Stay put'.

In truth the Sub-Regional Controller was himself somewhat cut off. Whilst his communication links with UKWMO/ROC and other SRCs remained open, only a single teleprinter line to just one of his four counties had survived EMP and blast damage.

It was under cover that the deficiency in public education showed up worst.

The broadsheet had told families to take with them enough water for seven days, at two pints per person per day. For a family of four this added up to fourteen gallons! And that was for drinking purposes alone.

Most families had either underestimated or been unable to obtain the amount of food necessary for a prolonged stay under cover. By the fourth day most were hungry.

Very few were prepared for the considerable stresses of remaining in a confined space for a long period. Families with children came under the greatest strain.

The County Controller was experiencing similar difficulties communicating with his districts. Below district level, communications were to remain almost non-existent for some time to come. It was clear that the village could expect little help from outside.

Combined with the failure to distribute radiac instruments, the breakdown in communications meant that very little local information was available on radiation levels.

It is true that the ROC, fire services and police continued to monitor with what equipment they had, but this information reached the County Controller only intermittently. The means to pass it on to the villages did not exist.

So it was not until the eighth day that the single steady note of the 'All Clear' sounded, and the people emerged.

Physically the damage appeared surprisingly light. Most of the survivors seemed shocked and weakened by their confinement. It was time to take stock.

The Parish Council met. Facing them were a number of conflicting priorities. Advised by the Volunteer, they decided to tackle the question of water and sanitation first.

To avoid pollution of the water supply and the spread of disease, it was decided to start with the digging of latrines and the burial of corpses. The Parish Clerk kept a register of deaths.

In their weakened condition, the digging took longer than had been anticipated.

Health care was also a problem. Dysentery began to sweep the village. The two former nurses counselled strict quarantine for anyone from an affected house. It was hard to distinguish the symptoms from those of radiation sickness.

In any event the absence of medical supplies prevented all but the simplest form of nursing.

Food was a further problem. It was clear from the blocked roads that it would be some time before buffer stocks could be distributed.

The Volunteer organised a special survey of resources and damage. These included fuel, building materials, water, bulk foods, crops, livestock and medical supplies.

They also looked at plant and equipment – this produced no less than three electric generators – firefighting equipment, chemicals and transport.

The village shop having been raided almost as soon as the All Clear sounded, the Parish Council decided to safeguard the remaining stocks and supplies from the start.

The peacekeeping force were properly sworn in as special constables, in the absence of the regular police. They were armed with stout sticks – firearms having been ruled out as likely to cause more trouble than they prevented.

In the event it was not long before the Specials were needed, some resistance being met to the council's attempts to requisition vehicles.

Casualties were counted and categorised as dead, those severely ill with radiation sickness, those likely to recover, sufferers from epidemic disease and those injured by blast, flying debris, etc. Overall the casualty rate was not high. There were, however, a number suffering from severe shock, and two attempted suicides.

A messenger was dispatched with this information to District Control. He travelled by motor bike.

During the first few days following re-emergence, the privations of life were suffered with some stoicism. Order was maintained, with only the evacuees seemingly sullen and unwilling to contribute.

This was perhaps understandable since most of them had lost their families in the destruction of the cities.

A billeting system was organised to cope with those whose houses had been rendered uninhabitable.

Being a dairy county, there was actually a surplus of meat, as cattle were slaughtered before they became too sick to be edible.

All of this changed on the eleventh day after the attack, when the first refugees arrived. At first they were welcomed, albeit with reluctance from certain quarters.

By the thirteenth day, the trickle had become a flood, bringing with it new disease, dissension and disorder. Homes were occupied, stores looted.

Matters came to a head when a gang of young men forced their way into an outlying farm; the farmer was killed resisting and his wife raped.

Reluctant to hear the case on his own, the village's one JP swore in two more magistrates. After a summary trial all three young men were found guilty.

Clearly the time had come for firm measures if order was not to break down irretrievably. After lengthy deliberation a capital sentence was handed down. The three offenders were shot that evening.

The effect was immediate, and although it subsequently became necessary to arm the Specials, no further death sentences were necessary – instead most punishments were corporal and immediate.

Regular patrols were now a necessity. Roadblocks were set up at the approaches to the village to prevent a further influx of refugees.

It was two and a half weeks before a representative of the District

Controller arrived across country in a Landrover, the roads being blocked by abandoned vehicles.

His report to the Controller states that due to the high degree of preparedness and the effective organisation, the proportion of casualties from radiation sickness, malnutrition and epidemic disease was uniformly lower in Manton than in the three adjoining villages.

Perhaps with a proper system of public education the damage, both human and material, might have been even less. It is clear that the only effective protection small communities have is the protection which an individual can draw around his family. To do so he needs education, advice and training.

Studies of the behaviour of those subjected to bombing raids in Dresden, Coventry, London and Hiroshima suggest that prior education and preparation are of key importance to survival.

It is doubtful whether a last-minute publicity campaign, even given time to mount it, can ever be as effective as a permanent co-ordinated public education scheme.

Given the likelihood of central Government consenting to such a radical change of policy, a scheme to train individual volunteers is probably the most realistic and effective alternative.

Come the day, such a scheme could save millions of lives.

Document 4

Here is the news on Northern Ireland?

Following the incident involving a *Panorama* team in Carrickmore, Northern Ireland, in the autumn of 1979, the standing instructions on coverage of Northern Ireland matters were reviewed by the Director of News and Current Affairs, Dick Francis, after consultations with the Director-General Ian Trethowan and the Board of Governors. The instructions represent a system of tight control exercised by senior BBC management, the greater part of which is appointed – directly or indirectly – by Whitehall. They set out the strict limits of reporting in Northern Ireland, the absolute discretionary powers of senior management as to who can be interviewed (even to exclude those not actually members of a terrorist organisation) and the list of proscribed organisations as it stood at the end of November 1979. It has not been possible to discover what additional unwritten guidelines operate within the BBC senior management. By implication, similar constraints apply to organisations within the rest of the United Kingdom, both in connection with the unrest in Northern Ireland and for other, quite distinct, political reasons.

Section 1 of the Standing Instructions sets out the process of referral from individual programme makers to Network Controllers; the final veto is reserved for Director, News and Current Affairs and for the Director-General. In appearance the Standing Instructions seem to represent an organisational arrangement that is an essential part of running a large and complex BBC bureaucracy. In practice, and especially in sensitive areas such as Northern Ireland, it is also a rigorous system for the vetting and possible censorship of programmes. In matters affecting coverage in

Northern Ireland the Standing Instructions are bluntly specific: 'Controller Northern Ireland must be consulted and his agreement sought to all programme proposals having a bearing on Ireland as a whole and on Northern Ireland in particular.' In cases of disagreement the matter is referred to London for a final ruling from DNCA and the Director-General.

These instructions provide a blanket control over programme content so that, in theory at least, any matter whatsoever can be vetoed if it impinges on an Irish issue, whether it be brass bands or cookery.

Paragraph 3 covers proposals by individual programme makers to interview members of terrorist organisations and those 'who are or may be associated with such organisations'. And here the Standing Instructions are framed to allow considerable discretionary powers to senior BBC management over who can be interviewed. The list of proscribed organisations is, presumably, updated on the advice of the official intelligence services. The discretionary powers are couched in terms that grant wide interpretation of a person's connections with a proscribed organisation: 'Interviews with individuals *who are deemed* by D.N.C.A. to be closely associated with a terrorist organisation may not be sought or transmitted – two separate stages – without the prior permission of the Director-General.' (Author's italics. In the Standing Instructions themselves, this entire sentence is picked out with heavy underlining.)

At the time of the review of the Standing Instructions, in November 1979, the list of proscribed organisations in Northern Ireland stood at eight:

Irish Republican Army
Irish National Liberation Army
The Cumann na mBan
Fianna Eireann
Saor Eire
Ulster Freedom Fighters
The Red Hand
Ulster Volunteer Force

In principle these Instructions are designed to give individual reporters in the BBC a broad freedom to investigate and to follow through on 'leads'. Section 2, for example, advises reporters that it is the instinct of the journalist to find out, and 'nothing in this revised instruction is intended, in these rare but real circumstances, to inhibit the reporter from finding out.' But the right to publish the results of those investigations is totally under the control of the BBC senior management; most BBC reporters are retained on freelance contributors' contracts which can be ended at short notice and which guarantee nothing about eventual publication through a broadcast programme. In this sense BBC current affairs programmes are not a forum for the publication of individual reports and documentaries prepared by skilled professionals, many with considerable expertise in their fields. Rather, those programmes are the result of carefully filtered material. And in the case of the Carrickmore incident the material was never remotely close to publication; the process of editing the filmed material had not even properly begun. The reporter had exercised his acknowledged responsibility 'to find out' by travelling to the village concerned. This is something commonly done by newspaper journalists in Northern Ireland; it is something actually endorsed by the BBC's own Standing Instructions. Nevertheless, from the reaction of the BBC management to the incident it seems clear that BBC reporters do not have the same freedom of investigation enjoyed by their professional colleagues in the newspaper industry.

Seen in this light the Standing Instructions are a monument to hypocrisy. In the words of the BBC, 'They are the framework in which our journalists are free to work in a difficult, contentious and dangerous area, backed by the fullest possible authority of the BBC.' In practice that freedom to work exists only within the most restrictive framework, designed to give discretionary power to a small group of senior people and vulnerable to direct political pressures from the government of the day. On the question of Ireland the BBC has been shown to be little more than a defender of the status quo; is it surprising that it is increasingly seen as a spent force in other, unrelated, areas where minorities are under threat or where the unchallenged power of the state poses real dangers of tyranny?

Document 5

Tapping the telephone

In July 1980 the Post Office Engineering Union completed a report on the extent of surveillance being carried out through the British telephone network. In that report the figures of the British government on officially sanctioned eavesdropping, as set out in the White Paper 'The Interception of Communications in Britain' (Cmnd 7873), are disputed.

It should be noted that, in keeping with a deep sense of official fun, this White Paper was made public on April Fools Day 1980.

The POEU report elaborated on the techniques of wire-tapping used by the British government, the victims of surveillance and the potential for greatly expanded surveillance in the future offered by new technologies. The following extract is an unabridged section of the report.

How is tapping conducted?

The warrant procedure

As far as telephone taps officially authorised by warrant are concerned, the procedure commences with a formal application to the Secretary of State. The procedure is summarised in para. 9 of the White Paper:

> Applications for warrants are sent by the police, by Customs and Excise and by the Security Service to the Home Office (the Scottish Home and Health Department for police and Customs and Excise warrants in Scotland). Applications are made in writing and must contain a statement of the purpose for which interception is requested and of the facts

and circumstances which support the request. Every application is submitted to the Permanent Under-Secretary of State at the Home Office or the Secretary, Scottish Home and Health Department (or, in their absence, nominated deputies) who, if he is satisfied that the application meets the required criteria, submits it to the Secretary of State for approval and signature of a warrant. In a case of exceptional urgency, if the Secretary of State is not immediately available to sign a warrant he may be asked to give authority orally, by telephone; a warrant is signed and issued at the earliest possible time thereafter.

We know Home Secretaries to be honourable and hard working men who take their responsibility for interception of communications very seriously and examine applications for warrants most conscientiously. Nevertheless we find the existing procedures disturbing for four main reasons.

First, the Home Secretary has limited time. As well as examining individually each application for interception of communications, he has to consider individually all the more problematical immigration cases, all the most serious parole cases and all detention orders under the Prevention of Terrorism Act. On top of this, he has all his Departmental responsibilities, his Cabinet work, his Parliamentary duties and his constituency case load. With the best will in the world (and we do not doubt that the will is there), it is impossible practically for one man to give the proper measure of scrutiny to an average of nine or ten applications a week.

Second, the Home Secretary has limited advice. On a matter such as the interception of communications, he will not consult more than a tiny handful of Home Office officials and he will not consult his Political Advisor, his Junior Ministers, his Cabinet colleagues or his Parliamentary Private Secretary or other MPs. Consequently, he is over-dependent on the information and advice supplied to him by his professional security advisors who, while obviously competent in their fields, have a limited political perspective and restricted practical knowledge of political and trade union activity.

Third, the Home Secretary does not have total control. Para. 10 of the White Paper admits that warrants may cover an organisation rather than an individual (although this seems contrary to the recommendation in para. 56 of the Birkett report) and that in some cases authority to change warrants may be delegated to the Permanent Under-Secretary of State. Furthermore, the Home Secretary has no control over tapping which may be authorised by the Prime Minister or the Secretary to the Cabinet or by the Foreign Secretary or the Defence Secretary (see 'Inside Story', page 144). No Minister has control over official tapping which is performed without the need for a warrant.

Fourth, there is no Parliamentary accountability. The Home Secretary is exercising a power on behalf of the state, not himself, and, as with the exercise of any power by any Minister, a democratic society requires that there should be a measure of accountability to Parliament. The sensitive nature of this power is such that the accountability cannot be as open and

detailed as in most other cases but the present absence of any accountability whatsoever is disturbing and unacceptable.

As well as telephone taps officially authorised by warrant, there is
'official' tapping which does not require a warrant. This derives from an
'institutional' relationship between the police (or CID and Special Branch)
and the Post Office and the arrangement is set out in a Home Office
circular of 1969 (cited by L H Leigh in 'Police Powers in England and
Wales', page 215).

A senior official at Post Office Headquarters can authorise tapping in
certain cases without the need for a warrant and it is understood that in
1978 15 police requests for interception concerning serious criminal cases
were made and the information was provided in six cases. Additionally, in
urgent cases local telephone managers have the authority to allow the
police to listen in on calls

How easy it is for the police to intercept calls without a warrant must be
a matter for conjecture but, on page 161 of the (now unavailable) book
'Operation Julie , the head of the operation, Inspector Dick Lee, explains
how he avoided routine police channels and persuaded an unnamed
organisation to tap a suspect's telephone.

How the Post Office taps

Most official tapping – whether authorised by warrant or not – is carried
out on behalf of the relevant agency by specially selected Post Office
personnel. These personnel volunteer for the task and are drawn from
grades represented by a number of trade unions (including of course the
POEU). During their time on tapping duties, they are under the operational
control of the Home Office.

These men are unknown to their other Post Office colleagues and
operate out of their sight and in most cases without their support. The
ordinary Post Office engineer has nothing whatsoever to do with telephone tapping and has the same mixed feelings about the practice as most
members of the community.

The actual mechanics of telephone tapping cannot be described in
detail, but most members of the public would be amazed and concerned
by the range and sophistication of surveillance technology which now
exists, although we hasten to add that most of the techniques are not used
by the Post Office and only a tiny proportion of the population are actively
at risk from the application of the techniques.

The essential point to grasp is that technically a telephone conversation
can be intercepted at virtually any point in the link between subscriber and
subscriber. (Optical fibre cable – which is now being introduced in small
quantities in the British telecommunications network and is used in some
military applications – cannot be tapped but, even with this, at some point
the pulses of light have to be converted into electrical signals and at this
point tapping is possible.)

In practice, most parts of the transmission line plant would not be used
for tapping purposes, since in many cases tapping circuits would present

formidable technical and practical problems and interfering with a cabinet, pillar or distribution point in the local network would be too open to public view and too liable to discovery by Post Office engineers on normal duties. Therefore most tapping takes place in the local telephone exchange or in the customer's premises.

In the case of official tapping, virtually all of it is liable to be based on the exchange since, compared to a home or office, access is easy and detection is unlikely. It is likely that such official tapping is based on the main distribution frame (MDF) where each individual circuit is wired across by means of a jumper wire.

The main points to note about this procedure are that it is possible to gain easy access to the exchange outside normal hours and work in reasonable comfort with little chance of being observed, the basic technical operation is simple and quick, it is easy to pass the tap to the monitoring centre (which may be any distance away) via a trunk or junction circuit by the use of one jumper, no attention is drawn to an extra jumper since there are already so many, and there is little prospect of discovery by staff on conventional duties.

Other surveillance techniques

The techniques which can be used to intercept or overhear a telephone call or a conversation in the room of the telephone include the following:

1   A conventional tap on a telephone line which may be a metallic contact or an induction device which picks up the pulses in the line – these draw an almost undetectable amount of electricity from the telephone wire and give no betraying noises.

2   An 'infinity transmitter' which is a device inserted into a telephone handset which, when activated by dialling the number and giving an ultrasonic note on the last digit, prevents the telephone ringing and transmits over the dialler's line all the sounds in the room where the telephone is situated whether the handset is on or off the telephone – this can be installed in a matter of minutes.

3   An induction device to pick up telephone conversations from the stray magnetic field of the telephone itself – this must be within about four feet of the telephone.

4   A microphone using a wired link, the wired link either being specially laid or using an existing pair of wires or a single insulated wire – the range and sensitivity is unlimited depending on the size of the microphone.

5   A microphone using a radio link with a transmitter – the sensitivity is great although the transmission range is limited.

6   An electronic stethoscope of high amplification with wall-listening microphone and socket for connecting pin-hole microphones or the spike-mike for inserting into plaster walls – this requires access to adjoining walls.

7   A directional microphone concentrating a beam of sound from a
    distance on to a sensitive microphone and so hearing across inter-
    vening noises – the range is only about 25 yards.
8   Reflection of a laser beam off a window-pane or an object in a room
    to pick up the vibrations generated by the speaker – this is a recent
    development.
        (Note: much of this information is taken from the Younger Report
    on Privacy, Cmnd 5012, page 155.)

Many of these techniques are used by the police and the security
service. No warrants are needed to employ bugs in a police investigation
(in the Metropolitan Police, bugging is normally authorised by a Deputy
Commissioner). Substantial use was made of bugging in the sieges at
Spaghetti House, Balcombe Street and the Iranian Embassy.

Furthermore, most of these techniques are practised by those organisations and individuals concerned with industrial espionage or private
investigation. The laws against their use are few and weak. There are only
three laws in Britain that relate to private surveillance. They are the
Wireless and Telegraph Acts 1949 and 1967 and the Theft Act 1968. The
Wireless and Telegraph Acts make it necessary to have a licence for all
radio transmitters and forbid listening to non-public broadcasts. Licences
for radio transmitters are very rarely granted and there are an average of
about 80 prosecutions a year under these Acts, but they are usually against
pirate radios and hardly ever against those using bugs. Under the Theft
Act, a person can be prosecuted for stealing electricity for the operation of
a tap, but this is not a serious limitation on professional investigators and in
any event the constraint can be avoided by using battery-powered bugs
and other methods. Another serious problem is that there is no registration
or regulation of private security firms and investigators in this country.

The result is that private bugging and efforts at de-bugging are now big
business. Equipment is easily available and last year an American company, Communication Control Systems, actually opened a London shop
selling a wide variety of specialised devices. The shop is called Counterspy
and is located at Park Street in Mayfair.

Besides these taps and bugs, all of which are operated as covert
operations, there are a couple of other additional invasions of privacy of
telephone communication which are practised (in the main quite properly)
by the Post Office:

1   Service observation – This involves the Post Office making random
    monitoring of calls to test the quality of service. It is understood that
    some 300,000 calls are monitored every week by 600 observers
    throughout the country and around 10,000 of these are said to be
    monitored from beginning to end ('New Statesman', 9th February
    1979). Of course this practice is necessary to ensure good service
    but it is nevertheless an infringement of privacy.
2   Meter Check Printer No. 2A – This is a device for recording on paper
    tape the number, destination and duration of any calls made from a

particular telephone, although there is no record of the content of the calls. Its main use is to check the accuracy of telephone bills where the customer disputes them, but it has been used to obtain information to assist police enquiries (see 'Operation Julie'). Estimates of the number of such meters range as high as 18,000. ('Rights', August 1978)

The effect of new technology

All this demonstrates vividly that telephone conversations are open to many kinds of interception or surveillance and the advance of technology is ensuring that the threat is growing. Even the White Paper admitted that 'one of the reasons for the present concern about interception is the fear that technological changes have made it easier to intercept telephones' (Para. 25), yet it made no attempt to deal with the point.

One kind of technological advance that is relevant is the production of smaller, more sophisticated and (in some cases) cheaper and more obtainable bugs and other surveillance devices as a result of the development of micro-electronics.

Another development is computerised voice recognition. Duncan Campbell scared many people when he wrote:

The equipment at Ebury Bridge Road was designed by GCHQ, the government's code-and-cypher centre at Cheltenham. This has access to the latest US know-how, including computerised voice recognition techniques. According to one tapping centre employee, voice-recognition operations have reached an advanced stage – given the availability of good-quality lines – and by 1978 speech on many lines could be transcribed automatically and printed-out almost 'on demand'. ('New Statesman', 1st February 1980)

However, the consensus in the electronics industry is that this capability simply does not exist at present:

One British ex-army source, now doing consultancy work in narrow band communications and speech processing, said that none of the authorities with whom he had come into contact had even hinted that direct transcription was possible. He even cast doubt on the possibility of accurate voice identification which would be certain enough for the purposes described in the report. ('Electronics Weekly', 13th February 1980)

Nevertheless, the capability of automatic transcription of voice messages is certainly being developed:

Experts who dismissed the idea of an automatic machine which could transcribe phone calls were shaken this week when IBM revealed details of advanced work on natural language speech recognition. IBM researcher Fred Jelinek, head of the team at IBM's top laboratory in the US, described an automatic dictation machine which has already reached the point where it can transcribe the vast majority of English language words from continuously spoken input. ('Computing', 17th April 1980)

Still another important development – and much the most important in the sense that eventually it will affect all telephone subscribers – is the progressive introduction by the Post Office Telecommunications Business (and its successor British Telecommunications) of a new generation of switching equipment known as System X. The first System X exchange is due to open in July 1980 at Baynard House in London (this is a junction tandem exchange). Then the first local System X exchange will open at the end of the year at Woodbridge in Suffolk.

In May 1979, the POEU published a detailed review of the plans of the Post Office Telecommunications Business in a study entitled 'The Modernisation of Telecommunications'. Pages 17–23 describe the exchange modernisation programme and the future deployment of System X. We explained then the nature of the system:

System X (TXD) is a family of new systems using microelectronic technology, integrated digital switching and transmission and stored programme (software) control. The system is designed to be modular, enabling each switching system to be assembled from a range of basic modules, and evolutionary, enabling continuous development and improvement.

Some concern – which we share – has been expressed about the enhanced capacity of a computer-controlled exchange like System X to monitor what should be private telephone communications.

Malcolm Peltu, former editor of 'Computer Weekly', has written:

The new System X computerised telephone exchanges do not, a Post Office spokesman said last week, make telephone tapping any easier. This may be true in the sense that it is already easy enough to tap lines given the will (and, let's hope, the warrant). System X, however, does increase the potential use, scope and efficiency of telecommunications surveillance and to deny this is to deny some of the clever features of the system. One of the earliest services System X will provide to the public is the ability to bring more than two people into a conversation wherever they are located. If this is possible at the customer's request, the same capability could clearly bring a silent 'mole' into a conversation. System X is essentially a computer controlled by software programs; it is a relatively easy matter to modify the software to provide comprehensive and detailed monitoring of the destination and duration of all calls. ('New Scientist', 24th April 1980)

Duncan Campbell has expressed similar views:

A new generation of British telephone exchanges, known as 'System X', is about to come into service. This, if not regulated, can be turned into a tool of mass-surveillance far more readily than our present cumbersome electro-mechanical exchanges – and there is another shrouded department of the Post Office which appears to be working on just that project. In today's exchanges, large cables enter from the street, spray out onto distribution frames and are connected to long racks of switching equipment. Everything is highly visible, and comprehensible even to uninstructed eyes. Every aspect of System X's operation will be concealed inside miniature electronic devices. Its overall operations will be controlled by inaccessible computers, themselves subordinate to regional control centres. Complex facilities for channelling calls through exchanges will anyway be required, and adding a few programmes to monitor 'target' lines will be simple. No dangerously visible extra wires will be required to be attached during semi-clandestine visits: there will be no warning lights, and rather fewer people around each exchange to notice what may be going on. ('New Scientist', 1st February 1980)

This is a matter which the POEU has taken up with the Post Office. It has been admitted by the Post Office that stored programme control exchanges change the method by which the routing and control of calls is brought about and that it will be easier for individuals to gain access to customer lines from a remote point. However, we have been assured that access to control areas of software will be limited strictly by protection protocols. Nevertheless, it is obvious that official tappers would have access to these protocols.

We intend to press this matter further with Post Office management. Ultimately, however, it is not simply the POEU which must be assured but the general public and the kind of enquiry into telephone tapping which we have in mind would cover this issue.

The case for an enquiry

The omissions of the White Paper

As the first stage of our case for a full enquiry into telephone tapping, we intend to establish the serious inadequacies of the White Paper, 'The Interception Of Communications in Great Britain' (Cmnd 7873), and the statement to the House of Commons on 1st April 1980 and of the associated appointment of a judge to perform a monitoring role.

At a mere seven pages of text for a price of £1, the White Paper is hardly value for money. It adds little to the Birkett report and indeed on many occasions it simply repeats Birkett.

We believe that the White Paper contains three major areas of omission. First, the White Paper omitted some of the basic statistics on the interception of communications:

a   Although it purports to bring up-to-date the Birkett report, the figures for the number of Home Secretary warrants for both telephones and letters in the year 1957 are inexplicably missing and the figures for the number of Secretary of State for Scotland warrants for both telephones and letters for the entire period 1957–S6 are missing as well (this omission is noted but not explained).

b   Even when figures are given, it is not made clear whether the number of interception warrants is cumulative or not. This particular point was picked up by Clement Freud after the Commons statement when he asked: ' . . . whether the number of interception orders listed in the White Paper are cumulative – that is to say, those currently in force – or is the number given simply that of the new orders that have been published?' ('Official Report', 1st April 1980, Col. 212). But the Home Secretary did not deal with the question.

c   Although Birkett broke down the figures for each year into the two broad categories – Police, Customs, Post Office and Security on the one hand and drugs, lotteries, and obscene publications on the other – there is no breakdown whatsoever in the recent White Paper. Again this point was picked up by Clement Freud after the Commons statement when he asked: 'Will he consider subdividing the number of interceptions into those instigated by the Police, those by Customs and Excise officials and those by the security forces?' ('Official Report', 1st April 1980, Col. 212). But pointedly the Home Secretary did not answer this question either.

d   Even when some kind of statistical analysis is given, it is suspect. Para. 22 of the White Paper suggests that interception of communications led to the seizure or played an essential part in the case of 62% of the heroin and 56% of the cocaine seized in 1978. However, David Clark has written that, 'the claim . . . is demonstrably untrue' since 'as far as heroin seizures are concerned Mr. Whitelaw was talking nonsense' ('New Statesman', 2nd May 1980). Apparently in 1978 Customs had an all-time one-off record seizure of a large consignment of heroin following vigilance by Customs Officers.

Second, the White Paper omitted any substantive reference to Northern Ireland. This omission was understandable if regrettable in the case of the Birkett report, since in 1957 Northern Ireland had its own Government and Parliament, but since 1972 Northern Ireland has been governed by direct rule from Whitehall and Westminster. Commenting on the omission of Northern Ireland from the White Paper, the previous Home Secretary, Merlyn Rees, said: 'I believe that it would be the height of folly to give numbers of any kind about Northern Ireland – much as I am assured of them – because terrorism is established in Northern Ireland in a way that we do not experience in the rest of the United

Kingdom.' ('Official Report', 1st April 1980, Col. 209–210). However, on the same occasion, James Kilfedder, a Northern Ireland MP noted for his anti-terrorism views, stated:

> Because of the evil terrorist campaign that has been waged in Northern Ireland for the past 10 years or more, it is naturally assumed that a far greater number of telephone tappings will take place in the Province in proportion to the rest of the United Kingdom, but that does not justify the Home Secretary's refusal to give the figures. Is the right hon. Gentleman aware that his refusal to do so, and his refusal to extend judicial monitoring to Ulster, will create greater concern in Northern Ireland where many believe that phone tapping, conducted by the Army, takes place and extends to those who are not engaged in criminal or terrorist activities? ('Official Report', 1st April 1980, Col. 218)

In these circumstances, the situation in Northern Ireland must be reviewed. Certainly the POEU's Union Regional Council for Northern Ireland has expressed particular concern that the ordinary Post Office engineer be cleared of any involvement in the practice of tapping telephones on behalf of the Army or the Police.

Third, the White Paper omitted any reference to surveillance of communications conducted by official organisations other than the Police, Customs and Excise and the Security Services. Principal among these is Government Communications Headquarters (GCHQ). According to Duncan Campbell, GCHQ designed the Post Office tapping centre in Chelsea, provided much of the Centre's equipment and receives much of its intelligence ('New Statesman', 1st February 1980) and GCHQ or the Americans' National Security Agency (NSA) intercept on a routine basis much international telecommunications traffic, that is radio, telegrams, telex and telephone ('New Statesman', 2nd February 1979). However, other agencies believed to be involved in tapping but not covered by the White Paper include the Foreign Office (that is, Military or Defence Intelligence 6) and the Ministry of Defence (that is, Service Intelligence).

Reservations about the proposed monitoring

Associated with the publication of the White Paper came the announcement of the intention to appoint a 'senior member of the judiciary' with the following terms of reference:

> To review on a continuing basis the purposes, procedures, conditions and safeguards governing the interception of communications on behalf of the Police, H.M. Customs and Excise and the Security Service as set out in Cmnd Paper 7873; and to report to the Prime Minister. ('Official Report', 1st April 1980, Col. 208)

Subsequently, Lord Diplock was appointed to the position.

We do not regard the appointment of a judge on the basis announced as anything like an adequate safeguard in the circumstances. We have five main reservations.

First, Lord Diplock is an able and distinguished judge, but a man of 73 who has been Chairman of the Security Commission for nine years cannot be seen to have the required measure of independence from the Home Office and the Security Services to perform the task to the evident satisfaction of Parliament, the press and the public.

Second, it would appear that the judge will not have the power to investigate the detailed circumstances of particular cases and in any event it is difficult to see how such a senior member of the judiciary will have the time to monitor in sufficient detail the operation of a system of telephone tapping said officially to involve some 400–500 warrants a year (or an average of around ten a week).

Third, the judge's terms of reference only cover interceptions authorised on the warrant of the Home Secretary and the Secretary of State for Scotland and do not include interceptions authorised by other Secretaries of State (particularly the one for Northern Ireland) or interception by State agencies which have not received express authorisation (such as GCHQ).

Fourth, although the judge's first report will be published, his subsequent reports will be secret with Parliament being informed only of the findings of a general nature or of any changes in arrangements, so that secrecy will continue to prevail.

Fifth, there is no involvement of Parliament in the monitoring process (beyond being the recipient of occasional statements at the absolute discretion of the Home Secretary) and therefore there is still no real political accountability over what is essentially an exercise of political judgement by the Home Secretary.

Reasons for an enquiry

It is because of these serious omissions in the Government's White Paper and the grave reservations over the announced role of the judge that we must press our case for a full enquiry. We believe that there are four main reasons why a fresh enquiry is vitally necessary 23 years after the Birkett report.

First, the level of telephone tapping has increased significantly as evidenced by the Government's own statistics in its White Paper. The Home Secretary has said that there has simply been a 'modest overall increase' ('Official Report', 1st April 1980, Col. 206). However, the increase in warrants for telephone tapping in England, Wales and Scotland from 1958 to 1975 was from 129 to 468, a rise of some 260% although the figures have fallen a little in recent years.

Second, there have been many changes in technology over the past quarter of a century and many believe that current and coming technology makes telephone tapping easier and less detectable and therefore its abuse more likely. The principal changes are on the one hand the introduction of semi-electronic exchanges (TXE2, TXE4 and TXE4A) followed by fully electronic exchanges using stored programme control (System X) and on the other hand the use of micro-electronics to produce small and sophisticated bugging and surveillance devices.

Third, there is an urgent need to review practice concerning all forms of interception of communications, whether authorised or unauthorised, whether using tapping techniques or not. In 1957 the Birkett report devoted a mere 108 words to the subject of unauthorised tapping and wrote something which could never be said today: 'All the evidence we heard was to the effect that there is, and has been, no tapping of telephones by unauthorised persons in this country' (Para. 129). In 1972, Chapter 19 of the Younger report on Privacy (Cmnd 5012) dealt with some aspects of the problem but it was a partial study and one now somewhat out-dated technologically.

Fourth, there is growing public concern about the extent of the interception of communications by various agencies in various forms and the community is entitled to have its anxiety taken seriously and answered comprehensively. As Patrick Gordon Walker noted in his reservation to the Birkett report, 'One of the factors determining the evolution of policy in regard to the interception of communications has been the state of public opinion towards the exercise of this power' (Para. 173). He went on to argue that: 'Public repugnance to the interception of communications has, it seems to me, increased and there should therefore be a further restriction upon the use of this power . . . ' (Para. 174). Demonstrably, this is even more true today than it was 23 years ago.

We believe that individually these arguments are persuasive and that collectively they are compelling.

Notes

Unless otherwise stated, the place of publication is London.

2 BACKWARDS INTO THE FUTURE
1 Chatto and Windus, 1957.
2 Thames and Hudson, 1958.
3 Quoted in Tony Palmer, *The Trials of Oz*, Blond and Briggs, 1971.
4 *Poverty in the United Kingdom*, Allen Lane, 1979.
5 On 26 June 1978.

3 THE POST-INDUSTRIAL RIP-OFF
1 Daniel Bell, *The Coming of Post Industrial Society*: Basic Books, New York 1973, and Heinemann Educational Books, 1974, p. 109.
2 W. W. Rostow, *The Stages of Economic Growth*: Massachusetts Institute of Technology, Cambridge, Mass., and Cambridge University Press, Cambridge, both 1960.
3 Herman Kahn and B. Bruce-Briggs, *Things to Come*, Macmillan, New York 1972.
4 See the optimistic book by Charles A. Reich, *The Greening of America*: Bantam Books, New York 1970.
5 It is no accident that the 1980s began with news of the imminent bankruptcy of Manchester, said to face a city deficit in 1981–2 of some £94 million. The leader of Manchester council, Norman Morris, appropriately referred to the outlook as Manchester's Doomsday Crisis (*Guardian*, 20 June 1980).

6   Basic Books, New York 1975, and Heinemann Educational Books, 1976.

7   University of Texas Press, Austin 1978, and Macmillan, 1978.

4   A NEW DARK AGES

1   Bantam Books, New York 1975.

2   Thomas Conyngton, 'Motor Carriages and Street Paving', in *Scientific American* Supplement, New York, 1 July 1899.

3   Herman Kahn, William Brown, Leon Martel, with the assistance of the staff of the Hudson Institute, *The Next 200 Years*: William Morrow, New York 1976, and Associated Business Programmes, 1977.

4   The UN's Food and Agricultural Organization estimates that the world has 3·19 billion hectares of potentially arable land. Multicropping would increase this effectively to 6·6 billion hectares, roughly ten times the amount harvested today.

5   *Facing the Future*, OECD, Paris 1979, p. 29.

6   Ibid., p. 41.

7   R. H. Tawney, *Religion and the Rise of Capitalism*, Pelican, 1938, p. 50.

8   *Business Week*, New York, 19 May 1980.

5   DON'T SHOOT THE ECONOMIST

1   The phrase is borrowed from the book of the same name by Jude Wanniski, Simon and Schuster, New York 1979.

2   These observations are drawn from Jude Wanniski, *The Way the World Works*.

3   Revised edn, Penguin, Harmondsworth 1975.

4   Fred Hirsch, *Social Limits to Growth*, Routledge & Kegan Paul, 1977.

5   *Facing the Future*, OECD, Paris 1979.

6   DEATH TO INDUSTRY

1   In *The Theory of a Leisure Class*: reissued, Allen and Unwin, 1957, and New American Library, New York 1959.

2   Gollancz, 1937.

3   In 1976 Sir Harold Wilson was appointed chairman of a Committee to review the workings of Britain's financial institutions. It reported in 1980.

4   *European Economic Growth and the US Post-war Record* (highlights of *Why Growth Rates Differ* by Edward Denison

assisted by Jean-Pierre Poullier), Brookings Institution, Washington 1967.

5   In the United States, the figure was 64 per cent, which
    In the United States, the figure was 64 per cent, which
6   Again, the notable exception was the United States.
7   *The Government's Expenditure Plans*, HMSO, March 1980, pp. 36–7.
8   *Sunday Times*, 8 June 1980.
9   *Financial Times*, 31 May 1980.
10 Ibid.

7 DOMESDAY 1986
1   Including the cost of purchases for home use from the North Sea.

8 THE SIEGE OF 1990
1   In March 1979 the British customs and excise computer was paralysed by a strike of the Civil and Public Services Association.
2   W. A. P. Manser, *Britain in Balance*, Longman, 1971.

9 CASTLES TO THE POWER THREE
1   *Computer Age*, June 1980.
2   Brenda Maddox, *Communications: The Next Revolution*, The Economist, revised edn, 1969.
3   Alvin Toffler, *The Third Wave*, William Morrow, New York, and Collins, both 1980.
4   In *The Collapse of Work*, by Clive Jenkins and Barrie Sherman, Eyre Methuen, 1979.
5   Thorstein Veblen, *The Theory of a Leisure Class*, 1899: Allen and Unwin, 1957, and New American Library, New York 1959.
6   *Evidence to the Committee of Inquiry into the Engineering Profession*, 1978.
7   In *Equality*, Unwin Books, 1931, p. 2.
8   Chatto and Windus, 1957.
9   Routledge & Kegan Paul and University of Toronto Press, Toronto, both 1962.
10 Thames and Hudson, 1958.
11 In *The Coming of Post Industrial Society*: Basic Books, New York 1973, and Heinemann Educational Books, 1974, pp. 410–11.

12   Hans Berliner,'Computer Backgammon', in *Scientific American*, New York, June 1980.

10 THE NEW LAND HUNGER
1   Cmnd 7599, HMSO, 1979, p. 109.
2   Peter Kellner and Lord Crowther-Hunt, in *The Civil Servants: An Inquiry into Britain's Ruling Class*, Raven Books, 1980.

11 THE DOUBLE BLUFF
1   J. M. Keynes, *The Economic Consequences of the Peace*, Macmillan, 1919.
2   Gross domestic fixed capital formation as a percentage of gross domestic product fell from 4·1 per cent to 3·5 per cent between 1958 and 1979 for manufacturing, and rose from 0·4 per cent to 2·1 per cent for financial enterprises.
3   They were condemned as a cartel operating behind a screen of collectively arranged interest rates. The report recommended that this interest rate system should be dismantled. The net result would be to drive up the price of money borrowed by ordinary house-buyers; the greatest effect would certainly be felt by lower-paid mortgage customers. Cmnd 7937, HMSO, 1980, Ch. 8.
4   The amount would be more than enough to buy the entire list of UK-registered securities quoted on the London Stock Exchange at their 1980 value.
5   Northfield Report, Cmnd 7599, HMSO, 1979, p. 36.
6   Centre for Agricultural Strategy, *The Efficiency of British Agriculture*, Reading 1980.

12 MONKS WITH EXPENSIVE HABITS
1   *The Times*, 6 June 1970.
2   Eleventh Report from the Expenditure Committee 1976–77, HMSO, 1977, para. 13.
3   23 September 1979.
4   Hodder and Stoughton, 1971.
5   *Investors Chronicle*, 9 March 1979.
6   *Cambridge University Reporter*, Cambridge, 22 October 1969.

13 THE LEVERPEARSON EFFECT
1   Not surprisingly, the third-generation viscounts were both products of landfax education: Lord Cowdray went to Eton and Oxford, Lord Leverhulme to Eton and Cambridge.

2 The islands of Lewis-with-Harris cost £167,000, for some 350,000 acres and a population of 30,000, which comes to roughly £5·50 per person. The former owner threw in a set of Gobelin tapestries which now hang in the Lady Lever Art Gallery in Port Sunlight.
3 Quoted in W. P. Jolly, *Lord Leverhulme*, Constable, 1976, p. 224.
4 Judith Ennew, *The Western Isles Today*, Cambridge University Press, Cambridge 1980.
5 Quoted in *Port Sunlight Magazine*, summer 1967, p. 19.
6 Quoted in W. J. Reader, 'Impressions of Leverhulme,' Royal Academy of Arts, 1980, pp. 10–11.
7 Jolly, *Lord Leverhulme*, pp. 233–4.
8 Pearson's North American oil interests were consolidated from 1969 in cooperation with Ashland Oil.
9 S. Pearson and Son, Report and Accounts 1979, p. 6.

14 BLACK KNIGHT RULES OK
1 John H. Goldthorpe and others, *Social Mobility and Class Structure in Modern Britain*, Clarendon Press, Oxford 1980, p. 85. The statistical background can be found in this book and in a companion volume by Messrs Halsey, Heath and Ridge, *Origins and Destinations*, Clarendon Press, Oxford 1980.
2 Routledge, 1935.
3 *Financial Times*, 3 July 1980.
4 See Alistair Mant, *The Rise and Fall of the British Manager*, Macmillan, 1977.
5 A term from Britain's recent past, 'U' means 'Upper Class'. The fact that it has found its way into the *Oxford English Dictionary* is testament to the pervasive hold of class politics on the British mind.

15 CS ISN'T JUST A GAS; IT STANDS FOR CIVIL SERVICE
1 Peter Kellner and Lord Crowther-Hunt, *The Civil Servants: An Inquiry into Britain's Ruling Class*, Raven Books, 1980, p. 300.
2 *The Times*, 5 December 1977.
3 Hugh Thomas (ed.), *Crisis in the Civil Service*, Anthony Blond, 1968, pp. 25–6.

4   Quoted in Kellner and Crowther-Hunt, *The Civil Servants*, p. 123.
5   Ibid., p. 124.
6   Method 1, entry by written examination; method 2, assessment by a panel.
7   House of Commons, Paper 597, Seventh Report from the Expenditure Committee, Session 1975–76, Vol. I, para. 39.
8   Harold Wilson, *The Labour Government 1964–70*, Michael Joseph, 1971, p. 276.

16 PREPARING FOR THE FEUDAL PEACE
1   See Peter Laurie, *Beneath the City Streets*, revised edn, Panther, 1979.
2   Sidgwick and Jackson, 1978.
3   Published in 1976.
4   Bertrand Russell, *Portraits from Memory and Other Essays*, Allen and Unwin, 1956.
5   Penguin, Harmondsworth 1959, pp. 192–3.
6   Home Office Circular No. ES 1/1972.

17 HERE IS THE NEWS?
1   The history of British magazine and newspaper publishing is replete with noble names: Lord Thomson, Lord Matthews, Lord Rothermere, Lord Hartwell, Lord Drogheda, Lord Northcliffe, Lord Beaverbrook.
2   See Richard Collins, 'Television News', BFI Television Monograph No. 5, p. 46.
3   *Wall Street Journal*, New York, 27 May 1963.
4   Anthony Smith, *The Shadow in the Cave*, Quartet, 1976.
5   Glasgow Media Group, *More Bad News*, Routledge & Kegan Paul, 1980, p. 20.
6   Tom Burns, *The BBC: Public Institution and Private World*, Macmillan, 1977.
7   Ralph Miliband, *The State in Capitalist Society*, Weidenfeld and Nicolson, 1969.
8   *The Times*, 31 July 1980.
9   *Financial Times*, 31 July 1980.

18 SHHHHHH . . . YOU KNOW WHO
1   The trial of Crispin Aubrey, John Berry and Duncan Campbell in 1979.

2   J. R. Clubberley and D. Blakey,'*The Police National Compu-ter System in the United Kingdom'*– a Home Office conference on the use of computers in police operations, November 1976, p. 56.

3   Report of the Committee on Data Protection, Cmnd 7341, HMSO, 1978, p. 82.

4   *Security Gazette*, April 1979.

5   *Policing the Police, Vol. 2*, Peter Hain (ed.), John Calder, 1980.

6   Official figures are disputed by officers of the Post Office Engineering Union – much official tapping needs no warrant and other tapping is done by 'friendly' intelligence services. See Document 5 of the appendix.

7   *Daily Express*, 9 June 1980.

19 GOOD NIGHT, KNIGHT

1   Blond and Briggs, 1973.

2   Methuen, 1971, p. 5.

3   Routledge, 1942.

Suggested reading

Unless otherwise stated, the place of publication is London.

Bell, Daniel, *The Cultural Contradictions of Capitalism*, Basic
  Books, New York 1975, and Heinemann Educational Books,
  1976
Cambridge Economic Policy Group, *Review*, Vol. 6, No. 1 and
  other issues
Cooley, Mike, *Architect or Bee?*, Langley Technical Services,
  Slough 1980
Fromm, Erich, *The Fear of Freedom*, Routledge, 1942
Goldthorpe, John H., and others, *Social Mobility and Class
  Structure in Modern Britain*, Clarendon Press, Oxford 1980
Halsey, A. H., and others, *Origins and Destinations*, Clarendon
  Press, Oxford 1980
Hirsch, Fred, *Social Limits to Growth*, Routledge & Kegan Paul,
  1977
Hoggart, Richard, *The Uses of Literacy*, Chatto and Windus, 1957
Kellner, Peter, and Crowther-Hunt, Lord, *The Civil Servants: An
  Inquiry into Britain's Ruling Class*, Raven Books, 1980
McLuhan, Marshall, *The Gutenberg Galaxy*, Routledge & Kegan
  Paul, and University of Toronto Press, Toronto, both 1962
Mant, Alistair, *The Rise and Fall of the British Manager*,
  Macmillan, 1977
Organisation for Economic Co-operation and Development,
  Facing the Future, Paris 1979
Townsend, Peter, *Poverty in the United Kingdom*, Allen Lane,
  1979

Veblen, Thorstein, *The Theory of the Leisure Class*, reissued, Allen and Unwin, 1957, and New American Library, New York 1959

Wanniski, Jude, *The Way the World Works*, Simon and Schuster, New York 1979

Wilson, Sir Harold, and others, *Report of the Committee to Review the Functioning of Financial Institutions*, 2 Vols, HMSO, Cmnd 7937

Young, Michael, *The Rise of the Meritocracy 1870–2033*, Thames and Hudson, 1958

Index

academic knowledge, bias towards, 102–3

Africa, southern, students from, 135–6

agriculture, *see* farming

aircraft carriers, 184–8

allotments, 126–7, 238

alternative technology, 236

architectural design, 95–6

aristocracy: correct way of addressing, 164–5; elevation of Lever and Pearson families to, 144, 149, 152, 154; management of financial institutions, 167; *see also* landfax aristocracy

artificial intelligence, 96–7, 106–7

BBC: chairmen, 206–7, 218; preparation for nuclear war, *200*; *see also* broadcasting

banking, 84–5, 100, 122, 155

Binary Thought, 170, 171–4

bio-technology, 91–3

Black Death, 204

'black economy', 51

Bradfield, John, 138, 141

Bretton Woods conference, 48

brickmaking, 63

British Leyland, 40, 41

British Steel Corporation, 220

broadcasting: control over content, 209, 216–17, 251–3; domination by landfax aristocracy, 208; government control over, 217–20; during nuclear war, 199–202; study by sociologists, 210–12, 213–14; *see also* news broadcasting

Brookings Institution, xii, 62

Buddenbrooks, 6

bugging techniques, 257–8; *see also* telephone tapping

building societies, 123

C3 revolution, *see* high-technology revolution

Cabinet, social and economic background of, 132, 135, 168, 169

Cambridge Livingstone Trust, 135–6

Cambridge Science Park, 140–2

Cambridge University, *see* Oxbridge; Trinity College

capital formation, 128–9

car industry, crisis in, 38, 39–41

cargo cults, 166–7

Carrickmore incident, 216–17, 219, 253

Central Policy Review Staff, 182

Chrysler Corporation, 38, 39

Church, medieval, 112

Church and Chapel, 172–4

City institutions: earning power, 83–4; failure to invest in industry, 61, 67–8

civil defence, 193–4, 197–8, 204–5

civil liberties, loss of, 201, 222–3

Civil Service, 177–88; approach to procurement in defence sector, 183–8; attitudes and principles, 178–9; creation of, 177; lack of technical specialisation, 181–2; Oxbridge bias, 103, 132–3, 167–8, 179–81; recruitment to, 179–82; size, 183

class structure: failure to reduce inequalities of, 163–4; held together

IReLand
a hISTORY
ROBERT KEE

the book of the major
BBC/RTE Television series

'A careful, well-balanced, sensitive book, the fruit of
long, fascinated reflection over its subject matter; it
is warmly to be recommended, not only to those who
know little or nothing about Irish history, but also,
and especially to those who think they know a lot
about it . . . an excellent book.'
Conor Cruise O'Brien, OBSERVER.

'His achievement is to explain, lucidly and vividly,
the bloodiness of the conflict . . . he is twice the man
in print.' SUNDAY TIMES.

In the book of the successful, and often controversial, television series, Robert Kee examines the
'prison of Irish history', going back to its very
beginnings to identify the principal groups involved
in modern Ireland. He traces the emergence of each
group and their links over the ages, establishing how
past facts have bred present myths.

HISTORY   0 349 12081 1   £5.95

THE SCHUMACHER LECTURES

Edited with an introduction by Satish Kumar

With contributions from:

LEOPOLD KOHR   HAZEL HENDERSON   R. D. LAING

EDWARD de BONO   AMORY LOVINS   IVAN ILLICH

JOHN MICHELL   FRITJOF CAPRA

The Schumacher Lectures embraces economics, psychology, physics, linguistics, history and philosophy and brings together eight remarkable and original thinkers with an astonishing range of ideas, which stand as a testimony to the immense influence of E. F. Schumacher's work. The contributors share a common conviction that our society can no longer accept the demands of technology and 'progress' – we must actively determine our destiny and our own real needs.

Satish Kumar is the Chairman of the Schumacher Society and Editor of *Resurgence*, with which Dr Schumacher was closely associated. After Dr Schumacher's death in 1977, *Resurgence* launched the Schumacher Society, which now holds an annual series of lectures in honour of the bestselling author of *Small is Beautiful*.

'A thought provoking and sometimes inspiring taste of the current ideas of some influential thinkers, it is to be recommended.' *Time Out*

PHILOSOPHY   0 349 12118 4   £2.50

PATRICK MARNHAM

DISPATCHES FROM AFRICA

'We fear Africa because when we leave it alone, it works,' says the author of this provocative book. Patrick Marnham shows how outsiders – British, Russian, American, French and Chinese – have repeatedly tried to alter a land they do not understand. The relief workers, scientists, businessmen, tourists and conservationists all roam through Africa wreaking havoc as they go, attempting to mould the continent into their numerous images and ideals. Here are the elephants of Kenya and their predators, the game wardens; the West African outposts and their swollen populations of refugees; the tourists of Africa, who come to enjoy the 'primitive life' by observing a tribe which is desperately trying to flee from them; the citizens of Bamako, building their houses at night only to watch them being bulldozed the next morning; and Gambia, a country of eight barristers and no psychiatrists, where the British Ambassador's grant ignored the inadequate hospitals and instead equipped a new cricket team.

DISPATCHES FROM AFRICA reveals a country beset by illogical boundaries, horribly mismanaged financial aid and comically incompetent government structures. But the true brilliance of the book is its ability to allow still another Africa to seep through. The Africa of powerful ideas and raw energy which, for reasons of politics and ignorance, have gone awry. This Africa is a land of Northern ineptitude superimposed on an inherent native harmony.

'This shrewd, acrid book is an excellent antidote to the usual guff written on Africa' *Sunday Telegraph*

WORLD AFFAIRS   0 349 12280 6   £1.95

THE WAPSHOT CHRONICLE

John Cheever

THE WAPSHOT CHRONICLE brings us the
fortunes and foibles of the Wapshots – the
splendid patriarch Leander, his wife, Sarah, their
two sons, and Aunt Honora. Their story moves
from a small New England river town to New
York and Europe, and from the early twentieth
century to the 1960s.

'The book is written with an apparently inex-
haustible flow of inventiveness, and incidents
follow each other – bawdy, whimsical, or uproari-
ously comic – in an order apparently unrelated,
but in fact most carefully devised. For the zest
and vigour and sheer skill of Mr Cheever one can
have nothing less than very warm admiration.'
Times Literary Supplement

A GERMAN Love Story

ROLF HOCHHUTH

This is the poignant story of two very
ordinary human beings whose natural
instincts proved stronger than their fear
of the inhuman penalties decreed by
Hitler and imposed by Himmler and his
Gestapo. It is also a razor-sharp and
ironical study of Nazism as a worldwide
phenomenon not specific to Germany
alone.

Rolf Hochhuth is already known for
the controversial nature of his plays; and
A GERMAN LOVE STORY, his most
thought-provoking work, can best be
described as a documentary novel. He
has met and interviewed the survivors of
the true and brutally tragic story – the
woman whose love sent her lover to the
gallows, the men who built the gallows
and watched his execution, the local
Nazis who denounced the ill-starred
couple and who still live and prosper in
the idyllic South German village where
Stasiek Zasada, a Polish prisoner of war,
was judicially strangled nearly forty
years before.

FICTION   0 349 11698 9   £1.95

ABACUS

DANCE OF THE TIGER

BJÖRN KURTÉN

DANCE OF THE TIGER plunges us into life 35,000 years ago, when two completely different species of human beings existed: *homo sapiens* and Neanderthal man.

This is the story of Tiger, son of the Chief of a peaceful village inhabited by Cro-Magnon man. It is also the story of the struggle for survival between two species in Europe during the Ice Age.

The only survivor of a savage attack against his tribe, Tiger roams wild, hunting mammoth and sabre-tooth tiger, determined to track down the brutal warrior who killed his father. Alone and badly wounded, he is rescued by a Neanderthal clan — the troll-like creatures he has heard of but never seen. Far in the north, on the clan's island, Tiger learns the Neanderthal language, falls in love with their leader, and discovers the deeply human side to a people branded as barbaric. Finally he hunts down his prey. And *we* discover what may be the solution to prehistory's most puzzling mystery: the disappearance of the Neanderthals from the face of the earth.

FICTION   0 349 12121 4   £1.95

(ABACUS)

GOD ON THE ROCKS
Jane Gardam

A hot, seemingly endless summer between the wars, in a small seaside town in north-east England: this is the background to Margaret Marsh's slow awakening to the world around her. A child caught up in the drama of the dance of life and death, Margaret observes the sexual rituals of the adults who are part of her daily life. Her father, preaching the doctrine of the Primal Saints; her mother, bitterly nostalgic for what might have been; Charles and Binkie, brother and sister, atrophied in a game of words like flies in amber; and, the inevitable catalyst, Lydia, the Marches' maid, given to sateen and the smell of Devonshire Violets and the vulgar enjoyment of life: all these contribute to Margaret's shattering moment of truth when the dam breaks. It is not only God who is on the rocks at the coming of summer's end . . .

FICTION   0 349 11406 4   £1.95

A SELECTION OF TITLES AVAILABLE FROM ABACUS

NON-FICTION

PRISONERS OF PAIN	Dr. Arthur Janov	£3.50 ☐
OTHER WORLDS	Paul Davies	£2.50 ☐
THE SCHUMACHER LECTURES	Satish Kumar	£2.50 ☐
THE OLD STRAIGHT TRACK	Alfred Watkins	£2.50 ☐
SEX IN HISTORY	Reay Tannahill	£2.95 ☐
SMALL IS BEAUTIFUL	E. F. Schumacher	£1.95 ☐
TOUCH THE EARTH	T. McLuhan	£3.95 ☐
THE ARABS	Thomas Kiernan	£2.95 ☐
TO HAVE OR TO BE	Erich Fromm	£1.75 ☐
IRELAND: A HISTORY	Robert Kee	£5.95 ☐

FICTION

A STANDARD OF BEHAVIOUR	William Trevor	£1.95 ☐
THE EMPEROR OF THE AMAZON	Marcio Souza	£2.50 ☐
THE WAPSHOT SCANDAL	John Cheever	£2.50 ☐
GOD ON THE ROCKS	Jane Gardam	£1.95 ☐
A GERMAN LOVE STORY	Rolf Hochhuth	£1.95 ☐
JACK IN THE BOX	William Kotzwinkle	£1.95 ☐
DANCE OF THE TIGER	Björn Kurtén	£1.95 ☐
KINDERGARTEN	P. S. Rushforth	£1.95 ☐

All Abacus books are available at your local bookshop or newsagent, or can be ordered direct from the publisher. Just tick the titles you want and fill in the form below.

Name _____

Address _____

_____

Write to Abacus Books, Cash Sales Department, P.O. Box 11, Falmouth, Cornwall TR10 9EN.

Please enclose a cheque or postal order to the value of the cover price plus:

UK: 45p for the first book plus 20p for the second book and 14p for each additional book ordered to a maximum charge of £1.63.

BFPO & EIRE: 45p for the first book plus 20p for the second book and 14p for the next 7 books, thereafter 8p per book.

OVERSEAS: 75p for the first book and 21p per copy for each additional book.

Abacus Books reserve the right to show new retail prices on covers which may differ from those previously advertised in the text or elsewhere, and to increase postal rates in accordance with the P.O.